"This is a beautiful story from start to [...] one very special human/canine team an[...] have had on so many human lives. *Ric[...] read that will not only make you laugh and cry, but [...] what great love, trust, and dedication can achieve."

—**Victoria Stilwell**, author, *Train Your Dog Positively*

"If you've ever loved an animal, this book is a must-read. It will lift your heart and keep you turning the pages with its insights about love, loss, keeping your faith, making a difference, and the intangible but incredible connection we have with our animals."

—**Dr. Marty Becker**, America's Veterinarian

"Ricochet's awe-inspiring story is a celebration of the healing power of the human/animal bond. Judy's personal journey with Ricochet is a moving story of hope with a four-legged champion of compassion who continues to touch many lives. This is a must-read tribute to real American heroes on both ends of the leash!"

—**Robin R. Ganzert, Ph.D.**, president and CEO, American Humane Association

"*Ricochet* is a must-read for everyone who wants to be inspired in a challenging world in which inspiration is much-needed. I've never met a dog like Ricochet and I hope one day to do so. Thanks to Judy Fridono for sharing this wonderful story of a most amazing savior. Ricochet is a very special dog whose story must be circulated and shared globally."

—**Marc Bekoff**, author, *Why Dogs Hump and Bees Get Depressed*

"What a wonderful story! Ricochet is everything anyone could hope for in a dog—friend, coworker, and surf buddy—to name a few of her many qualities. This amazing dog and her incredible human partner found their purpose in life together. They will make you want to spring into action with your own natural talents. This book is a blessing!"

—**Allen and Linda Anderson**, founders of Angel Animals Network and authors, *Animals & the Kids Who Love Them*

"Ricochet will bound right into your heart. Her story inspires us all to find our purpose!"

—**W. Bruce Cameron**, author, *A Dog's Purpose*

"Judy Fridono recounts story after story of lives forever changed, her own included, with the help and presence of her furry canine companion, Ricochet, whose *soul* purpose is to encourage and comfort anyone who dares to dream of riding the perfect wave. Profound and uplifting, the story of Ricochet is not so much about a dog who surfs but about the impact she has in the lives she touches, one paw at a time."

—**Susan Sims**, publisher, *FIDO Friendly* magazine

"Inspirational. Profound. Enlightening. A brilliant memoir about universal love."

—**Jennifer Skiff**, author, *The Divinity of Dogs*

"*Ricochet* is an inspiration to millions. Whether making a splash in the water or on land, her story will grab the heart strings of any animal lover."

—**Seth Casteel**, author, *Underwater Dogs*

"Surf Dog Ricochet is just the most amazing and compassionate dog who has given so much to help others with her charity and fund-raising events. Ricochet has made such a positive difference in the lives of people with disabilities and continues to paw it forward daily to help others. Ricochet is truly an example of courage, hope, motivation, and inspiration to people all over the world."

—**Jamie Downey**, publisher, *American Dog Magazine*

"There isn't a more inspiring testament to the amazing positive life changes that can be experienced through a loving friendship like Judy and her dog Ricochet's story. Each page reveals more about this amazing pair, and their beautiful life together. Judy and Ricochet are a revelation, and their story reveals how love and respect for animals can change the world."

—**Wendy Diamond**, Chief Pet Officer, Animal Fair Media, Inc.

# Ricochet

## Riding a Wave of Hope with the
## Dog Who Inspires Millions

Judy Fridono
with Kay Pfaltz

Health Communications, Inc.
Deerfield Beach, Florida

*www.hcibooks.com*

**Disclaimer:** Some of the names have been changed to protect the privacy of the individuals.

Permission to excerpt the lyrics to *Dios Esta Aquí* granted by Raul Galaeno. Copyright 2007 © Dios esta aquí. U.S. All rights reserved. www.diosestaaqui.us.

The Library of Congress Cataloging-in-Publication Data

Fridono, Judy.
  Ricochet : riding a wave of hope with the dog who inspires millions / Judy Fridono, with Kay Pfaltz.
     pages cm
  ISBN 978-0-7573-1772-9 (hardback)
  ISBN 0-7573-1772-3 (hardcover)
  ISBN 978-0-7573-1773-6 (epub)
  1. Fridono, Judy.  2. Dog owners—United States—Biography.  3. Service dogs—United States—Biography.  4. Human-animal relationships—United States.  I. Pfaltz, Kay.  II. Title.
  SF422.82.F75A3 2014
  636.73092—dc23
  [B]

                                                            2014013038

HCI, its logos, and marks are trademarks of Health Communications, Inc.

Publisher: Health Communications, Inc.
          3201 S.W. 15th Street
          Deerfield Beach, FL 33442-8190

*Cover image of Ricochet © Tamandra Michaels*
*Cover image of boy surfing © KillerImage.com*
*Back cover photo © Barbara McKown*
*Cover design by Larissa Hise Henoch*
*Interior design and formatting by Lawna Patterson Oldfield*

In memory of Mommy,
our time together was much too short.

To Rina and Ricochet,
when I needed a hand, I found your paws.

To every dog, big and small.
Some dogs are extraordinary and destined
for greatness by touching the lives of millions,
while others who are no less extraordinary
are destined for greatness by
touching the life of one.

To all those who have walked beside us
on this journey, as well as everyone getting ready
to take the first step on their own journey.

In honor of Caleb,
your light shines forever
in our hearts.

## A Note from the Author

*If Ricochet's life can serve as just one example of truly living one's purpose, if her life can open just one mind or heart, if we can raise consciousness or "paw" this gift forward to even one person through this book by giving them hope, or if one animal is saved from being relinquished to a shelter, abused, or worse, then we've succeeded in our purpose for writing this book.*

*I hope my experiences act as your vehicle, driving you to your own place of thought-provoking revelation and empowerment as you have the opportunity to embark on your own spiritual journey and emerge into the beauty of your own true self and unique life purpose. I hope you further explore how your own animals can teach you valuable lessons. May your spiritual partnerships open new doors and new relationships, and inspire you to forge new ground in the interconnectedness of all beings.*

"... The problem with pounding a
square peg into a round hole is not that
the hammering is hard work.
It's that you're destroying the peg."

—*Paul Collins*

# Contents

# Foreword

Like almost everyone on the planet, I became aware of Ricochet, the surf dog who helps people with special needs, because someone sent me a link to a video. Like everyone, I shook my head in wonderment. How is this even possible?

Ricochet can surf. *I* can't even surf! And how can a dog look deep into the soul of a person and know just what that person needs and then provide it? This story, Ricochet's story, explains it all. You will find yourself astounded.

Of course, dogs consistently amaze us with what they can do. Dogs guide, they rescue, they warn of danger, they detect illness. They bond, they love, they cuddle and comfort. And they do it for one simple reason: to please *us*.

Around 30,000 years ago, our species forged a partnership with one of our natural enemies. Wolves were our competition for prey animals and most likely also hunted us, so the alliance was not a natural one. But wolves and people are both very social beings, and once the canine/human bond was formed, it proved to be the most successful interspecies partnership in recorded history. And as the relationship evolved, the foundation for it all was clear. Love.

Humans tinkered with dog breeds, creating dachshunds and Dobermans, bulldogs and beagles, shih tzus and spaniels. We put them to work, we took them hunting, we taught them tricks. They put up with all this not, as one might assume, because only humans know where to get fried chicken, but because they love us. Everything they do, they do for us.

That is a dog's purpose: to love humans and give to them without condition.

Ricochet's ability to balance on a surfboard is impressive, but as you read her story, you'll probably find yourself more enthralled with the way she intuits the needs of the people she meets. In a way, Ricochet is the culmination of 30,000 years of a symbiotic partnership between man and dog. So we should be amazed by her, but not surprised. Because where there's a need, there's a dog. And that's how it should be.

—**W. Bruce Cameron**
author of *A Dog's Purpose*

# Prologue

## September 24, 1995

Fourteen-month-old Patrick Ivison toddled through a parking lot with his mother, Jennifer Kayler. Patrick, a beautiful, vibrant, blond boy, smiled up at his mom with glee. He'd started walking at just ten months, which was a blessing because his mother couldn't afford a car. Struggling financially, Jennifer had recently moved into her parents' home while they were stationed in Spain. She was hurrying home to call them, and had just set Patrick on the ground to rest her weary arms.

Up ahead in a parked car, Jennifer noticed a driver gesturing wildly as he argued with a woman in the passenger seat. But she kept walking with Patrick alongside her. Suddenly, without warning, the angry driver threw the car in reverse, screeching backward without looking behind him.

Jennifer scrambled frantically but she wasn't quick enough to grab her son from the lurching mass of metal. The back bumper clipped her son and knocked him down, a rear tire rolling over his little body. In the horrible, surreal moments that followed, an incredulous Jennifer saw her son lying pinned under the car, his blond hair sticking out.

*It's impossible*, she thought. *That can't be Patrick lying there.*

But it was.

Frenzied with panic, she ran to the driver's side of the car and tried to lift it with all her might. She was desperate to pull Patrick out, but he was wedged—stuck under a half ton of metal. And it was then when she began shrieking uncontrollably, maniacally, causing people to come running to help when they heard the urgency in her screams. Death hung in the air, and a tiny life hung in the balance. In the desperate chaos that followed, bystanders lifted the car and Jennifer yanked Patrick free.

As she held his limp body in her arms, her relief turned to horror as his lips, then his face, began to turn blue. He lay deathly still, making no sound. Not a cry or a cough. In the blink of an eye, every mother's worst nightmare had become real for Jennifer.

In that terrible moment, she knew her son was gone.

# Introduction

*"When your life is on course with its purpose,
you are your most powerful."*

—Oprah Winfrey

Ricochet would be the first to admit she is not a perfect dog. She digs holes, chases birds, stalks gophers, and climbs up trees after squirrels. She still barks at the garbage truck and has a panic attack if a balloon pops.

And that's okay. We are all a little quirky, broken, strange, or different. That's what makes us special. Ricochet's journey is about what we all want: to be accepted for who we really are. To be encouraged and celebrated for what makes us unique and not chastised for what we can never possibly be. To embrace the notion that we are all imperfectly perfect.

But even though Ricochet is an ordinary dog—perhaps as "ordinary" as any dog in a shelter right now—Ricochet possesses and radiates an extraordinary spirit. Hers is a spirit of purity, compassion, kindness, and an incredible ability to reach into the souls of others. Even as a puppy she was the silly one, the exuberant one, the confident one. But complementing this playful, goofy side is an uncanny knowing that seems to exist just beyond time, just beyond the normal day-to-day life most of us are trying very hard to control. And it's in that place that I find Ricochet.

I've always loved animals. But it was Ricochet who taught me that dogs can be wise teachers and animal messengers, offering us profound lessons if we only stop to listen.

Many times they know what we don't know or perhaps what we once knew but reasoned or rationalized away. Their divine nudges are often disguised in wet noses, wagging tails, loving looks, and pensive stares, and they can push us back on the right path to knowing, but only if we open our eyes and hearts to their intuitive messages. And the truth is, we could all use a little guidance.

Life is not always easy. Sometimes it's messy. Despite our efforts to control our lives, in reality, we have absolutely no control. When our carefully constructed plans unravel, we are left at a crossroad. That was the reality for many of the people you will read about in this book, including me. They were coasting through the calm waters of life when a crashing wave blindsided them and took them under. When they emerged from the shock and opened their eyes, they felt the sting of salty tears and saw on the horizon a future different from what they had ever imagined. They were forever changed.

But these resilient souls prove that times of struggle can reveal our strength; that we can emerge from whatever the obstacle to find joy and purpose again. Ricochet has been blessed to cross paths with these amazing people, and in her unique way, she helps them to be free, to heal, to be whole. Through their stories, mine, and Ricochet's, I hope you'll realize that there's always hope, no matter who you are or where you are in your journey.

Ricochet came into my life on a wave of serendipity. The truth is I fought it instead of riding it, coming close to emotionally drowning myself. But when I finally embraced the wave and accepted that a higher power was charting this remarkable dog's course and taking me along for the ride, my world began to change.

When bad things happen to you, you can retreat into the darkness alone or you can open your heart and reach out to others with trust and vulnerability. I think you know in which direction Ricochet would nudge you. With a wagging tail and a look of love, she would probably tell you to "Go with the flow, keep your paws up, and face the wave, no matter how high."

# Chapter 1

# The Catalyst

*"Life begins where fear ends."*

—Osho

### Chicago, 2003

I sprang upright in the darkness.

My eyes popped open wide to see the glow of my alarm clock: 4:48. *Phew,* I heaved a deep sigh of relief, my heart still racing. It was just a nightmare—*the same nightmare.* I was safe. Nobody was chasing me. No one was trying to kill me.

Taking a measured breath to calm my nervous stomach, I wiped the sweat from my forehead and rubbed my eyes, slowly adjusting to the dark room. It was as good a time as any to greet the day; there was much to do in anticipation of my new houseguest. I still had training treats and other puppy supplies to buy. Making my way to the coffeepot, I smiled thinking that I was already spoiling this little girl who I hadn't even met. I had applied and was accepted to raise a service-dog puppy. According to the paperwork, I'd be caring for a female golden retriever/Labrador mix named Rina. I wasn't quite sure how to pronounce her name at first, but this eight-week-old cutie had stirred something within me that had been dormant for some time. Looking down at the photo of her sweet puppy face, I already felt a responsibility to this little

5

yellow bundle of fur. Rina would live with me for a little over a year. When the time was up, she'd return to the organization for advanced training, and then she would be placed as a service dog for a person with a disability.

I'd always wanted to make a difference in the world. In fact, my favorite movie of all time was *It's a Wonderful Life* by Frank Capra. James Stewart plays George Bailey, a distraught man whose imminent suicide attempt on Christmas Eve is interrupted by his guardian angel, Clarence. Clarence shows George how different—and worse off—life in his community would have been if he'd never been born. I often wondered if I'd ever made a difference in anyone's life. I didn't want to leave this earth without truly helping at least one person, and I thought that raising a service dog would be a good opportunity. And, since my husband had moved out, I not only had the time, but I had the space, too.

That afternoon, on June 20, I pulled into Chicago's O'Hare Airport, my eyes searching out the cargo area. I wasn't a fan of dogs flying in cargo, but I had to abide by the rules of the training organization. I wondered what it would feel like to be an eight-week-old puppy separated from her mother and littermates for the first time. The dark and rumbling belly of an aircraft had to be a scary place for a tiny puppy nosing her way into the world on a solo flight.

I paced in the waiting area, wavering between anticipation and concern. My heart thumped a little faster when an airline employee appeared, carrying a crate. I was expecting to comfort a shivering and nervous puppy, but when I looked inside the crate, I locked eyes with a confident young pup who was on her feet, vibrating with energy and ready to bound into my life.

And when I jiggled open the latch, that's exactly what she did, jumping into my arms. She was so small, so precious, and so perfect. Her chocolate eyes and dark nose stood out against a soft, pale yellow coat. Even through her puppy-cuteness, her wise and thoughtful face might have seemed very serious if it weren't for her busy pink tongue lapping at my eyes, nose, and mouth. I felt an immediate connection with this little pup!

"Look at the puppy," a passing woman exclaimed, as she quickly turned and made a beeline for us.

"She's a service-dog-in-training," I answered proudly, already feeling protective as this stranger moved in to pet Rina's head.

"Well, if her job is to be cute, she's already doing great work," the woman said with a laugh as Rina licked her hand. "I could fall in love with her."

*So could I,* I thought.

Rina would be my canine charge until she was about sixteen months old. I'd be responsible for giving her a safe home, taking her to obedience classes, providing socialization, and, most important, loving her. Sure, I knew I'd have to return her to the training organization, and I knew, too, that I could easily get attached to her. Just thinking about it, I felt the first poignant twinges of my decision already. But I also believed that eventually Rina would be a faithful companion who would change someone's life for the better. Little did I know at the time that she would play a bigger role in my life than I could ever imagine.

Back at my house, I carried her up the wooden steps onto the porch overlooking the lake.

"You and I are going to have so much fun out there," I said, motioning to the backyard.

Holding her gingerly, I unlocked the deadbolt and turned off the alarm. Once inside, I set her on the floor, and she was off in a flash, sniffing around the house, checking out corners, and pawing at the new toys.

Watching her explore her new world with such joy was more fun than I'd had in a long time. As the weeks progressed, I enjoyed watching her learn and grow. She loved to scout out the nooks and crannies of the lakeshore, scrambling over logs and nosing her way through the grass like a great lion cub in the wild jungle. Such an adventurer she was. The first time she crept up to the water's edge, she gazed down at her reflection in the water and her tail began wagging furiously. She looked up at me eagerly, as if to tell me that she had spotted a new friend to play with. At night, we'd play endless games of fetch, and then we'd cuddle. The fuzz of her fur would tickle my nose as I sat with the pooped-out puppy sleeping in the crux of my neck. The two of us had a wonderful time playing, but we worked hard, too.

A star pupil in her puppy kindergarten class, Rina passed her obedience 101 class with flying colors, and we coasted on to adolescent classes. She adored playing with other dogs, especially her best friend Zoe. She'd pull me and pant excitedly whenever she spotted a potential friend, so we worked to tone down her display of enthusiasm. Tugging on the leash is not acceptable behavior for a service dog because it could potentially yank a disabled partner into a harmful fall.

I'd been instructed to use a "gentle leader" with her, a collar-and-leash system that wraps around the dog's neck and rests loosely around its nose. This was the organization's collar of choice, as it would allow the trainer to steer the dog's nose and thereby the dog's body. Unfortunately, Rina was not a fan of this contraption. After brief, unsuccessful struggles to free herself, she'd shut down, lying on the floor looking defeated. I hated seeing her like that.

Rina had other idiosyncrasies, too. In particular, she was an unabashed Kleenex thief, scouting out tissues no matter where they were hidden, even in my purse. She didn't tear them up or eat them, but she loved to proudly carry her find around in her mouth. I'd just laugh and hold out my hand. "Give," I'd say, and she would drop the tissue in my hand with obvious disappointment.

"I know. I never let you have any fun, right?"

Later, she graduated from Kleenex to shoes. I loved coming home from work to see my front entry, which now resembled a small shoe store, with flip-flops and sneakers lined up from where Rina had grabbed one in excitement and dropped it. I couldn't help but smile when I'd find the odd, single shoe in the yard, delivered by Rina and forgotten. Her own canine calling card: Rina was here.

Her footwear fetish notwithstanding, she was making great progress. She was full of energy, and I was sure she was on the right track to success. She went everywhere with me so that I could expose her to as many experiences as possible. She needed every opportunity to meet different people, children, and animals so she would be comfortable and well behaved in a wide variety of environments. Rina had a wonderful demeanor and sense of humor, often looking up at me and laughing. She'd smile and wag her tail, wiggling her whole body back and forth. Our bond grew stronger every day, but I never lost sight of the ultimate goal of returning her to the service-dog organization—even when someone suggested that maybe Rina had a different purpose.

On that day, I had an appointment with my energy healer, Linda, who was treating my arthritis. I brought Rina with me, of course, and Linda looked us over thoughtfully. I wondered if she was feeling the energy between us.

"This dog is meant for you," Linda said emphatically.

"No," I corrected her. "I'm raising her for someone else."

Deep down I was flattered, but I didn't want to admit that she might be right: I was growing attached. But Rina was going to make a difference to someone who truly needed her, and I'd make sure of it.

Linda stopped what she was doing and smiled intuitively. As she resumed my treatment, she kept stealing glances at Rina but said no more. I dismissed what Linda said at the time, but I never forgot it.

As the green of the trees and the buzz of cicadas gave way to fiery red leaves and the honking of migrating geese, Rina enjoyed our outdoor romps, especially when it snowed. She looked like a miniature polar bear, sticking her head into the fluffy white stuff, then shaking it wildly to be rid of the flakes that made her nose twitch. One day I took her to the edge of the now-frozen lake and stepped onto the shimmering surface. She stood at the shore and looked at me quizzically as if to ask, "How are you walking on our lake?"

"Come on, Rina!" I scuffed my feet and she followed, the two of us slipping and sliding our way along the edge. Just then her legs splayed outward and she skidded.

"It's okay, I got you!" I laughed. But this time, when I tried to scoop her up into my arms, it wasn't a neat fit like it had been months before. She had grown so much!

"You're such a big girl now," I said, helping her scoot onto the snow-dotted ground as I looked into those big brown eyes. The eyes that now held my heart.

When Rina was fourteen months old, we went to the training center where she and I would soon part ways for her advanced training. I hoped to give her a chance to acclimate to where she would train next, if only for a short visit. I didn't want Rina to feel like I was abandoning her on turn-in day, and I thought an overnight stay might make the transition easier. When the time came, we said our good-byes, and I didn't worry much about it. She was in good hands, one step closer to her career as a service dog and a lifelong home.

Just like a mom who drops her youngest child off at the first sleepover, I couldn't wait to see her the next morning. But when I arrived to pick her up, I knew at once that something was wrong. She wasn't excited to see me. Her normal energy and buzz of excitement were gone. She looked dazed and out of sorts. Since she'd never stayed in a kennel before, I figured she'd snap out of it, so I put her in a sit/stay while I talked to one of the trainers. That's when I noticed that Rina was peeing, peeing, and peeing some more.

Dark, concentrated urine puddled around her on the floor. She had *never* done this before and looked mortified. When she continued urinating for much longer than seemed possible for a young dog's bladder, I was stunned. It was obvious that she hadn't relieved herself for the entire twenty-one hours I'd left her at the center!

The trainer didn't think anything of it, which infuriated me.

*Poor Rina!* As I glanced into the kennel, I wondered if anyone had even bothered to show her how to use the doggie door. Obviously not. We didn't have one at home, so she didn't know how to use it. Like the good trouper she was, she'd held it. She wanted so badly to do as she had been trained and not have an accident. No wonder she wasn't excited to see me—she probably thought if she moved she would lose all bodily control! Now here she was, peeing with her head hanging and eyes averted.

I fumed as the trainer droned on about leash corrections, which is when a trainer snaps a loose leash with a quick tug to demonstrate that a dog has done something unacceptable. Frankly, I hated leash corrections, and this was the first time I realized they used this training technique. It seemed to me there were more positive ways to teach behaviors without being so heavy-handed.

"You have to snap the leash quickly," the trainer demonstrated, yanking Rina's leash with a forceful tug.

A large woman with a brusque manner, she would have intimidated most humans, let alone a little dog. When she jerked the leash again, my eyes grew wide. *Rina isn't doing anything wrong! Why is she demonstrating a correction?*

Then she commanded Rina to sit straight, a simple behavior but one Rina wasn't able to process in her mounting intimidation. Her ears were back as she crouched and desperately tried to disappear into the floor. All the while, Oblivious Trainer Lady ignored Rina's cues, continuing to jerk the leash and stressing her further.

When I mentioned that Rina didn't like the gentle leader, lo and behold, the trainer went to get a gentle leader! She wanted to show me how to "fix" the problem. I knew Rina would hate it, and I winced involuntarily as I watched the woman put it on her.

Rina fought against it, but only a little, too unsure of herself to do anything more.

"Let's tighten it up so we can see how she reacts," the trainer suggested.

*How do you think she will react?* I thought, furious yet holding my tongue. Why couldn't I speak up to this lady? Why couldn't I say something to defend Rina?

Rina was so confused about why she was being punished that she simply melted. She locked into a down/stay, too afraid to move or turn her normally attentive gaze to see who was entering the room. Hoping to rescue Rina from the clutches of this insensitive canine commando, I improvised.

"Do you want to observe her in a play situation?"

Thankfully, the trainer thought this was a great idea, clapping her hands and releasing Rina to go play. "See, now she's wagging her tail," she said.

*She should have been wagging her tail this whole time!* I thought, but again I bit my tongue.

When I fetched Rina from the playroom, I noticed that she had pooped in the middle of the floor. Again, this was something she hadn't done the entire time she had lived with me. While I didn't blame Rina for her actions—after all, nature calls—I just wished she'd chosen a better spot for her deposit . . . like the trainer's shoe!

Hundreds of questions raced through my mind when we got home. *Am I overreacting? Being too sensitive?*

If this was how service-dog training had to be done, maybe I wasn't cut out for it. I'd heard warnings from other puppy raisers that if a dog was released from service-dog training for whatever reason, the pup would sometimes return with a broken spirit. The thought of this happening to Rina broke my heart. I wanted her to keep her vibrant spirit, not become a robo-Rina.

I couldn't stand the images in my mind of how Rina looked—so sad and scared. But maybe I needed to stop thinking about her temporary discomfort and consider the person with the disability whose life Rina would change for the better. I knew how hard it was to live with a debilitating condition like arthritis, but I could only imagine what it must be like for people with much bigger challenges. I tended to think more about the animal than the person, and it occurred to me that maybe my perspective needed to change. Perhaps the end justified the means.

All the same, my mind kept drifting back to the fear in Rina's eyes. I recognized fear. I wrestled with it almost every day.

*"Don't worry; you're safe," my husband would try to reassure me. "No one's trying to attack you."*

*But that's what I felt deep inside. I was finally in a nice home, on a lake, and in a safe neighborhood, but I had this irrational, foreboding sense that someone would drive up, come into my house, and attack me.*

*As night fell, the panic would set in. "Please," I'd beg him. "Please, just sleep with the fireplace poker under the bed. I don't feel safe. Please, just in case."*

*When he went out of town, I was constantly on edge—even when daylight came. If the doorbell rang, I'd have a full-blown panic attack. I'd stand frozen, too afraid to move to answer the door because whoever was behind it would kill me, but terrified that if I didn't answer, they'd break in and kill me. Either way I was in danger.*

*I knew my thoughts were irrational, but I couldn't stop them, no matter how hard I tried.*

My mind continued to race over Rina's future despite my efforts to distract myself. Our time together was running out. I tried to convince myself that maybe it wouldn't be so bad for her. She would ace the training and become a service dog to a wonderful person. But part of me no longer wanted her to go through training. Part of me wanted her to just stay with me. I felt guilty for having such a selfish thought, but I couldn't help it. Rina was a sensitive dog, and the strict training environment worried me.

Hoping to settle my conflicting emotions, my energy healer Linda suggested that I contact a reputable animal communicator she knew named Rebecca. Apparently the communication could be done over the phone, and I would be able to ask questions and get answers from Rina. It seemed like a long shot, but wanting to tame my uneasiness, I figured it couldn't hurt. What did I have to lose, except a few bucks?

While I was on the phone with Rebecca, I watched Rina lying in the living room, happily gnawing on a chew toy. There were no visible changes in Rina's calm demeanor nor did I feel any odd sensations. Even so, I listened intently and was floored by Rebecca's insights.

"She says she's nervous about going to school," Rebecca revealed. "She thinks she's in trouble and that is why she is going."

"Please tell her she's not in trouble," I said. "Tell her that she is going to live with a wonderful family afterward. She just needs to train for a little while longer."

"She doesn't know if her head has more room to remember," Rebecca explained after a brief pause. The response broke my heart.

Apparently Rina also thought that the people at the school were too strict. *They were.* She didn't understand why they couldn't "just have fun." *Me neither.* Although I agreed with Rina's observations, I asked Rebecca to explain her purpose and why she was born to do this very important work for someone—it just wasn't going to be me.

By the end of the conversation, Rebecca assured me that Rina said she would go, but reluctantly. I didn't know what to do. She was never supposed to be *my* dog. Then I had a thought. "Please tell her one more thing," I implored. "Please tell Rina that if things are too much for her to handle, and if she really doesn't want to be there anymore, then she should growl."

For a service dog in training, growling means immediate release. It would be Rina's "Get Out of Jail Free" card. I felt guilty for suggesting such an extreme tactic, but I wanted to protect her in case it became overwhelming for her. I knew that Rina could make the decision on her own if only she had the tools.

True to her nature, sweet, gentle Rina told Rebecca that she couldn't do that.

Two months later, on August 15, 2004, the time came to drop Rina off for advanced training. This was it . . . our good-bye. But when I got to the center, I couldn't bear to let her go. I called the office from the car and did what any honest pet-lover would do—I fibbed.

"I have a friend who wants to see Rina before she goes," I said. "I'll bring her in tomorrow."

They didn't sound too thrilled, but they agreed.

I soaked up every minute of our extra day. We cuddled and played fetch. I took her to a park and set her loose to run between the dense trees. The sun filtered through the canopy and danced across her coat as she crashed through leaf litter on a wild expedition. She was fearless and full of curiosity, her nose sniffing and her tail wagging wildly. Watching her made me smile, and I hoped that she would be this happy again sometime soon.

The next morning, outside of the center, I hugged Rina tightly to my chest in the car.

"It's going to be okay," I promised. My words were meant to reassure her, but I was really talking to us both. I ran my hands down both of her silky ears and put my nose into her coat, sniffling back tears.

"This is what you were meant for," I told her, crying into her ruff. "And you are going to be so good at it."

She looked up at me with the deep chocolate eyes I knew so well by then, and I wished with all my heart that she didn't have go. The image of her cowering under a correction flashed through my mind, and I cried even harder.

Wiping my tears, I led her into the building. An assistant showed us through the offices and into the kennels, which seemed to take forever, and yet it was over in a painful flash. As I opened the door and sent her into the kennel, I struggled to stifle the tears. I wanted Rina to believe that staying there was a good thing.

I bent down to meet her eyes one last time.

"I promise you, I will find a different way to train service dogs, Rina," I said. "I promise I'll find a more positive way." And I meant it.

As I turned to walk away down the hall, I made the mistake of looking back over my shoulder. Rina cocked her head and her pleading eyes locked with mine. *Why are you leaving me?* I could almost hear her begging, *Please don't leave me.*

Everything within me fought against running to her, grabbing her, and bringing her back home where some part of my heart and soul knew she belonged. I wanted to tell her I wasn't abandoning her, but we both knew the truth: I was.

But I was obligated to give her back. There was nothing else I could do.

My throat clenched as I relived the pain of letting go and the sting of knowing that, once again, I was losing someone I loved deeply.

# Chapter 2

# Loss and Fear

*"The worst prison would be a closed heart."*

—POPE JOHN PAUL II

## Chicago, 1968

"Good boy, Rajah," I said, breaking off a piece of my pretzel and placing it in my outstretched palm.

The sweet golden retriever mix lowered his head and ever so gently took my offering. Patting his soft fur, I sat down on the sidewalk outside our brick apartment building. Beside me, I could see Rajah's body panting happily in the shadow cast above my eleven-year-old frame.

I was oblivious to the police cars wailing in the background, not only because they were a common occurrence in our neighborhood, but I was focused on perfecting our next trick—luring Rajah to step through my hula-hoop. I'd already taught him to sit and fetch. He was a quick learner, and I knew it was only a matter of time before he mastered jumping through the hoop. When my mom rescued him from the Anti-Cruelty Society, she was looking for a watchdog with a loud bark to deter robbers. She got a guard dog; I got a friend.

Growing up in the gang-riddled inner city of Chicago, gunshots rang out like fireworks on the Fourth of July and sirens screeched throughout the night. But even so, it was home.

My grandparents on both sides lived across the street from each other in our predominantly Italian neighborhood. An assortment of aunts, uncles, and cousins lived in the same building we did or in other buildings on the same block.

Both sets of grandparents were from the "old country" and retained their old ways. Grandpa Fridono was a gruff man who rarely smiled and was always afraid of getting robbed. Grandma Fridono had long, blond hair that she wore in a bun. They had four sons, including my father. When their boys were young, my grandfather physically and verbally abused them all in the name of "tough love." There was also a dark family secret: mental illness—paranoid schizophrenia, depression, anxiety, hypochondria, or just the aftereffects of living with abuse and fear on a daily basis.

Although we weren't an affectionate family, and hugs were few and far between, we were close. Grandma Fridono cooked us Italian dinners sometimes then rapped on the floor with a broom handle to summon us upstairs to pick up the pot or plate.

My maternal grandparents were from Poland. My grandfather died when I was five, and my only memory associated with him is standing on the kitchen table as someone dressed me for his funeral. Grandma Mydlowski was a round woman who wore babushkas and did jigsaw puzzles at the kitchen table. She wouldn't let us eat Popsicles for fear we'd catch colds, and she'd "take the chill out of the milk" before she let us drink it. Whenever we walked by, she'd cover her ear because she thought she could get a cold from the "wind" that reached her as we passed.

I had two older siblings, Maria and Frankie, and a younger brother, Bobby. Our father was a chain-smoker. And a drug addict.

He always had a cigarette tucked behind his ear, ready to be lit by the one dwindling to ash between his lips.

Together, my father and I would hunt the neighborhood for empty pop bottles to redeem, cashing in the money for a trip to Kiddieland. Those outings were some of my favorite times as a child, although as I got older he would only promise to take me, but never follow through.

I was a charitable kind of kid, always eager to help people. When I was eight, I learned that a close family friend's young son had recently been diagnosed as being deaf, so I brought over my piggy bank full of change and gave it to his mother.

"Here," I offered, "you can use this to buy him a hearing aid."

I have many good memories of growing up, like the smell of Gonnella bread baking, running through the spray from the fire hydrants in the heat of the summer, and riding my bicycle to the nearby lake.

But I also remember the fighting. My father and mother argued constantly. Once, when I was about eight, I cowered behind a chair as my enraged father upended a table and slammed it into a wall. Another night, as I lay next to my mother, trying to sleep, my father screamed at her from the bedroom doorway, threatening to put scissors in her heart. It was the drugs that fueled his rages, but the cause didn't matter. The only thing I knew was that I was scared.

When I was ten, my mother had finally had enough of the fighting and my father's erratic behavior, so she moved us across the street to live with Grandma Mydlowski. I could see my father anytime I wanted, but he became less and less emotionally available as the drugs continued to take a toll on his mind. Not only was he doing drugs, he was also dealing them. Although we didn't know it at the time, sometimes he'd take my brother Bobby and me on drug runs. We'd sit at the drugstore counter sipping ice-cream sodas while my father collected narcotics from the pharmacist. Or we'd go with him to the neighborhood bar, where we'd play pinball games and eat pretzels. I didn't know what he was dealing, but I'd look in his medicine cabinet and count the bottles of red and blue pills all lined up. Sometimes his "customers" would play poker and gin rummy with us when we were at his house. We liked them because they gave us quarters and we'd run to the candy store.

Many nights my father would call my brother Bobby and me on the phone from across the street, and we could tell he was high. His conversations were incoherent, with my father babbling on about things we could barely understand and changing topics in mid-sentence. Sometimes we'd set the phone down on the table and walk away, maybe finish watching our TV shows. After a while, when it seemed he should be talked out, we'd pick up the phone again and end the one-way conversation. "Okay, Dad," we'd say. "I've got to go." He never knew we weren't listening.

Shortly after we moved into a second-floor apartment in Grandma Mydlowski's building, one of the first-floor apartments was burglarized. Although I had grown up modeling the fear I saw in my parents and grandparents, this time a robber was actually in our building. I was terrified. My sister was so nervous that she pressed clay onto our windowsills and armored it with thumbtacks, believing the sharp points would keep burglars out. But I knew better: Nothing would keep them out if they wanted to get in badly enough.

From that day on, I was petrified to walk in the front door because I'd have to pass that first-floor apartment. I always had this feeling that someone was in there ready to burst out and grab me. Going through the middle entrance terrified me, too. There was a door under the steps that led to a storage area, and I was sure someone would pop out when I walked up the stairs. The mailboxes were down there, and I was always anxious when my mother asked me to get the mail, running as fast as I could down and up the stairs again.

My fears cropped up in other places, too. Even though nothing happened in my father's building, I was afraid to walk up the long gangway to my father's apartment in the back. I'd sprint as fast as I could to get in the door because I feared someone was lurking in the backyard to harm me.

Just before my sixteenth birthday, my fears became reality on a summer evening in August of 1974. My friend Terri and I were walking another friend home, and as we were returning to Terri's house, we noticed a car cruising by slowly. A bunch of guys inside were watching us. Stalking us.

I'd been told in grammar school by Officer Friendly: "If a car moves in one direction, you run in the other." So that's exactly what I did. Little did I know that two of the guys had gotten out of the car at the corner and were following us on foot. I turned to run, but it was too late. I wasn't fast enough.

They knocked me down to the sidewalk. I never saw their faces, just four feet with high-top sneakers standing over me. Everything became a blur. I understood only later that their intention was most likely to get Terri and me into their car to commit unspeakable crimes. But my only concern at the time was just trying to breathe. I heard the chains of the nunchucks, but my body was in shock. As the wood and chains lashed my body and thumped against my head, again and again, all I felt were faint taps. Everything was numb, and I began to black out. Then, as if from far away, I heard a muffled scream. Maybe Terri's, maybe mine.

Fortunately, our neighbor Eddie was sitting on his front porch across the street, and he heard the scream, too. He didn't know who was in trouble, but it didn't matter. In our tight-knit neighborhood, we followed an unwritten code to protect one another. And that's what Eddie did. He began yelling into the darkness, startling my assailants. They leaped over my bruised body, ran to their car, and screeched away.

With adrenaline coursing through my veins, I jumped up and ran toward Eddie's familiar voice. In a daze, I saw Terri standing on the other side of the street near him. As I approached them, Eddie reared back to punch me—an unidentified stranger in the shadows.

"It's me!" I yelled, rubbing what I could feel was a huge lump forming on my head.

*Thank goodness I was safe.* Shaken, more frightened than ever, but safe. When I think back now, I realize that Eddie's shouts had probably saved my life.

By now, other neighbors had darted outside to see what had caused the commotion; a few raced off in their cars after the attackers, who ended up getting away.

Our mothers quickly showed up on the scene, hugging us tight.

In the days that followed, nothing much was said about the incident, as if by not talking about it we could push it to the back of our minds and pretend it never happened. My diary entry from that night seems to confirm this. It read simply: *Tonight me & Terri got jumped. We were walking down Huron Street and I got hit in the head. Terri got away.*

Such a nondescript entry could have described a casual night of going out for ice cream, not enduring a vicious attack. Although I pushed the experience far back into my subconscious, I still felt the pain of it deep inside me. The physical blows left their marks in my muscles and bones with bruises and aches, but they lessened over time, yet the damage to my soul and psyche was permanent.

Shortly after this incident, I developed juvenile rheumatoid arthritis, and I have been in pain every day since. Maybe the stress and fear of growing up or the attack caused my joints to start hurting. Perhaps the pain on the inside needed to get out and manifested itself as arthritis. At first the pain radiated through my joints. My knees hurt in particular, and I felt aches in my hands, wrists, and elbows. Sometimes the pain in my legs was so extreme that it was impossible to walk. Some days the pain was so bad that I missed school. Of course, I was sidelined from participating in any kind of sports.

The combination of physical pain coupled with emotional anxiety brought me to a place of depression. I'd sit on my bed, and my faithful friend Rajah would watch me like a sentinel, his muzzle on the covers, his deep, dark eyes looking into mine. While Rajah couldn't take away my pain, he was still good company.

There had always been gangs in our neighborhood, but the bloodshed seemed to intensify in the months after Terri and I were jumped. Gang members from other neighborhoods would search our streets, driving slowly with headlights off, looking for rival gang members to shoot. The turf wars were never-ending, and friends of mine were casualties. The first was my friend JT.

One night, JT just disappeared from his house. Some say he'd been lured out by some guys who claimed his friends were in trouble; others guessed he was abducted at gunpoint. The details didn't matter. The next morning his barefoot body was found in a junkyard, shot six times in the head and once in the shoulder. JT's gruesome murder was followed by several more: one friend was purposely mowed down by a car, two others were shot in drive-by shootings while they were just hanging out on separate occasions, and a friend's brother was mistaken for a gang member and was shot to death near a playground. Even our priest got shot while fending off a purse-snatcher after midnight mass on Christmas Eve.

While teens in nearby suburbs were dressing for proms and dances, we were dressing for funerals. The deaths resonated throughout the community like a horrible version of the game Telephone, leaving my friends and me looking over our shoulders, fearful of who might be next.

As if losing friends to gang violence wasn't enough, I lost two of my grandparents within three years of each other: Grandma Fridono died in 1975, and Grandpa Fridono died in August 1978. I almost lost my brother Frankie that year, too. On Thanksgiving, Frankie was at a bar playing a pinball game against another guy for a dollar. Frankie lost the game, so the guy went to the bar to retrieve the winnings, but the bartender told him that another guy had taken the money. Tempers flared between the winner and the guy who took the money. My brother tried to break it up and stepped in between the two guys.

"If you're going to shoot someone, shoot me," he said jokingly. My brother didn't think the guy would do it because they had gone to school together, yet before he could even move out of the way, a bullet blasted through his lower chest, just below his heart.

I was asleep at home, unaware of the tragic turn of events until, in the early morning hours, a police officer knocked on our door. As he explained to my mother what had happened, a piece of my heart turned cold. The familiar feeling of dread. Almost everyone I knew who had been shot had died . . . and I was sure the same fate awaited my brother.

We rushed into the hospital as they wheeled Frankie into surgery. My mother ran to the gurney. For a few seconds, Frankie came to and looked into our mother's eyes. He had been in a deep depression with thoughts of suicide for months, but seeing the concern in her eyes, he felt incredibly loved. That's when he decided he wanted to live.

The same surgeon who took care of our priest when he was shot the year prior was taking care of my brother. I don't know if it was my prayers, the priest's, or the amazing surgeon who didn't give up on him, but my brother pulled through. Never mind that the bullet ripped through his small intestine, pancreas, and spleen, and that he would stay in the hospital for more than a month, *he was alive.* Frankie was one of the fortunate ones.

In 1980, when I was twenty-one, my father's drug abuse hit its peak. Chicago winters were frigid, and heating his cluttered apartment was expensive. To battle the cold, he bundled himself in his parka. One night, he leaned over the range to light a cigarette from the stovetop burner, and his parka ignited in flames. He was so deeply burned that he required skin grafts and weeks in the burn unit.

I sat across from him on a hospital bed, looking at his bandaged, raw, red face. With tubes in his mouth and still attached to machines, he struggled to talk. As he reached for me, the image coming toward me was horrifying. He looked like a monster from *Night of the Living Dead*, a memory that would sear in my brain for years to come.

The following year, Grandma Mydlowski was diagnosed with pancreatic cancer. She fought the disease valiantly for months. My mother took a bus to the hospital every day after work just to be with her, returning home exhausted every night. When the doctors said there was nothing more they could do—that they would make her as comfortable as possible—my mother must have felt so helpless. She was going to lose her mother and there was nothing she could do, yet we never discussed her grief or fears. I never asked.

My grandmother lost her battle with cancer, passing away on Mother's Day in 1981. I only saw my mother cry twice, both times only briefly, and once again she did her best to remain strong for us. Even though she must have been heartbroken and lonely, she set about the work of settling our grandmother's affairs and finding us a new place to live. Somehow we all missed the strain that was being put on her.

Five months later, on October 17, my father died alone in his apartment. One day his heart just failed, which was no surprise to us. The years of drug abuse had finally caught up to him. He'd been dead for two days before someone stopped by, probably to score drugs. When he didn't answer the door, the visitor broke in and found his body, which was too decomposed for an open-casket funeral. I wanted to see him at the mortuary, but his friends discouraged me, saying my father wouldn't want me to see him like that.

Despite all these deaths, I did not yet understand what real grief was. I was about to find out.

A week before Christmas that year, my mother was having trouble breathing. She'd already had a heart attack two years before. This time, she was admitted to the hospital, where doctors got her breathing under control. Four days later, she was released, but the doctor advised her to rest and take it easy. Of course, my mother didn't know how to take it easy, but we weren't worried. She seemed fine. So when I ran out the door for work on Christmas Eve, I didn't remind her to be careful or see if she needed anything. I only asked if she would brush the cat's hair. It was the last thing I ever said to her.

Christmas Eve was our most important holiday. Normally, we'd put up a tree and decorate, but since we'd only been in our new apartment for three weeks, we agreed not to exchange gifts or put up decorations because the year had been too tumultuous. We planned a quiet family dinner instead: just my mother, brother, sister, her husband, and me. The true spirit of Christmas.

Unbeknownst to us, my mother had called a friend of hers that morning and told her she felt bad that there was no Christmas tree. Wanting so much to add some holiday cheer to our home, she dressed and walked eight blocks to the drugstore in the bitter cold and snow. There she picked out a festive tablecloth, which she thought would lend some color and Christmas spirit to our apartment. On the way back, she was only a half-block from our building when she collapsed in front of a funeral home.

My brother Bobby arrived home to a simple note taped to the door: "Your mother had a heart attack and fell over in the street. She's at the hospital."

A few minutes later I walked through the door as Bobby was hanging up the phone. I couldn't see his face, but something must have registered in my subconscious that the news on the other end of the line was dire.

I was barely inside before Bobby blurted out, "Come with me! Mom's in the hospital."

As Bobby and I sped through the city streets, I didn't think for a moment that anything bad would happen. It was Christmas Eve after all. The nurse led us to a private waiting room where a priest waited. I suppose I should have been prepared for the worst, but the thought of my mother dying never even crossed my mind.

"Your mother has had a heart attack," the nurse explained in a gentle voice. "Her vital signs are very low. The doctors are trying to revive her now. She's unconscious, but we're doing everything we can to save her."

I called my sister and brother-in-law, who rushed to the hospital to meet us. But despite the gravity of the situation and everything that had happened that terrible year, I still believed with all my heart that my mother would live. She was only fifty-four. Of course she would survive.

Two hours later, with the rest of the family gathered in the small room, the same nurse and a doctor returned. Very calmly and slowly, the doctor explained that my mother had died. I didn't hear anything after that. I just started crying uncontrollably. I was in shock.

"How could this happen? How could this happen?" I demanded. *Why? How?* My mind screamed, begged, cried out hysterically. *No, no, no!*

My brother Bobby punched his fist against the wall. I vaguely recall the nurse, now a faceless void in my hazy memory, asking me if I wanted a sedative.

"She doesn't need a sedative!" my brother-in-law, Terry, snapped at her.

Then the nurse asked if we wanted to see our mother. My siblings went, but I didn't. I couldn't. It was Christmas Eve. How could God take my mother from us on Christmas Eve? I thought I'd known pain, but this was a visceral ache deep within my soul; the shock and disbelief were beyond knowing. My entire world had shifted. I felt completely empty.

We left the hospital in a daze and returned home different people. We were orphans. Alone with our grief, we were unable to arrange our mother's funeral until after Christmas, and we didn't dare call friends to tell them because we didn't want to darken other people's festivities.

Our lives as we had known them were destroyed, and in our despair, my brother and I gathered all of the Christmas ornaments, decorations, and cards, and we destroyed them, too. Somehow seeing all of the brilliantly colored bulbs smashed and shattered into bits gave us an image to match our broken hearts.

I stripped the house—and my heart—of Christmas. My mother had died buying something festive, and I never wanted to celebrate that holiday again. Not only did I get rid of every ornament, but I discarded the entire notion of Christmas as well. From that day forward, Christmas celebrations ceased to exist for me. I would despise the holiday season, overwhelmed with a sense of depression and dread whenever it rolled around.

My heart was sealed. I was just a kid in many ways, and I still needed my mother. But she was gone. Irrevocably gone. The one person I loved most, the one person I needed most, and perhaps the only person I'd ever been able to count on. She was not going to be there for me ever again. She would not be there for my wedding, crying soft tears of joy in the background, someone with whom I could confide my fears and who would offer her strength. It was selfish to think these things, but I had no idea how I would move forward without her. I could do nothing but grieve, even opening one of her old jewelry boxes from time to time just so I could smell her.

My grief had many facets, but the one that cut the deepest was realizing that I had failed my mother, the one person who had always been there for me. Yes, I loved my father and I thought about him, too, but he had been leaving me in bits and pieces my entire life. My mother had seemed so indestructible. Now I understood how hard her own mother's death must have been on her. I wished that I had told her I loved her more often. My brother Frankie shared the same regrets. He said that our mother was there for him when he was dying, but he wasn't there for her. Our guilt was all-consuming. Our mother had always said that she lived for her children, and now I wondered if she had died for us as well.

My brother Bobby and I stayed in the apartment and nothing got easier. A few weeks after she died, I was carrying a load of laundry back home from the cleaners. As I set the laundry down in the hallway, I barely saw a shadow in the corner before the stranger lunged for my neck. We struggled and I screamed, my glasses flying to the floor. With the room a fuzzy blur, I groped around to find my glasses while the man grabbed my purse and ran. No one came to help me. Alone and frozen with fear, the memories of my attack as a teenager came flooding back into my mind. The police found my purse the following day, relieved of its contents. That was the end of my time in that apartment, even though it held memories of my mother. I was too afraid to live there anymore, so I found a new place in a safer neighborhood.

The months passed, and I went through the motions of having a life, but I was just existing. Because my heart had shut down from all the losses, I was emotionally numb for many, many years. As a result, I had two failed marriages. When I walked down the aisle each time, I still believed in a "happily ever after." I hoped that I'd have children of my own—start my own family traditions—but it never happened.

So I did what I had to do to survive emotionally. I became bitter, angry, negative, and depressed. Unable to bear any more heartache, I built walls and detached myself from people. Time marched on, but I stayed stuck, certain that life was precarious and unpredictable. I was convinced that bad things would always happen to me; it wasn't a matter of *if*, but *when*.

# Chapter 3

# Loss and Fear Interrupted

*"If you love something, let it go. If it comes back to you, it's yours. If it doesn't, it never was."*

—RICHARD BACH

The house was empty without Rina.

My heart ached to hear her nails clicking on the floor and her tail thumping in the shoe-lined corridor when I walked through the front door. Vowing to keep my promise to her, I left my healthcare job in the corporate world, and I enrolled in a service-dog training school. I'd spent hours poring over my options, finally deciding on an associate degree program that seemed to align with my philosophy on positive training methods. But there was a catch: The school was in California. If someone had told me that one day I'd just pack up and move to California for a four-month program, I would have said, "You're crazy." It just wasn't the sort of thing I did, the control freak that I was, but I was determined to keep my promise to Rina.

I found an apartment near the school, a quiet place with its own entrance above a family home. What made it especially appealing was the dog run on the side of the house. The training program required students to care for their service-dogs-in-training 24/7, so having access to a dog run was a bonus. The owner, Paul, helped me carry a few things from my car into my new home.

"So you're going to school," he said with an appraising look, seeming to note that I was a bit older than the usual coed.

"Yes, I'm getting my associate degree in service-dog training," I answered. "I just raised my first service-dog puppy."

"A puppy," he remarked. "What's her name?"

There was a moment's pause before I could even form the word. "Rina," I choked out.

"Isn't *that* something," he said. "The woman we bought this house from was named Rina. What a coincidence."

Rina was such a unique name, one I'd never heard in my life prior to caring for my Rina. I wondered if somehow Rina had something to do with the synchronicity of me finding this particular apartment out of all of the other possibilities.

"It's great that our dog run is going to be put to good use," Paul said, motioning toward the side yard.

There wasn't a lot of time to explore since school started right away. What I loved the most about working with the puppies was how they were like little sponges—clean slates, eager to learn, and always surprising me with what they were capable of doing. The more they learned, the more I pushed the envelope. I wondered what I could teach a puppy that no one else had taught at such a young age. My first success was teaching a puppy the complex task of turning on a light switch when it was only six weeks old. As far as I knew, no one at the school had taught that behavior to a pup so young.

One night when I returned from school, I noticed that I had a voice mail. I was only half-listening until I heard a woman say,

"Rina is being released from the program." The voice on the message gave a couple of reasons, but one term resounded through my mind: "assertive fear."

I stood still a moment, letting the weight of the message sink in. Then the tears came. I was smiling, then laughing—and all the while crying. Beautiful, wonderful tears. It was only later that the thought came to me: *assertive fear . . . had Rina, possibly . . . just maybe . . . growled?*

*Could I believe it? Rina was really coming back to me?* Puppy raisers get first dibs if the dogs they raised are released. *Yes! Rina was coming back to me!*

The next day, I called to find out exactly what had happened. The woman who answered the phone shuffled through papers as she read me a list of Rina's shortcomings in a voice that sounded like she was reading a bad report card.

"Assertive fear: She refuses to perform behaviors when she is uncertain. Avoidance assertiveness: She has resistance to following commands," the woman said.

"But what did she *do* exactly?" I asked.

"It looks like she refused to walk by a stationary vacuum cleaner even though it wasn't turned on," she answered. I heard more papers shuffle. "She refused to walk on an unsteady table and to step across a grate."

The woman paused and sighed. "In short, she just shut down."

It'd been one month since I'd dropped her off, thirty days that felt like an eternity.

"When can I pick her up?" I asked, trying not to laugh.

It was never my intention for Rina to fail the program, of course, and despite our differences in training philosophies, I would be forever grateful to this organization for the opportunity to raise a puppy and for gifting me with such an incredible dog.

I drove to the San Francisco airport to pick up Rina, my patience wearing thin in the crawling traffic. I kept imagining how our reunion would go. I could envision her entire body wagging and I could practically feel her tongue on my face and how soft her fur would be when I hugged her. As soon as we saw each other, I'd tell her that she was coming home to stay with me for good.

At the airport, I called into her crate, "Rina!" expecting her to explode with excitement and relief when she saw me.

But the dog inside didn't. Instead of wagging her tail and smiling with her wide Rina grin, she kept her head down and wouldn't meet my gaze. I was crushed. She seemed muddled, her face ashen. Over and over, I apologized for what she'd been through. I knew that during training they would do many things to intentionally stress a dog to see how it would cope in a service situation. And yet the dogs are already stressed from being in an unfamiliar environment, away from their caregivers. Some dogs do poorly under these circumstances, and it appeared that Rina was one of them.

She was not the dog I'd left at the kennel. She was not her normal self. As I walked her out of the airport, she balked when a tall man with shaggy hair passed us, then she slunk closer to me. She didn't trust people anymore, and I knew I had some work to do to get her back to feeling safe. Safety and trust are paramount for both animals and people, and traumatic events can invade our very souls. I knew what it felt like to have my trust completely shattered, and I would do my best to make sure Rina would feel safe once again.

A few days later, during a break from school, I took Rina to the beach to celebrate her homecoming. She'd always loved romping in the Chicago snow, and I was sure she'd adore the miles of shoreline, sand dunes, and crisp salt air even more.

Near the waves, I took off her leash and released her to run. I wanted her to know that she was free.

She paused, leery of someone walking in the distance, and belted out a few quick barks in that direction. Then I watched as she relaxed, and I squinted as she morphed into a bounding flash of yellow, bright against the steely overcast sky and its reflection in the waves. In the blink of an eye, she was sprinting down the shoreline chasing waves. I caught glimpses of the puppy she had been, as well as the best friend she would continue to be. Reaching down, I found a seashell, and I wrote her name in the sand. *Rina.* I wiped my eyes. I was still going to keep my promise to her, but now she and I could find a positive way to train service dogs together.

Linda, my healer, was right: Rina was my dog after all. And now she'd be living in a home that was once owned by a woman named Rina, and she would use Rina's dog run, aptly named just for her.

Once Rina came back to me, I relished our time together, especially our weekend expeditions. We traipsed along dusty river trails and walked through redwood forests, her nose sucking in and sneezing the aromas. We visited dog parks and we waded through the waves at the nearby beach. As I completed my degree, I taught

Rina everything I was teaching the other dogs. She was a fast learner and loved to work. To me, she was the perfect service dog.

At night we'd fall into bed exhausted, and I gladly gave up my legroom for her. One night I watched her sleeping, her body heaving in and out in a steady rhythm. She was doggie-dreaming, her legs twitching, eyes flitting, and her throat grumbling a muffled *grrff.* Was she running through the canyon? Wrestling with her best friend, Zoe? Whatever the inspiration, it was clearly a wonderful dream.

The next morning, as the sun beamed through the blinds, I awoke to see Rina sitting upright on the floor, her tail swishing side to side. As I sat up, her tail-swish became a drumming *thump, thump, thump.*

"Morning, Rina," I yawned. I couldn't believe it: I had actually slept through the night. Unlike the organization that released her, I appreciated her "assertive fear" because she would bark if anyone came near our home, and that gave me a much-needed feeling of security. My nightmares had abated just knowing that Rina was watching out for me while I slept.

My once-in-a-lifetime dog was finally home, bringing with her a sense of safety that I'd never known.

# Chapter 4

# The Birth:
# The Universe Delivers

*"There is no greater gift you can give or receive than
to honor your calling. It's why you were born.
And how you become most truly alive."*

—Oprah Winfrey

"Okay, Rina," I said, "we've got a lot of work to do today." From the way she cocked her head and smiled, it seemed she was already two steps ahead of me. We had the lavender, the ribbons, and the scale to weigh the puppies.

"Rina, look." She began to scan the room to see what I wanted her to retrieve. Her eyes came across a notebook on the coffee table.

"Yes," I coaxed, "get it." She walked over to the table and gripped it in her mouth.

"You're such a good helper. Bring it here." I could hear her nails, *click, click, click,* as I watched her carry it from the adjacent room into what was now our puppy nursery.

We were getting ready to welcome a litter of puppies into the world, and it would be any day now. Everything had to be perfect.

After earning my degree, I decided to stay in California. The warm weather was much better for my arthritis and I really didn't have anything tying me to Chicago anymore. Rina and I moved a bit farther south to San Diego so that I could volunteer as a trainer for the service-dog organization Paws'itive Teams, whose positive training philosophy was very similar to mine. While working with them, I put the finishing touches on my own nonprofit service-dog training organization, which I called Puppy Prodigies.

Firmly believing that every dog is exceptional and deserves the best chance, our mission was to help puppies achieve their full potential by focusing on their early weeks, which are crucial to their training success. The philosophy of Puppy Prodigies is that puppies begin learning the moment they are born. In fact, the puppy's first seven weeks are the critical window during which the greatest changes take place, physically and behaviorally. Research shows that in moderation, stress stimulates the brain at this most important time in its development. When a puppy is properly stimulated during this time, his brain matures faster and he will grow up to have a larger brain with more and bigger cells, and more interconnections between them. What's more, because the puppy's brain is still in such a formative state, the experiences it undergoes at this early age will have a tremendous impact on his mind. Early training, socialization, and positive experiences result in a well-balanced dog with a wonderful temperament.

I contend that if you bring puppies into this world, you are responsible and accountable for their entire lives. Sadly, many dogs are relinquished to shelters every day. My hope was that Puppy Prodigies could also help counterbalance the negative experiences of these shelter dogs and give them the best chance at adoption. But regardless of what kinds of dogs we would ultimately help or under what circumstances, I was excited when Puppy Prodigies received its nonprofit status in July 2007. We were official! Through

Paws'itive Teams, I connected with a program that offered me a
chance to whelp (help birth) and raise a litter of puppies. This
would be my first opportunity to raise a generation of dogs using
the Puppy Prodigies principles.

Josie, a beautiful, red-coated golden retriever, was the dam of
this litter. She was a sweet and quiet dog, and her dark coloring
was my favorite shade. She had a wonderful smile and loved to be
stroked, gently placing her front legs in my lap to crawl up, asking
for more attention, *please*. While I had helped whelp puppies at
school, this time I would be on my own. I had a wonderful team
of volunteers to help, but it would be my responsibility to make
sure mother and pups were healthy and safe, and that they received
the best possible care.

One night I lay down next to Josie and put my hand to her
belly, soaking up the miracle of the tiny movements inside of her.
All night long, the puppies kicked and moved. Carefully resting
a prenatal baby monitor up to her abdomen, I listened in awe to
the prominent beating of ten small hearts. Just weeks earlier, an
ultrasound showed ten tiny spinal cords. I couldn't resist resting
my hand against Josie's soft fur to feel the amazing thing that was
happening inside of her . . . the miracle of so many new lives—so
many possibilities to make a difference.

One thing was certain: I would keep a girl for the Puppy Prodigies program. I envisioned this little puppy growing up to become
a service dog and being matched to a person with a disability when
she neared her second birthday. While I knew Josie would have
a large brood, I wondered how many boys versus girls there'd be
in the litter, and I pondered what "my" puppy would be like—the
puppy I would shape for a meaningful life as a service dog.

On January 25, 2008, Josie began to show signs of labor. Her abdomen was hard and the contractions rippled through her. She was resting in a whelping box, a low-sided structure that kept her contained but gave us both room to move about. As she lay comfortably on layers of bedding, I gathered towels and other supplies so we had them close at hand. My friend Charli from Paws'itive Teams came to help with the delivery, and from looking at her, it was obvious that she took her assignment most seriously.

"I'm your midwife," she stated with intensity as she stood before me, wearing a bandana decorated with brightly colored paw prints in honor of the occasion. She was ready to assume her nurse's duties, which involved catching and cuddling the first puppy.

With my trusted assistant by my side, I put on soothing music, a CD called *Protected by Angels* by Stephen Rhodes, which was not only relaxing for me but I hoped for Josie as well. The mellifluous harmonies resonated with sounds of serenity, enveloping the room with a feeling of protection and love, which is what I hoped to evoke during the births. I wanted to create a cocoon of safety—a perfectly peaceful atmosphere for the new lives we were ushering into the world.

But Josie was on her own time schedule and didn't bother to tell us exactly when her first puppy would appear. While we watched her like a pot, she just wouldn't boil. We'd been waiting for what seemed like hours, restless, and, quite honestly, a little bored. I fixed my attention on the computer while Charli took a restroom break. But when I turned around to glance into the whelping box, I gasped and yelled for Charli.

"There's a puppy!" I called, and then laughed at Charli's frustration that we had somehow managed to completely miss the first birth. So much for our planning! The tiny puppy was slippery, wet, and dark brown from the protective membrane sack. It looked like a little sausage with itty-bitty legs.

A few minutes later, Charli was brave enough to whelp her first puppy while I talked her through the process. She gathered up the tiny body and held it up to Josie.

"What do I do? What does she do?" Charli asked.

"Let Josie lick the umbilical cord and sever it," I coached her.

Charli held up the puppy and Josie cleaned it, licking it gently and then biting through the cord.

"Make sure she doesn't eat the placenta," I warned.

"But she wants to!" Charli said, turning to Josie. "No, sweetie, you can't do that," Charli warned with a more serious tone that matched her expression. "I'm scared," she admitted, her attention focused on the tiny body in her hands. "I don't think it's alive."

I told her to put her finger in the puppy's mouth, assuring her that if the puppy was sucking, it was okay. Charli's worry rose when she realized it wasn't sucking, but just then we noticed that the puppy was moving and we both exhaled sighs of relief.

"Here, rub the puppy with the towel until it squeaks," I instructed, watching Charli gently stroke the pup with a towel, as if she were holding something very delicate and precious. And she was.

"Try to do it briskly," I said, hoping she didn't feel overwhelmed. "You have to make the puppy squeak."

Still nervous about whether she was doing it right, Charli rubbed harder. Suddenly the puppy gave one long squeal, announcing its entry into the world. Charli looked up from the pup with amazed eyes and a big, proud smile.

I've never witnessed a human birth, but I can tell you there is something infinitely wonderful about a new tiny life and watching anxiously as you will the palm-sized body to take its first breath. The world stops for a moment as you feel life begin in the palm of your hand.

I think many of us believe we have to go to cathedrals or sacred sites to feel holiness, to feel the magic of a moment. But when we open our hearts, there is magic in every moment. If I wasn't consciously thinking these thoughts—because at the time I was only aware of wanting ten healthy births and perhaps a few girls—I know some part of me felt it.

Josie delivered three girls and five boys without any complications. After each delivery, Charli or I would dip the puppy's umbilical cord in iodine and tie it off with thread to avoid infection. We'd then weigh each puppy and document the time of birth. After that, we'd tie a different colored ribbon around each tiny neck, which enabled me to identify the puppies as I weighed them and made notes about their physicality and behaviors. Their ribbon colors would also be their names for the first eight weeks: Purple, Pink, Black, Teal, Tan, Blue, Green, Orange, Yellow, and Red.

As the puppies made their way into the world, they seemed at once so fragile and tiny, so tender and vulnerable, yet at the same time feisty and full of vigor. Their eyes were tightly shut and their pink noses seemed huge in proportion to their squished brown faces. When each membrane sac was removed, their little legs moved back and forth. I loved each one, but had no time to stop and bond with them. We had work to do. A misstep could mean a tragedy. Then suddenly, all around, I heard another type of background music—the music of tiny puppies crying . . . and it was music to my ears.

Sweet, beautiful Josie was such a wonderful mother. If either Charli or I held a puppy away from her for too long, she'd look up at us with her panting, tired smile and anxious eyes.

"You worried, sweetie?" I murmured gently, lowering a little boy puppy back down for her to lick. I knew she was getting tired as her sides heaved with each labored breath in and out.

After delivering puppies for three and a half hours, I saw that Josie's kind face was crumpled with exhaustion and her eyes had a faraway gaze. She only had two more puppies to deliver, and I crooned soft words of encouragement to her. Although I hoped she'd add two more girls to the litter, more than anything else, I just wanted the puppies to be healthy and for all of us to finally get some rest. I wasn't really thinking about what I said to her, but I kept talking to keep her engaged. Taking her muzzle in my hands, I gazed into her weary eyes. Suddenly an image of a puppy with a white marking on her chest flashed in my mind.

"Make the next one a girl, Josie," I said, "a girl with a white patch of fur on her chest."

Minutes later, at 10:07 PM, Josie lurched with another contraction. I reached down to catch the puppy. The newborn slid into my hands, warm and still cosseted in its membrane sac. I pinched open the protective sheath to allow the puppy to breathe, and I held its head up to help drain the fluid from the puppy's airways. A faint puff tickled my fingertips—its first breath of life. I felt incredibly blessed.

Slipping the tip of my pinky into the puppy's mouth to ensure it would suckle, I felt the miniature mouth tug against it.

"What are you?" I whispered, as my eyes traveled past its belly button. "You're a girl! You're a girl!" I marveled, hearing the joy in my own voice. As I rubbed her with a towel to stimulate her lungs, I said softly to myself, "A girl. *A girl.*"

She began to squirm and talk, speaking to me in babbles and gurgles, a language unique to puppies.

"She sure has a lot to say!" I laughed. I had no idea what she was trying to convey to me, but it didn't matter. She had captured my full attention, as well as my heart. As I look back now, I'm sure she was speaking directly to me. In fact, she would have much more to tell me when I finally decided to listen.

As I gazed upon the miracle of this perfect little being, I glanced at her chest and felt my breath catch. My jaw dropped in disbelief. It didn't seem possible, but there it was—a discernible white patch of fur, right in the middle of her chest.

"Oh my gosh. She has a white patch on her chest!" I said, holding the little puppy out for Charli to see.

Charli's jaw dropped, too, mirroring my own.

"Look at that!" she said, equally excited by the surprise. She moved in to take a closer look. "It kind of looks like a butterfly," she mused.

In that miraculous moment it seemed unmistakable: This puppy was meant for me. I had asked for her and she had appeared as requested. A cosmic custom order. Some may consider it coincidence; however, it was anything but. I was awestruck to have witnessed or maybe even to have willed such a miracle. The beautiful little puppy with the white mark had announced herself with a flourish of serendipity, and as I cuddled her in my hands, I had no idea that her momentous birth was just a hint of the synchronicity that was yet to come.

I tied a yellow ribbon around her tiny neck. For the puppy who came into the world in the most profound manner, the world was just beginning, a future replete with possibilities. And although the internal battle I fought for three decades was still smoldering, a new world was beginning for me, too.

# Chapter 5

## Que Será, Será

*"What's meant to be will always find a way."*

—TRISHA YEARWOOD

After four hours, Josie had given birth to six boys and four girls—ten wiggling, nursing, squirming, beautiful little puppies. This was the closest I'd ever get to having children, and I was thrilled to have witnessed the miracle of life.

Relieved to know all of the puppies were healthy, I began thinking about the significance of the dark-red puppy with the white mark on her chest. I had asked for such a puppy, and that's what was given to me. I wondered if somehow she was destined for me. Of course, whichever puppy I chose would need a name. Since I didn't know where this puppy would be going after her two years of training, I thought the name *Que Será, Será* would be a fitting one, meaning "whatever will be, will be."

Josie was a dedicated mother who didn't like to leave her puppies for a moment, and she watched them around the clock. However, the first night of puppy music kept both Josie and me from a good night's sleep. Thankfully, a trip to the vet the next day confirmed that Josie and the pups were fine, but the vet gave her a shot of oxytocin to stimulate more milk flow and to pass any retained placentas. That night, we all slept soundly.

Two days after the birth, life around the house began to return to the new normal. Quiet music, low lights, and the scent of lavender filled the puppy nursery.

It amazed me that each of the little puppies had already started displaying unique characteristics, and I could differentiate certain things about them at such a young age. Yellow, with her white patch of fur, was the darkest red of all the puppies, and her glistening coat was as smooth as silk. She was quiet and laid-back—so relaxed, in fact, that she sometimes nursed upside down! But she was also submissive: She'd try to get a nipple, but if she couldn't, she'd give up, unlike some of her other littermates who'd attach and refuse to let go. I reasoned that maybe Yellow was just being magnanimous—a portent of the altruistic dog she'd grow into.

Yellow proved to be very smart, and she and I bonded quickly. I'd often find her lying in a way that allowed her full tummy to be off the floor. "What'cha doing?" I'd kid her as she'd squirm her way to the raised bar of the whelping box, looking like a fat, little seal. Sometimes she'd crawl onto a stuffed animal to relieve the pressure of her full belly. She loved to be petted and responded like she was ticklish, kicking her legs back and forth when I petted a certain spot. But I noticed that she'd sometimes lie in the whelping box by herself, not cuddling with her littermates as much as some of the others did.

Because I was spending all of my energy on the puppies, Rina's routine was severely interrupted. During the puppies' birth, Rina stood silently by. Josie wouldn't let her near her babies, and to honor Josie's protection of the pups, I kept Rina out of the room.

Yet it was hard for me to exclude her because she was a part of everything in my life, but on some level I'm sure Rina understood all that was happening. She accepted that her role was to stand by quietly. I'd set up a baby gate at the doorway to the room and she would lie or stand right there, peeking inside. Josie couldn't see her but I could. And as I looked into her questioning eyes I could feel her asking, "What's that?" Pangs of guilt gnawed at me. I needed to spend time with this new little family, but Rina was my family, too. After all, we were going to be in this together. I hoped Josie would grow more tolerant in the days that followed because, not only did I miss having Rina involved, I knew she would have enjoyed helping to retrieve some of the puppy items I needed. But more than anything, I just wanted Rina to be a part of it all.

I had a growing feeling I'd be keeping Yellow to continue training in the Puppy Prodigies program. I was sure this serendipitous gift from the universe would not only meet my expectations but exceed them. She would be the perfect service dog and would complement our small family nicely for the next couple of years. Therefore, I became determined to foster a relationship between Rina and Yellow. I started by placing a towel in Rina's bed each night, and the next morning, I'd place the same towel in the whelping box so that Yellow could imprint on Rina's scent. After a couple of days, when Josie was out of the room, I brought Yellow to Rina and let her sniff her.

At first, Rina wouldn't make eye contact. Her ears were back, and she walked away. *Was she afraid of the little thing that was almost, but not quite, like a dog?* I realized her apprehension probably came from me not allowing her in the room; now she associated the puppy with something hazardous. It appeared I had some work to do in fostering their bond.

At thirteen days, the puppies were beginning to look more like dogs than aliens from Planet Sausage. While their eyes had started to open, they couldn't actually see or focus yet, so they were solely dependent on Josie and me to help them navigate their world.

I bottle-fed the pups, even as Josie nursed, just as another way to bond with them. I shouldn't have been surprised to find that Yellow was the only one who figured out bottle-feeding the first time. I wanted the puppies to associate people with something positive, like food, so I used drops of goat's milk on my fingers to imprint them on me.

Since I had done so much research on puppy brain development, I was eager to see what Yellow was capable of at this early age. Placing an orange bath towel on the floor, I set a small bowl of goat's milk on it and started the video recorder. I scooped Yellow from the whelping box and placed her on the towel. Even though her ears weren't open yet and she couldn't hear, I spoke to her the entire time. I dipped my finger into the goat's milk and put it in front of her mouth. Catching the scent of a familiar smell, she didn't hesitate to latch on to my finger. As she slurped the milk, I started moving my finger very slowly to see if she could follow my finger with the lure of the milk.

Could she ever! I had to keep dipping my finger in the milk because she was devouring it faster than I could replenish! She was urging her little body to move itself in the direction of the milk, not wanting to miss a drop.

As she took a couple of wobbly steps forward, I tried to lead her in a circle. Very slowly, very patiently, and very determinedly she moved herself around. With her tiny nails on her baby paws catching traction on the towel, her belly was still flat on the towel, so she looked like a sea lion in an amusement park, working for a fish. This pup was clearly food-motivated already, and I was certain she'd be a great student.

Smiling at her, I asked, "Do you want to try to drink this?"

I put the bowl of goat's milk up to her mouth so she could catch the scent. I never expected her to take a drink, but to my surprise, she dunked her face into the milk and began taking big slurps, lapping it up with vigor. *No more sucking now!* A big white mustache dripped from her face.

"Look at you!" I said in disbelief, as puppies don't typically start lapping until they're three weeks old.

She had quite the appetite, diving farther into the bowl.

"Oh my goodness, you just put your whole face in there!" I laughed at little Yellow. Moving the bowl away, I dabbed more milk on my fingers. Now she was really following them and latching on. She was actually sucking my fingers into her mouth!

"There go my fingers!" I couldn't help but giggle as I felt her soft gums. She dunked her head in the bowl and slurped, and then I lured her around in a circle again. This time, she rotated around much more quickly. Yellow was proving that puppies begin learning right away.

Free-spirited and confident, Yellow splashed the milk everywhere, dousing her legs and face. Once she licked all of the milk off her legs, she pressed her nose to the towel, seeking out the scent of milk. I dipped my finger back into the bowl and lured her in the other direction. She obliged quite skillfully for her third try. I ended the session by petting her back with two long strokes.

"Good job, puppy," I told her, and she responded by lifting herself onto all four legs. She could feel the vibration of my fingers tapping and went toward them in a waddling motion. Then all of a sudden, she rolled over and softly fell on her side like a piglet rolling in the mud. She had aced her first training session at just thirteen days old!

Later that night, I brought her to my bedroom to watch television with Rina and me—another good bonding exercise. But when I put Yellow on the covers, Rina fled from the bed; it seemed she was still quite uncertain about this undeveloped version of a dog! With our trio minus one, I sat back with Yellow, who lay quietly on my chest, breathing in unison with me.

On the seventeenth day, I upgraded the goat's milk to beef-flavored baby food, and Yellow absolutely loved it. She was now able to recognize me when I walked into the puppy room and she'd rush toward the door of the whelping box to greet me. Seeing this little body trying to be a big dog was so darn cute!

By this time, Josie allowed Rina to come into the room, which made life much easier for all of us. While Rina liked to watch me work with the puppies, when Josie nursed, it seemed to perplex Rina, as if she might be thinking that the puppies were aliens sucking the life out of Josie. I could almost hear Rina saying, "Run, Josie, run!"

Josie would sometimes stand while she nursed, teaching her puppies the valuable lesson of working for rewards. The uncoordinated pups had to reach up and stand on their back legs, which was quite a challenge. Many of them would miss the mark and topple over. Yet on the nineteenth day as I watched them nurse, I was startled by a coughing sound, and looked to see milk spewing from Red's nose. Knowing she was a voracious eater, I assumed she had just gotten overzealous. Even so, I watched her closely for the rest of the day. She seemed fine, but when evening approached, I was dismayed when she began to wheeze. Rushing her to the emergency vet, I held her close as we waited in the sterile room, and she wiggled her way up to my neck for warmth and security. I talked to her the entire time, trying to soothe her. "Hey, little one, you're going to be okay."

The vet tech took x-rays, which revealed fluid in the right middle lobe of Red's lung. Apparently, she had aspirated milk into her lungs and had developed pneumonia. The doctor treated her with an injection of antibiotics and said I could take her home with specific instructions for her care. Red and I were up three times in a steamy bathroom as instructed, and she had two private nursing sessions with Josie. Her appetite was still strong, which was a good sign.

Thankfully, by morning she was doing better. Her breathing was no longer raspy and she was playing with the other puppies. Josie wasn't spending as much time in the whelping box anymore, so when she arrived on the scene, the pups launched into their normal canine frenzy, trying to get to her for what they must have thought would be their last meal.

Being an aggressive eater, Red was on a nipple almost immediately. Because all ten pups were competing for eight nipples, I had to alternate them to ensure they all got enough to eat. My sense of calm turned to dread when I pulled Red off the nipple and saw milk pouring out of her nose and mouth again. But this time, it was even more than before, shooting out onto her face, my hands, and the floor!

I wrapped her in a blanket, put her in a small crate, and rushed her out to my car once again. By the time I got to the vet, she was shaking uncontrollably. As we sat again waiting for a doctor, I snuggled her close to my chest, doing my best to give her the comfort she so desperately needed. Feeling the vulnerability of her tiny body, I spoke to her softly, promising her I would do everything I could to help her.

When the doctor arrived, he took her temperature and palpated her lungs. From his grave expression and the way he shook his head, I knew the news wasn't good. He told me he could feel fluid in Red's lungs. She was in serious condition and needed to stay in the hospital over the weekend. He estimated the cost to be around a thousand dollars.

"That's fine," I said, not knowing where I'd get a thousand dollars, only knowing what I had to do. I couldn't *not* help her. Then the doctor gave me the next blow: He told me Red had a 50/50 chance of survival. Those odds were not high enough for me.

I couldn't let Red die. I'd suffered too many losses in my life, and Red couldn't be another one. I would do everything I could to save her little life. I drove home, picked up a blanket from the whelping box, and returned to the vet's office. I wanted Red to have something familiar in the incubator with her when she became aware of her environment, which is usually around twenty-one days. As I placed the blanket down next to her I whispered, "Fight for your life, Red. I know you can do it." I left the hospital hoping she would fight this illness as hard as she fought for her food.

Back at home and consumed with worry, I thought about how I felt holding her shivering body against my chest at the vet's office, about her in the incubator at the hospital, and about how these days and nights would be some of her earliest memories. Poor Red would become aware all alone in an incubator, without her mom or littermates. This wasn't the peaceful start I had planned, and I felt desperate to help, yet there was nothing I could do. I called the hospital every day to check up on her, and it was touch-and-go.

"She has a heart murmur," the doctor explained to me over the phone on the third day. "It's unrelated to the aspiration. I expect it will go away as she grows."

*As she grows.* Did that mean she would make it, or was I reading too much into the doctor's words?

Then, after four long days and nights, I breathed a huge sigh of relief when I got clearance to bring her home. Reunited with her mother and littermates, she made a beeline to a nipple. I was overjoyed; Red was going to be just fine.

Because I had comforted Red and she fought hard to live, I felt a newfound connection to her. This intense bonding experience planted a seed of doubt in my mind over my decision to keep Yellow, and I found myself comparing the two puppies as the weeks passed, wondering which one of them would be the better choice.

At three weeks old, the puppies' eyes and ears were open, and their teeth were breaking through the gums. They'd all found their voices and I loved hearing the symphony of their combined puppy barks. Their new favorite pastime was jumping on one another, tumbling and wrestling like big dogs.

On one occasion, I placed my friend's crated cat into the whelping box to socialize the puppies to cats. Yellow seemed to be the most interested and actually fell asleep in front of the crate. When the cat wasn't physically in the whelping box, a pillowcase the cat had slept on took its place. Among all of the puppies, it was Yellow who chose to curl up on the cat-scented cloth.

At four weeks, the puppies were too big for the whelping box, so I moved them to a puppy pen in the living room. Since their eyes and ears were completely open now, they were becoming more aware of their surroundings, and they were much more active. They were ready to graduate to the puppy playground in the backyard. To motivate them to explore this land of the unknown, I put their food bowl right outside the door. Opening the puppy pen gate, I watched to see who would venture out first.

Yellow it was! She was definitely the boldest and most adventurous of the litter, always eager to explore. She had already tried to get out of the whelping box, interested in whatever the world had to offer. One day I took her out of the puppy pen and let her walk in the living room where Rina was lying. Despite the slick hardwood floor, she took off, undeterred and unafraid of being away from the security of her littermates. She stayed awake for about ten to fifteen minutes, playing with full-out enthusiasm, and then slept for a couple of hours, only to repeat the sequence.

I taught the puppies that the only way they could be picked up from the puppy pen was to sit. Yellow caught on quickly, showing her intelligence even at this early age. Whenever I approached, as if on cue, I'd hear her crying to get out. I'd look over and she would sit very nicely. I couldn't resist picking her up for some cuddle time while I watched television. But she had other ideas. I'd lay her on my

Rina, 8 weeks.

Rina in the snow.

Rina before she left for advanced training.

Rina with some of her shoe collection.

Rina at Dillon Beach after she came back to me.

©Barbara McKown

Ricochet,
one week old.

©Barbara McKown

Ricochet,
15 days old.

Ricochet, early training.

Early training, flipping a light switch on.

Ricochet at the beach.

Ricochet, 8 weeks old, first time on a boogie board.

Jessica Hecock

chest, but after a few seconds, she would climb down and waddle over to Josie so she could be treated to a private nursing session. She knew I was her ticket out of the pen! She was using me to get what she wanted. What a brain this little pup was developing.

While she was very high energy and playful, she could also be very mellow at times, resting calmly to recharge her batteries before scurrying through the play equipment. She loved all of the equipment, scampering through the yard to explore every inch of it. With her adventurous spirit, Yellow was definitely my kind of girl. Ripping up paper with her little paws and budding teeth was, by far, one of her favorite activities.

Yet even with my growing love and appreciation for Yellow, I was still drawn to Red as well because we'd bonded during her ordeal. Unlike Yellow, Red was very affectionate and loving. Whenever I'd take her out of the pen, she loved to just lie on my chest, content to stay there and cuddle, enjoying the quiet time instead of using the one-on-one time to sneak down and get a snack from her mom. It was becoming easier to envision myself keeping her instead of Yellow.

When the puppies turned six weeks old, much of their day was spent outside in the puppy playground, a veritable treasure trove of enrichment toys and equipment. The puppies had no choice but to climb over, go under, or jump through. This prepared them for the real world by exposing them to novelty so they wouldn't fear it in the future. At this point, their distinct personalities were evident.

Once again, Yellow was the most confident pup in the litter. She was very agile, independent, and curious about moving objects, unsteady platforms, challenging walkways, uneven surfaces, and anything else she could find. She enjoyed investigating the hose, playing with bubbles, and, of course, nipping at her littermates. A quick problem-solver, she liked to interact with people. But rather than retrieving an object for someone, she would run off with it! She was, by far, the most energetic of all the pups. But at times I wondered if perhaps she had too much energy for her own good—and mine.

Her favorite toy was a "giggle 'n rock" ball, a ball with knobs on several sides that bounced around. When it stopped bouncing it emitted a giggle sound. As Yellow tried to grab the ball with her mouth, her entire head would vibrate. Then she'd bark and it sounded like she was vibrating under water. It was quite the sight to watch her charging at the ball, barking and attacking it.

Red, on the other hand, had a more relaxed way about her. She was curious, too, but moved more slowly among the obstacles. Red tended to steal people's hearts with her sweet, gentle demeanor, preferring to cuddle up with and kiss the kids who visited the puppy yard over playing with toys. Red's temperament reminded me so much of Rina's, and I felt the tug of love and familiarity. I knew that Red would grow to be a very special puppy. She had to fight for her life, and I truly think that makes a difference.

I began rotating the one-on-one time I spent with the two puppies for the next two weeks. Each night, I'd invite either Red or Yellow onto the bed with Rina and me to watch TV. Yellow refused to sit still and would always try to steal Rina's toy. Red, however, was content to hang out with us on the bed, and Rina even initiated play with her. Rina clearly liked Red better than Yellow.

What's more, as the pups grew, Red's even temperament, mild manners, and calm demeanor in the face of various stimuli seemed much better suited for service-dog work than Yellow's. While Red's traits met all of the criteria, she couldn't be placed as a service dog with her heart murmur. But since I'd grown so fond of her, there was nothing against me keeping Red for myself.

By the forty-ninth day, a puppy's brain has finished develop-ing, making the puppy neurologically complete with the brain of an adult dog. At this point, a temperament test can be helpful in assessing certain qualities, skills, or characteristics. Temperament can be described as the dog's outlook on life. Temperament is both inherited and innate, but environment plays a significant role as well. Like any test, a puppy temperament test isn't absolutely comprehensive, but it can reveal particular qualities, skills, or char-acteristics at one point in time. The test is typically performed by a stranger in a strange room. That way, the puppies are away from what's familiar, and their behavior can present itself without the comfort of their littermates, their mother, or their human family. But the results confirmed what I already knew: all of the puppies, including Red and Yellow, had desirable traits.

It was time for me to make a decision once and for all. The rest of the puppies were spoken for—some would go on to become trained as therapy dogs and others would go to loving homes, including Red, who had a potential home in San Diego if I decided not to keep her.

Since I had successfully used an animal communicator in Rina's situation, I decided to set up a conference call with Asia Voight, another well-respected animal communicator. Input from Rina, Yellow, and Red would help me decide which pup to keep. While some people might balk at the idea of animal communicators, this was an important decision and I wanted to remain open-minded to all options. I hadn't told Asia any of the details of Yellow's birth, so she knew nothing on her own.

"Okay," she agreed. "Let's see what they have to say. . . . Red says that the two of you have a close connection because you are both survivors."

Since I hadn't told Asia about Red's brush with death, I felt a tingle travel up my spine. Asia continued, "She may not be the smartest of the puppies, but she is definitely the sweetest. She says Yellow has dibs on you."

Next, Asia turned her attention to Rina. "Which puppy would you like to live with, Rina?"

I could almost hear Asia smiling on the other end of the phone when she conveyed the answer: "She says she likes Red best, but she likes Yellow best for you."

Of course Rina would be thinking of me.

"She is showing me images of a very busy mind," Asia continued. "Yellow never stops thinking. It freaks Rina out. That's why she runs away from her." Then Asia laughed. "Rina says she sometimes tells Yellow to be quiet. She tells her that she knows too much."

Yellow was the last to weigh in on the matter. After a brief pause to connect with the yellow puppy, Asia said, "Yellow would be sad if she didn't stay with you—but she doesn't want to be a pet dog." I was moved by that, but it was what Asia revealed at the end that gave me goose bumps and left me with a strange sense of wonderment: "Yellow tells me that she was predestined for you."

Predestined. For. Me.

I hung up the phone in awe, slowly digesting what Asia had said. Perhaps I'd known it all along, but there it was, plain as day. Yellow, Red, and Rina . . . these beloved dogs were telling *me*. And yet, if I was going to keep the yellow-ribboned puppy, I couldn't go on calling her Yellow. She needed a proper name. That evening I called my sister, Maria, to help me decide.

"What name feels right in your heart?" Maria asked.

"I don't know. I've just been calling her Yellow. I've still been thinking about calling her *Que Será, Será* . . ."

"Probably in light of not knowing what her future will be," Maria agreed. "Sometimes the universe provides in different ways, and it's not always what we think it should be but something even better."

"Yes," I said, pausing to think. "And she could be *Será* for short."

We bandied about a few options—Chance, Destiny, and Karma—yet none of the names seemed quite right. But as I stood in the puppy yard with my cell phone in hand, a whirling ball of red flashed past me. Yellow had bounded into the play area and jumped into the kiddie pool. There wasn't any water in it, but she literally leaped in with all four paws off the ground, a wild, whirly dervish of a dog—pure energy in motion.

"Crazy puppy! She bounces off the walls. It's like she's ricocheting around the play yard. . ." I paused, as the brilliance dawned on me. "*Ric-o-chet-ing*! That's it!"

And then and there, despite my grand plans to give her a cosmically meaningful name, at seven weeks old, she named herself. The name stuck. While it would be some time before I realized how truly appropriate her name was, for now she was like a ricochet, the energy that rebounds through a room and changes the course of everything.

I am convinced that animals come into our lives for specific reasons, and I hold true to the notion that they are much wiser than we are. So I decided to listen to the musings of three incredibly wise beings: Rina, Ricochet, and Red. More than anything, though, I went with my heart. I knew there was a reason Ricochet came into the world the way she did. I was certain the universe meant for us to be together. I had no idea what our future would hold and decided whatever will be, will be: *Que Será, Será.*

Ricochet was staying with me.

# Chapter 6

# Expectations:
# Control Creates Separation

*"We must be willing to get rid of the life we've planned,
so as to have the life that is waiting for us."*

—JOSEPH CAMPBELL

"Good girl, Ricochet," I said, patting her head as she wiggled excitedly toward me to retrieve her reward. I had never seen a dog so motivated, so focused, and so eager to please.

"Give," I'd cue, and her jaw would immediately release the wooden block into my hand. "Light," I'd say, and she'd tap the black knob on the wall with her nose. Then I'd praise her in my most excited cheerleader voice: "Excellent, Ric!"

I always ended our training sessions on a high note with a reward and a tummy rub. While stroking the soft and silky white fur on Ricochet's chest, I'd often think about how interconnected our lives had become these past few weeks. Since placing all of the other puppies in wonderful homes, all of my time was free to devote to Ricochet and Rina, and the three of us settled back into a less chaotic lifestyle.

One day, while running an errand, I left Ricochet in her puppy exercise pen to give her room to move around while keeping her safely contained. I'd been gone for only about a half-hour, but when I got back, the pen was empty. Suddenly, Ricochet bounded out from the bedroom where, thankfully, it seemed she hadn't gotten into any trouble. But I was curious to learn how she escaped from Pawcatraz.

I placed her back in the pen and then set up my video camera to record her while I stepped outside for a few minutes. The recording revealed that Miss Independent had spotted a toy outside of the pen and reasoned that the easiest way to retrieve it was to climb over the side. As I watched her scamper her little body up and over the gate, it dawned on me that I'd need to put a cover over the top of the pen from this point on. She was too smart for my own good.

Ricochet instantly grasped and excelled at every training challenge, bucking the conventional wisdom that you can't teach puppies complex tasks until they are at least six months old. I was excited by how quickly she learned to unzip clothing, retrieve laundry, pull a sock off of a person's foot, and open cabinets, among a dozen other behaviors—all at just eight weeks.

Ricochet proved intelligent beyond my wildest dreams. She was progressing through my neatly constructed service-dog plan with the infectious enthusiasm of a thriving puppy and a willing student, always eagerly awaiting the next learning adventure.

"Tug, Ricochet!" I cheered, pointing to the pink braided rope hanging from our fridge handle. Ricochet wiggled around in a circle, barking excitedly at Rina.

"Rina, show her how!"

Faithful, reliable Rina—three times Ricochet's size and fluffier in her full coat—dutifully walked by her little sister, grabbed the rope with her muzzle, and yanked, pulling the door open. *See, that's how it's done.*

"Good job, Rina. Now you try it, Ricochet!" She inched closer. "Come on! Tug!"

Ricochet grabbed the rope in her mouth, her little body wiggling with all the strength she could muster to open the door. Rina dashed to help her, and then the two dogs did something I could not have choreographed if I tried: they both grabbed the rope with their mouths, and backed up in unison, pulling the door open in complete canine camaraderie.

"Yes! You two girls are tugging!"

These were the moments that made training so rewarding, and I shook my head, still clapping and marveling at how the two dogs had worked together. Ricochet's swishing tail showed me she had this behavior down. With Ricochet, it often only took one time, and she would commit any behavior to memory. Sometimes it seemed as if she was reading my mind and knew what I was going to ask her.

"Ah-choo!" I'd pretend to expel a great sneeze, and at just eleven weeks old, Ricochet had learned to retrieve a tissue in a single training session. Even as I lowered the intensity of the mock sneeze to a mere whisper, she got the cue.

One day, when I exploded in an actual sneezing fit, Ricochet came running with the entire tissue box in her mouth, dropping it and pulling out tissue after tissue. "Thank you, Ric," I cooed, patting her silky smooth head.

Basking in the attention, she crinkled her eyes and wagged her tail enthusiastically.

"You are such a good girl, Ricochet. You are going to do great things, you know it?"

Once Ricochet had learned basic behaviors, we would continue to hone them so that she would be solid in all situations. A well-trained service dog doesn't waver in her task no matter the surroundings, noise, confusion, or chaos. There was still plenty to perfect by adding distractions, duration, and different environments, but with her natural aptitude, I was confident she would carry out her service duties regardless of the occasion.

In addition to her quick mind, Ricochet had an uncanny sense of balance. She loved to climb into our kiddie pool, so one day I invited her to get on a boogie board, not expecting much. But, true to her nature, Ricochet surprised me. She climbed onto the board and balanced like a pro, her eyes bright and curious. Luring her with dog-training treats, I enticed her to turn all the way around while balancing on the unsteady board. Even with four legs, the confidence and focus required to do a complete 360 on a floating board was more than impressive. She truly was a prodigy.

From my experience, I am certain that dogs know far more than we'll ever know they know. However, I had never seen a puppy learn as quickly as Ricochet. She was performing additional behaviors, including Hit It, High-Five, Hold, Retrieve, and Speak. As if her big sister's obsession had rubbed off on her, Ricochet found shoes irresistible, and I could no longer leave them lined up by the door. So many toys, yet shoes and newspaper were still the number-one playthings! When supervised, she also enjoyed watching a modern marvel of motion: the toilet flushing, which provided lots of free entertainment.

I worked on exposing her to everything and anything. Every day was a new adventure. I wanted Ricochet to meet all kinds of people and to be comfortable around wheelchairs, crutches, and anything else she may encounter as a service dog. She was doing very well, but sometimes her boldness got the better of her. One day we were at a barbecue by a boat launch. Rina and Ricochet were swimming in the water when a woman paddled by them in a kayak. Unflappable and curious, Ricochet saw this novel thing in the water, and rather than avoid it, she put one paw up on it, then the next ... then all four! In an incredible display of balance, she walked across the kayak and right into the woman's lap, where she proceeded to sit as comfortably as can be. The woman was a good sport about the antics of her uninvited copilot, and we all enjoyed a good laugh.

With Ricochet's keen sense of balance on the kayak, and her eagerness to crawl on the boogie board in the kiddie pool, I decided to try her out on a surfboard, curious to see if she'd get on it. One day, I brought her to Fiesta Island, a dog-friendly beach with gentle waves from the speedboats just off the shore. Ricochet and I waded ankle deep into the chilly water while Rina happily nosed through seaweed and explored her surroundings. As I steadied the board, Ricochet jumped on with a squirt of Cheez Whiz as her incentive. Spying a small wave from a passing jet ski, I asked Ricochet if she was ready. With her paws firmly placed, I said, "Go," and I released the board, watching Ricochet ride the entire wave with an easy grace.

"Great job, Ricochet!" I yelled. But she didn't hear me. She had leaped off the board at the shore where Rina waited, and the two buddies were off, tearing through the shoreline, making crazy eights in the sand, leaving a cloud of dust in their wake, and having fun together doing what dogs do best.

When they returned, I wanted to give Ricochet a try on another wave, so I put her leash back on and started walking toward the water. But she put the brakes on and simply wouldn't move. When a dog stops and refuses to move, I call the behavior "planting" and consider it a form of communication. Some people may interpret it as a sign of stubbornness, but I knew Ricochet was trying to tell me something. I believe in partnerships with dogs, so I took her feelings into consideration. She obviously didn't want to go back in the water for whatever reason. Maybe it was too cold. Maybe she was tired. I wasn't sure why, but I respected her decision and wasn't going to force her to get back on the surfboard.

The weeks passed with Ricochet excelling at almost everything she did. However, one day when she was about sixteen weeks old, we were working to retrieve a leash, and something suddenly changed. She seemed distracted and was slow to respond. I didn't think much of it at the time. After all, every dog can have an off day. But I soon realized it wasn't just one day—it was *every* day after that for many, many months. Despite my efforts to motivate her, she had zero interest in anything, including training which was previously fun.

Without any warning or apparent reason, she lost her spark. The fire was out, and only the ashes of her mind's brilliant firework remained. She was apathetic, unresponsive, subdued, and indifferent. As time went on, it seemed like depression set in for her, and frustration set in for me. We were at a standoff. A wedge had been driven between us, and the more I pushed her, the more she resisted. I knew what she was capable of, but she refused to be the exceptional dog I knew she could be.

"Come on, Ric! Go get the can!" I encouraged.

She normally loved pulling the garbage can down the entire length of the blacktop driveway, holding a rope in her mouth that was tied to it with a determined look on her face. This time, instead of bolting up with enthusiasm, she simply lay in the grass and looked up at me.

*What's going on?*

As her lack of interest continued, desperation launched me into the full-time role of activities director, trying different approaches on a rotating basis. The focus of my days grudgingly became how to motivate Ricochet. I tried training in environments where she was most confident. I changed rewards and incentives. I bought high-value treats, like liver and cheese, as well as Frisbees, squeaky toys, and stuffed toys. But Ricochet kept walking away from training sessions and was content to play alone. None of the things I would normally use to motivate a service-dog-in-training worked on her. There were plenty of possibilities, but even with my training background, I couldn't find the right one.

I felt like a guilt-ridden mom, afraid to admit out loud that my child was driving me crazy. The milestones we should have been checking off given Ricochet's enormous potential read instead like a diary of dysfunction:

**January 15:** I think Ricochet might have attention deficit disorder. She has no attention span whatsoever. She used to love the pool. Today she spent about a minute jumping in the water and then took off to chase a bee. Other dogs her age can stay focused on toys and tasks for much longer than she can. She doesn't even have a favorite toy or anything that interests her.

**February 5:** Ricochet is not cuddly or lovey like Rina was. Many times she's happiest wandering off by herself. Service dogs need to be with people, not alone.

**February 8:** Prima-dogga? Today she wouldn't get in the car when we were going out. She takes her own sweet time to do things the way she wants to!

The only thing that interested Ricochet anymore was digging. And gophers. Or digging to get the gophers. My yard looked like a mini Grand Canyon, with mounds of dirt and holes where there was once a lush green lawn. Ricochet's landscaping work was a daily visual reminder of the upheaval that she was causing in our lives. I couldn't leave her unsupervised for five minutes or she'd unearth a pile of fresh dirt. Poor Rina couldn't play freely in the yard because I had to fence it off. There was dirt everywhere from the gophers and Ricochet's incessant digging. Every morning, I'd try to sweep the dirt off the driveway, but it kept coming, much like the exasperating routine with Ricochet that had me losing my patience on a daily basis. I hated to admit it, but my prodigy had become a problem. I was starting to resent Ricochet and missed having sweet, helpful Rina to myself. Rina had never been this troublesome as a pup. On the contrary, Rina was always excited to perform a task. She loved to work. I felt guilty comparing the two dogs—and I knew it wasn't fair—but I couldn't help it. My propensity as a pessimistic person was to see the glass as half empty, and my negativity was spilling over toward my feelings for Ricochet. Negativity had a stranglehold on me and it wouldn't let go.

Thinking a change of scenery might help, I took Ricochet and Rina to Del Mar Dog Beach for some fun. As I was setting up our gear on the sand, I noticed Ricochet was gazing intently at something down the beach. I watched, and she quivered with excitement, her gaze locked on the shoreline, her eyes following something. Then I spotted it: a sandpiper darting back and forth at the edge of the water, its beak poking holes in the sand.

There were always birds on the beach. This wasn't new, but it seemed a switch had flipped back on in Ricochet. Her red-tufted ears were pricked and alert, and her deep brown eyes were intently watching the sandpiper's every move. She was energized and entranced. It had been so long since I had seen her like this, barely holding back the energy coiled inside and ready to spring. This was the dog I was missing. This was the dog I wanted back. So I did something I shouldn't have. I took off her leash and released her.

She sprang into motion, hitting her top speed in three seconds. Her ears were blown back in the wind and her coat fluttered with her strides. Her mouth was open, with her tongue lolling to the side in an expression of bliss. She looked like freedom incarnate. This was the dog I remembered! She had come back to life.

She careened into the waves, the sandpiper popping up into the air and skirting around her. The little bird wisely decided to fly farther down the beach, but Ricochet had no intention of letting it go alone. I watched as she sprinted to catch up with the bird, only to bump it to a new place and another chase. I couldn't help myself, and I laughed and clapped, encouraging her on. "Go, Ricochet! Get that bird!"

She looked absolutely free in that moment, and it was a beautiful sight.

For a few minutes, I ignored the reality of the situation. I was so happy to see Ricochet engaged in something with all her heart again that I didn't want to think about it. I wanted to watch the dog I once knew and enjoy the moment. But I couldn't block my thoughts for long. The problem, of course, was that chasing birds is a dangerous pastime for a service dog.

"She can't chase birds," I said aloud, but without conviction. Then I spoke the words again and this time I felt their heavy weight: *"But she can't chase birds."* If she were attached to a wheelchair and was overcome with the urge to leap after an avian adversary, the person in her charge could be injured. My heart, which had felt so light for that fleeting moment—running and melding beside this spirited dog—now sank. I had a new challenge in front of me: I was going to have to train her to control her impulses.

Unfortunately, her love for chasing birds was not a momentary weakness born to that freak day. It was a full-fledged passion for anything that she could chase. From then on, if I took her to an off-leash park or anywhere she was off leash when we came upon birds, she would chase them.

With high hopes of curbing her chase drive, one day I sat Ricochet down in front of the parakeet cage at the pet store and settled in cross-legged in front of her. I'd give her the cue to watch me, rewarding her with a treat anytime she glanced in my direction.

"Watch me."

She did, but with resignation and boredom written across her expressive face.

Two of the parakeets squabbled, flapping and scolding each other.

"Watch me," I repeated when Ricochet's eyes shifted in the birds' direction. I noticed her eyebrow whiskers twitch as she looked back to me. "Good," I said and then gave her another treat. Gradually, she kept her gaze on me for longer periods without trying to sneak glances at the birds.

"No birds, okay?" One eyebrow went up. Her whiskers brushed out. I stared into her eyes. "What's going on in there, huh?"

If I could teach her to give me her full attention whenever birds were around, then we might get past the problem. We began to make some progress. In fact, I could feed pigeons at the beach right in front of her. However, when she was off leash it was a totally different story.

When the weather warmed, I got out our surfboard, thinking we could give surfing another try. One day my friend Sarah and I took her to Coronado Dog Beach, and with the sun breaking through the clouds, I motioned for Ricochet to turn around on the board while Sarah steadied it. With my arthritis I wasn't able to manage Ricochet in the water, but Sarah could in the knee-deep water. Ricochet was wearing a lime green rash guard and a focused look on her face. She had one great ride, coasting all the way into the shore before she jumped off. While she rode in standing backward on the board, at least she did it.

"Well, Ricochet, we'll need to work a bit on that part," I said with a laugh. "But I do believe you're getting the hang of surfing."

I turned her around to face the direction she would be riding and gave her a squirt of Cheez Whiz as a reward. We took her out again. Looking over our shoulders, we waited for the next wave. We were almost knee-deep in the water, and although it was a little rough, the waves weren't too big.

As another wave approached, I called out, "This is the one!"

With that affirmation, Sarah released the board, and Ricochet was on her way.

"You can do it!" I shouted, and that's when I saw the flock of birds gliding in overhead. I felt my breath catch.

"Leave it!" I called, but Ricochet was off the board in a flash, running at full tilt down the beach. There was no point in yelling at her; she would come back when she was too tired to chase birds anymore. When she got back, I put her leash on so we could attempt a couple more waves. But she stopped and planted herself and wouldn't budge. She obviously had the same lackadaisical attitude toward surfing as she did for her training. Since it was apparent from her behavior that our surfing session was over, I unleashed her. Sarah, with surfboard in tow, and I, with a heavy heart, trudged out of the water.

"I just can't do this," I turned and grumbled to the sand and sea. I looked down the beach and saw Ricochet leaping up in the air in sheer joy after the flying birds. I was mesmerized by her enthusiasm, but perplexed on how to transfer it to her training.

But something inside me was speaking, too. When I watched her streaking after the birds those few times when I let her loose, I felt a twinge of happiness to see her doing something she loved. I stood there on the beach watching the elation pulse through every fiber of her being. I saw her crouch and coil then leap after the birds. I saw the strength of her muscles and fit body as she streaked after the flock when they flew off. But this just frustrated me more. *Was there a career for the Fastest Bird Chaser?* I would most definitely have to release her from service-dog work if I couldn't curb her desire to chase.

Not ready to give up on her, I decided to take a break from service-dog training and try more sporting activities to motivate her through fun. I took her to fly ball, agility, and lure coursing—anything to bring back the dog I knew. Lure coursing was doggie nirvana for Ricochet. It's a sport in which a dog chases a mechanically operated lure—in this case a plastic grocery bag—that's being whipped around a grassy area at thirty-five to fifty miles an hour. I watched her take off from her mark with unbridled enthusiasm, galloping at top speeds, twisting, turning, and tracking the bag with intense focus.

The next morning I was hopeful that she would be receptive to training since her energy had been released and her mind had been focused on a task. Since Ricochet loved battery-operated toys, I bought one that looked just like a puppy. I knew her ears would perk up when she heard me say "Go!" But this time she raised one eyebrow and then the other, and gave me a look that said, "Really? We just bought that at Petco." She yawned and rested her head on the ground. Our routine was like a continuous loop of *Peanuts* cartoons where the teacher drones on: "Whaa, whaa, whaa, whaa, whaa, whaa." Ricochet wasn't listening to a word I said. She simply walked away from the task—and from me! What happened to the puppy who had once stared so attentively at every move I made? I missed Ricochet's eagerness to engage with me: I missed our connection.

Suddenly my mind raced back to my childhood. I was six or seven and my dad was giving me a "swingy ride." I loved when he lifted me up and whipped me around so I could try to kick the ceiling with my feet. When I was about ten he said to me, "You were my shadow." *Were.* I didn't ask why he chose the past tense. When had I gone from an *are* to a *were?* The same pattern was repeated with my husbands. We went from "I do" to "We did." One day I realized my husband had left for work and he hadn't even said good-bye. Had he the day before? I couldn't remember.

Why hadn't I noticed? I feared this was the same kind of divide that had eroded between me and Ricochet.

In another effort to introduce more novelty into Ricochet's training, I decided to try dock-jumping. I knew Red and her new family would be attending the event, so I thought it would be a good day in more ways than one. In this sport, dogs competitively jump off the end of a dock into the water for distance or height. Being the water-loving dog that Ricochet was, I knew it would be perfect.

But Ricochet didn't think so. Rather than leaping into the pool with wild abandon as the other dogs were doing, she came to a pensive halt at the edge of the dock. From very early on, she had displayed an analytical mind, thinking everything through before she did it. For instance, if I threw a toy into the pool, Ricochet would not immediately hurl herself in after it on impulse or for instant gratification; she would sit at the edge, calculating in her mind how far she had to jump, how much energy she'd have to expend, and in which direction the toy was floating. Rarely would she just react to something without thought, except to chase a bird. And here she was thinking once again.

"Aw, that's so cute," one woman mused. "Your dog is really thinking about the jump."

*Overthinking is more like it,* I thought. *Why won't she jump? Where's her drive?*

She finally threw caution to the wind when she spied Red in the water. Only then did she deliberately belly flop right on top of her sister, causing a commotion and distracting Red instead of retrieving the toy like she was supposed to. I apologized for my belly-flopping anti-prodigy who was now drying off in the sun instead of participating like the other dogs. Envy clouded my vision as I watched the other dogs and their handlers working together, jumping, laughing, and enjoying the day while Ricochet snapped at flies.

The most frustrating part for me was that Ricochet had so much innate talent and yet she refused to use it. She just sat there without any interest whatsoever, in activities that were supposed to be fun. The times I took her surfing, she did really well . . . on two or three waves, that is, and then she would plant herself and refuse to surf anymore.

The harder I tried, the more emphatically Ricochet refused to participate. Unfortunately, I didn't have the energy to clear the hurdle. My arthritis was flaring, making it extremely painful to even crawl out of bed in the morning. As I was making an appointment with my rheumatologist, I thought about my own limitations and how they affected me so greatly. It occurred to me that maybe Ricochet's lack of interest was a side effect of something physical. But after a detailed array of tests, the vet couldn't find anything physically wrong with her.

Desperate for an answer, I also tried a few alternative approaches with Ricochet, including chiropractic and energy healing, but nothing revealed anything significant. The only difference was that my wallet was lighter and my heart was heavier. On the day that Ricochet refused to get into the car again, I knew the situation was out of control. Thinking that maybe Asia, the animal communicator I had worked with earlier, could talk some sense into Ricochet, I set up a call with her. I sat on the phone, staring outside at the piles of dirt mounds that were now my yard.

"Asia, please explain to her that she needs to have more enthusiasm."

"She doesn't understand what you mean," Asia said.

"Tell her it's like when the other dogs jump into the pool to get toys. They do it every time without hesitation. That's enthusiasm," I explained.

Asia laughed softly, seeming to choose her words with extra care. "Ricochet says that's ridiculous. She doesn't understand why they are willing to do the same thing over and over. Once it's done, why would you do it again? Ricochet wants to do new and out-of-the-ordinary things, not the same dumb stuff again and again."

*The same dumb stuff? Dumber than digging fifty holes in my yard?*

This wasn't easy to hear because training involves repeating behaviors but for a meaningful end result. I was at my wit's end. It appeared that Ricochet had an infinite amount of ability and zero motivation to engage in anything that wasn't novel or exciting. I thanked Asia for her insights and put down my phone, finally admitting the painful truth: Ricochet and I were no dream team. My high hopes for an exceptional dog had come crashing down with a thud. The sense of disappointment and loss were all too familiar to me.

I had spent a year of my life trying to rekindle Ricochet's spark to no avail. But really, what did I expect? My life was a running loop of loss and disappointment—a déjà vu of discontent. Why did I think my relationship with Ricochet would be any different? Maybe I was the source of contagion, tainting this magnificent dog with my legacy of dread.

I had fooled myself into thinking that the white mark on Ricochet's chest was a sign of significance, but now I chalked it up to simple genetics. My heart ached with the realization that I had made a grave mistake in choosing her. And even worse: If destiny were at the helm, had Ricochet made a mistake by choosing me?

# Chapter 7

# Acceptance: Releasing the Spirit

*"The only thing that will satisfy you in this life is what you are born to do."*

—Shandren Reddy

The months went on and Ricochet continued to resist, refusing to fully participate in our training. She reminded me of the brilliant child to whom learning comes easily, the one who doesn't feel the need to study or practice because she already knows she can do it, but just *doesn't want to*, walking away, lying down, or simply quitting a training session. The word that often came to mind with Ricochet was *lackadaisical*; she just didn't care. What's more, she often sought out her crate as a place of refuge and seemed content to remain there.

Despite her lack of interest, my job was to motivate her to do the work. However, as Ricochet passed the year mark, nothing changed. On one occasion, I worked on training her to toilet on cue, something that all service dogs must be able to do. Even though Ricochet had been housebroken very young, she still didn't relieve herself at the appropriate time and place.

One day, first thing in the morning, I took her outside on leash and told her to "hurry," which is the cue to toilet. She ignored me.

She stared off toward the hill by the house. She looked down the street. She nosed around the grass, but she wouldn't go.

"Okay, then," I said and took her inside, putting her back in her crate. Showing her true lackadaisical self, she didn't even seem to care if she lay in the crate or on the patio in the sunshine. After a while, I took her back outside to try again.

"Okay, Ricochet. Hurry." But still she would not.

By the third time I had to put her back in the crate, I wanted to tear my hair out. This was such a simple behavior, and yet she wouldn't oblige. She had, without a doubt, become the hardest dog I'd ever trained. I didn't want to give up on her, but Ricochet seemed to have given up on me.

The pride I'd felt when she was a young puppy had evaporated. I couldn't even remember feeling proud. Instead, there was dark, defeated anger within me, and I felt only disappointment for a dog who wasn't good at anything anymore. As I watched her littermates excel in their training and activities, I silently harbored embarrassment as a professional trainer who had a dysfunctional dog as the face of her service-dog program.

As I look back now, I see that my control, expectations, and disappointment had damaged our communication, relationship, and bond. My inner critic was getting to the point of publicly denouncing her and our relationship continued to suffer. And unfortunately for us, I wasn't just running out of ideas and patience; I was running out of time.

I was successful in helping Ricochet manage her impulses while she was on leash, and she'd never tried to chase anything when she was with me. But the reality was that I couldn't guarantee that she'd never attempt to run after a bird if she was placed with a person with a disability. It was still too much of a risk.

These thoughts, coupled with the fact that she didn't have a very good work ethic, constantly plagued me. Although the idea tormented me, I began to think I'd have to place her with someone else. I wanted to do the right thing for Ricochet, and perhaps living with me wasn't in her best interest. I started contacting potential people in case I had to re-home her. One potential candidate, who sounded very interested, was a woman who offered animal-assisted therapy. Her therapy dogs would accompany her to crisis situations and comfort people during their trauma. And there were other potential homes for her as well, so I knew she'd be loved no matter where she was placed.

But one question continued to nag at me: *Why would such a brilliant dog shut down at sixteen weeks old?* She seemed depressed, and I couldn't understand why. In retrospect, it makes perfect sense. Of course I was ill-equipped to pinpoint her source of malaise: My heart had been shut down for so long, I couldn't possibly recognize that hers was, too. I was besieged with disappointment, but I couldn't postpone my decision any longer. I'd have to release her from the service-dog program.

I was pondering these disheartening thoughts when I received an unexpected email. Carson Events was producing the Purina Pro Plan Incredible Dog Challenge for Nestlé Purina Pet and they were including a surf dog contest for the first time. With film crews attending for national television network syndication, the event was already generating a buzz. According to the email, there would be about a dozen dogs competing, but one of the dogs, King, had to cancel because he needed surgery on a broken nail. This left an opening for another dog, and the coordinator was inviting Ricochet to fill in the spot.

I sat down to think, feeling a bit nervous. One voice in my head said, *Go ahead and enter Ricochet. She's done pretty well on the board.* Then another voice piped up: *What? I'll be lucky if she gets on the board more than twice.* The fear wasn't unfounded. Most days she'd only venture into the water a couple of times and then she'd plant herself on the beach, signaling that our surfing session was done for the day. What's more, she was going to be up against some of the most seasoned and mature dog surfers. Not only would she be the only novice out there, her performance would be *filmed*.

I tried to convince myself that she'd only be required to ride a few waves and that she'd spend a relatively short time in the water. If she did well, it could be a testament to how early work with puppies pays off and that young dogs can do amazing things. It might be a great opportunity to raise awareness for Puppy Prodigies . . . or it might be a complete disaster.

Yet, even with these concerns, I wrote to the organizers and accepted their invitation. But the competition was only two days away. How was Ricochet going to surf, especially in front of a crowd, film crew, and other dogs—not to mention the birds? *What was I even thinking?* She'd probably surf backward. I went to bed the night before the contest feeling sick to my stomach.

The morning of the event I was a bundle of nerves, but I was determined to see the day through. I told myself that a surfing competition was nothing to get worked up about. She'd either surf well or she wouldn't. Even so, I hated the spotlight. On the way to the beach, I rolled down the car windows, hoping the salt air would settle my stomach. Ricochet perked up as soon as her nose caught a whiff of the ocean, her gaze fixed toward the spot where the shoreline would soon appear. The parking lot was packed with cars, and the beach was already abuzz with participants, spectators, and dogs. Taking a deep breath, I gathered our things and walked with Ricochet into the middle of the melee.

The Purina Pro Plan Incredible Dog Challenge was a large event that took place at the Del Mar Fairgrounds. Even though the surfing competition was on the beach away from the main event, that didn't stop the crowds from forming already.

I looked out across the water and eyed the waves. They were definitely bigger than what we were used to and I tried not to be intimidated. *Oh confidence, I need you now.* The veteran surf dog participants were greeting one another as their canine companions sniffed and touched noses in recognition. Everyone seemed to be having a good time and they all appeared ready for action. Meanwhile, I couldn't have felt more out of place. Then I noticed that Ricochet was sitting calmly, taking in her surroundings as if it were an average day on the beach, and I relaxed a little.

Surfboards lined the shore and a wide variety of dog breeds milled around them. Part of the surf culture for dogs and people is expressing your own flair and style. Ricochet was wearing a bright pink rash guard that said "Surfer Girl," provided by the Surf Divas, the instructors who were helping with the contest. It matched the hot pink and orange lei around Ricochet's neck.

Sizing up the other dogs, I knew the Bernese mountain dog had won a few competitions, and I watched her weave through the boards with ease and confidence. There was also a bulldog and a cocker spaniel mix wearing sunglasses. Most of these dogs had no service-dog training, but they knew how to surf. All of them seemed excited to be on the beach next to their boards. Even so, I started to believe that if Ricochet could focus, she'd be able to hold her own. Unfortunately, focusing wasn't her strong suit.

The contest coordinators passed out goody bags and gave us instructions. There were twelve dogs in the competition and each of us had ten minutes to surf, riding as many waves as our dogs could catch. We'd be judged based on the distance the dog managed to stay on the board, the size of the waves, and the "incredibleness" of the dog. I wondered for the thousandth time how exactly one judges "incredibleness."

Rustling around in the goody bag, I pulled out a life jacket. My face must've asked the question because a coordinator walking by said: "All of the dogs need to wear life jackets. It's for their safety." The beach was full of people, cameras, and birds. There would be surf instructors who Ricochet didn't know helping her in the water. *Am I asking too much of her?*, I wondered.

Suddenly I heard the bullhorn blaring an announcement that the competition was getting underway. "It's start time, people!" the announcer called. "Get your dog ready and life jackets on. Prepare to hit the water. Surf's up!"

There were six dogs in the large dog category, and as we waited for our turn, I wondered how I might be able to help Ricochet once she was in the water. I watched as one of the other surfers, a six-foot-tall guy, maneuvered his Chesapeake Bay retriever's surfboard deeper into the water and farther behind the breaking waves. The farther out you could get your dog, the longer the ride would be. As frail as my joints were, I just couldn't take the pounding water farther out in the surf. I had to depend on the help of the surf instructors.

I wondered if Ricochet would struggle in this rougher surf as well. She was used to surfing in the light chop of Fiesta Island in water up to my knees. But these rolling waves were the real thing. Ricochet had only been out in surf this high a couple of times, including a practice run the day before. She was still learning, and here I was asking her to perform like a pro. My thoughts were interrupted when our helper Alyssa called out, "Ready, Ricochet?"

Alyssa helped me get the board out into the waves as Ricochet balanced on top of it. Despite wearing a wetsuit and a white rash guard from Purina, I shivered in the cold water. The ESPN cameraman was in the water next to us, his waterproof lens pointed right at Ricochet and me. At that cold and shivering moment, the waves volleyed us and broke in our faces, salty and stinging. Ricochet slipped back on the board but then steadied herself. I wondered if the only footage the cameraman would capture of us would be Ricochet getting knocked off the board and of me drowning.

"How you doing, Ric?" I asked, and the dark eyes that met mine were focused. So far she had gotten on the board, out into the water, and avoided all distractions. I hadn't even seen her look at one bird. My heart rose a little in my chest. *Maybe*, I thought. *Maybe.*

Alyssa was behind Ricochet's board and she looked over her shoulder to gauge which wave would be the best one. The board bobbed slightly, pulling back toward a cresting wave. It was the second in the set. Alyssa called out "Now!" and launched the board. All I could do was watch.

Ricochet leaned forward. The wave caught the board, propelling it toward the shore and Ricochet dug in. She rode perfectly, skimming the water with balance, grace, and ease. Then suddenly I saw her board wobble. The waves churned around her and broke. I sucked in a breath. *She's going to wipe out!* But instead, she adjusted her stance, rebalanced herself, and regained control of the board.

She did it! All of that balance work as a young puppy had paid off. Ricochet was surfing like it was second nature.

Behind Ricochet, Alyssa leaped through the white water with high steps, her ponytail bouncing beneath her baseball cap. She was holding a can of Cheez Whiz and was wearing a huge grin. As the board passed me, Ricochet looked over her shoulder, then artfully spun around and took the rest of the ride backward, like she'd been surfing since she was born and was now hamming it up for the TV crews.

After sailing into shore, Ricochet waited patiently for Alyssa to meet her. I watched from the shallows. Ricochet didn't glance around at the strangers who were talking and exclaiming and running to and fro. Not only did she seem oblivious to the commotion, she seemed completely at home and in her element. But just then a flock of shorebirds passed overhead. My jaw tensed. My eyes jumped to Ricochet, and I prayed under my breath she wouldn't break and run.

She didn't even glance up. I let out the breath I'd been holding. I was still a good thirty feet out in the surf, and she looked for me, but she stood steady on her board. Alyssa gave her a little squirt of Cheez Whiz and then took her leash to lead her up on the shore and give it another go.

Although Ricochet was unfamiliar with the people who were helping her, she was working well with them. She got right back up on the board and concentrated on making her way out to catch the next wave. We had seven more minutes in the competition. Peering out into the gray ocean, I felt pride budding in my chest.

I saw Ricochet in her bright-orange life vest, balancing adeptly on her surfboard, whitecaps and surf leaping up around her. Her red coat was soaked from spray and she looked rugged and capable, happy and excited.

Every time she rode a wave in, she got right back up on the board. I kept thinking it was too good to be true—that soon she'd plant herself in the sand and decide she was done surfing for the day, but she didn't. And with her head held high, her legs positioned solidly on the board, she looked regal, like a Big Kahuna. She wasn't quitting; she was having a great time. She was cooperating, focusing, and acting like the puppy I had first trained.

And then came the last wave. Alyssa was shouting something out in the surf and dogs were barking from the shoreline. I saw Ricochet glance over her shoulder as the sun was trying to peek out from behind a bank of clouds. I shivered once but had stopped trembling all over. Then the waves were rolling in faster and stronger than before. Alyssa launched the board, and I watched as Ricochet sailed in, balancing expertly on the board as it tilted first to one side and then to the other, her tail like a rudder, her ears lightly flapping in the ocean spray and air. And then she was cruising all the way to the shoreline, as easy and graceful as anything I'd ever seen. I was smiling and laughing, and suddenly quite comfortable in the water—wonderfully cozy and warm, from the inside out.

That looked more like the puppy I knew. Ricochet, the great and brilliant dog was back!

The horn sounded, signaling the end of the heat, so I walked eagerly toward the shore. Alyssa waited for my cue to release Ricochet, who was patiently standing on her board . . . backward. I raised my hand to let Ricochet go, and Alyssa pointed her toward me.

Ricochet sprang from the board and landed in the calf-high surf with a tremendous splash. Then, with ears flapping and face smiling, she crashed through the water to get to me. She was all forward motion, but somehow her tail was still wagging at full speed.

I dropped to my knees so that I could wrap my arms all the way around her wet body.

"You're such a good girl," I said.

She jumped up on me, and my smile felt like it was permanently etched on my face. I laughed as she wagged not just her wet, bedraggled tail but her whole body. As she wiggled back and forth, I could almost hear her thoughts: *Did you see me out there?* Pure glee shone in her eyes. Then she gave herself a good shake, spraying water all over me.

I ignored the water rushing around our ankles and the ruckus on the beach. I just wanted to keep embracing and praising her. I felt all those months of frustration lifting from my shoulders and shuttling off into the ocean breeze.

Suddenly I felt a pang of guilt over how hard I'd been on her for so long. I leaned my face against her wet ruff and said, "I'm sorry, Ric." It was a moment of reckoning. "I'm proud of you." *Ricochet was finally good at something again!*

I patted her soaking coat and hugged her again, thanking her because she had done something for me as well. I'd never been able to compete in sports because of my degenerative joint disease and immune problems, but today she had given me the opportunity to live vicariously through her, and I felt the rush of the moment throughout my body. *She was good at surfing!* I gave her another hug and didn't bother to wipe away the tears, which were running down my face, mixing with the incoming waves before being washed away.

Still basking in the glow of relief and pride, we waited to see how Ricochet would place in the contest. But the results didn't really matter; we had already won. All the same, she stayed on her board longer than some of the dogs I had seen, and I ventured to say she had a certain amount of "incredibleness," with her backward surfing and all.

I listened closely as the first- and second-place dogs were announced, and when I heard that Ricochet had placed third, I couldn't believe my ears.

I wanted to jump up and down. "Oh, Ricochet! You did it!"

At only seventeen months old, she was the youngest dog in the challenge. The closest dog in age to her was actually three and a half years old. She had proven that young dogs, when trained early, could achieve just as much as older dogs. The scores were fairly close, with the first-place dog at 43 points, second place at 41.5, and Ricochet at 40.5. She had kept up with the "big dogs" and was awarded a gorgeous pink and white plumeria lei.

Plumerias symbolize new life and new beginnings, and above the lei, I could see the spark and interest back in Ricochet's eyes. She was grinning and looking around the beach as if something wonderful would happen at any minute. And for me it already had. She would go on to wear many leis over the next few years, but this one would always be my favorite. The Purina Pro Plan Incredible Dog Challenge would always have a warm place in my heart because of the pivotal changes it brought about. It was more than a surf-dog contest to me; it was an unexpected and fortuitous awakening to Ricochet's potential.

It was only after Ricochet and I had driven home, tired and happy, that I began to replay the day's events in my mind and to feel with deep certainty that the little puppy I'd trained was, after all, very good at something. When I let go of my guilt for being so hard on her for all of those difficult months, that's when the thought began to take shape: Let go of focusing on what she *can't* do, and focus on what she *can* do instead. I would no longer try to make Ricochet be something she wasn't. Instead, I would just let her be herself and allow her to shine her brightest. I thought about parents and children and how, like puppies, infants exhibit personalities early in life, their spirits expressing themselves little by little. But what if a father pushes his son toward sports when he only wants to spend his time painting? Or if a mother expects her daughter to enjoy the latest dolls, when all she really wants to do is climb trees and be outdoors? These children become burdened with parental expectations at an early age, and those same parents attempt to persuade their children to fit molds that were carved out for them even before they were born—instead of paying attention to the spirit of the child and the path the child wants to take—and perhaps the path the child was destined to take. We all have expectations like this, and for our dogs, too. Some people want an agility dog, some want a service dog, and some want a pet. But how many people look at their dogs and think about what the dogs would want to do?

Coming to this realization was the turning point in our relationship. I knew then what I needed to do, and it was so easy. It always had been. I just needed to let Ricochet be who she was. No mold to force her into, no making her be something she wasn't. She was perfect the way she was. "Imperfectly perfect," I said, and smiled to myself. I think she had known it all along, staying true to herself and what she wanted to do, not giving in simply to please me and accommodate what I wanted her to do. I saw clearly then that when I let go of my expectations, her spirit was released, and things began to change.

That night I fell asleep to the rhythmic sound of Rina's and Ricochet's methodical breathing, and I dreamed of Ricochet running toward me through the waves, her red coat in its bright-orange life jacket outlining her against the vast, shimmering sea.

When I woke the next morning I did what I'd resisted doing all those long months. I released Ricochet from the service-dog program. But when I made the decision I'd been unable to make for so long, there was not one ounce of regret; just an unfamiliar feeling of optimism and a budding sense of hope.

# Chapter 8

# The Rebirth:
# The Splendor of Surrender

*"The two most important days in your life are the day you are born, and the day you find out why."*

—MARK TWAIN

After Ricochet's success in the Purina Pro Plan Incredible Dog Challenge, I found myself at an unplanned crossroad. With a new appreciation for Ricochet's undeniable surfing potential, I wondered how she might possibly make a difference in the world through Puppy Prodigies. As I was pondering this thought, a flash of inspiration flowed through me like a bolt of lightning, and I felt an overwhelming urge to take action. It was the strangest feeling I'd ever encountered. Suddenly my fingers were dancing away on my keyboard as if they knew what letters to hit before my brain had processed them. The thoughts weren't mine, but they were flowing like a raging river, as if I were channeling a rushing source of divine inspiration.

Before I knew it, I saw the words "Surfin' for Paws-abilities" staring back at me from the computer screen. *Ricochet could raise funds for humans and animals in need through her surfing.* Within a few hours, a Web site was created, and the initiative was no longer a thought but a plan of action ready to be executed.

The moment I made a conscious decision to let Ricochet be who she truly was, the floodgates opened, beginning a chain reaction of synchronicity. While some may say the next course of events was just a coincidence, I believe it was meant to be. And just as serendipitous as Ricochet's birth, it was perfectly orchestrated once I let go of my expectations of her. As I sought to find a recipient for Ricochet's fund-raising, in another home and life, almost right around the corner from us, a fourteen-year-old boy named Patrick Ivison was busy building his own dream—to walk across the stage at his high school graduation.

And, like an exclamation point from the universe to emphasize just how powerful letting go of my expectations was, Ricochet's and Patrick's paths would collide in a rippling effect of amazing proportions. . . .

On September 24, 1995, life changed in an instant for Jennifer Kayler. Her son, Patrick Ivison, was fourteen months old, a beautiful blond boy whose smile and joyful laugh could melt her heart in an instant. Patrick had started walking at ten months old, and Jennifer was grateful for that because she couldn't afford a car. As they walked through a parking lot on their way home to her parents' house, she set Patrick down for a minute to rest her tired arms.

Just then, she noticed a driver parked in a nearby car arguing with a woman in the passenger seat. She didn't think much of it, and kept walking with Patrick alongside her. Suddenly, without warning, the driver threw the car in reverse as Jennifer bolted to grab her son. Unfortunately, she wasn't fast enough. To her horror, she watched helplessly as the back bumper clipped Patrick and knocked him down. In the terrifying moments that followed, Jennifer saw her son lying pinned under the car, the tufts of his blond hair sticking out from below. *That can't be Patrick lying there,* she thought, as panic coursed through her entire body.

Jennifer ran to the driver's side of the car and frantically tried to lift it, desperate to pull Patrick free, but her efforts were futile: He was wedged. She began shrieking uncontrollably, alarming neighbors and strangers who came running to her aid. Amid the chaos and panic, bystanders lifted the car, and Jennifer yanked Patrick free.

Her momentary relief turned to horror as his lips, then his face, began turning blue. In the blink of an eye, every mother's worst nightmare had unfolded for Jennifer. In that terrible moment, she knew her son was gone.

But then she heard a calming voice. "It's just a cut. Lay him down and let me look at it. It's just a cut. . . ." It was her neighbor, Bob Misko, a military police officer and semipro baseball player. Normally he worked on Sundays, but because of an injury, he'd been at home icing his shoulder when he happened to look out the window when he heard the screams. He had leaped up and raced outside to help.

Bob told Jennifer that Patrick had received a degloving injury in which the skin of his forehead had torn away from the underlying tissue. He carefully placed Patrick on the dirt of the parking lot and crouched next to him to check his vital signs. But there were none. Patrick wasn't breathing. Bob leaned over the tiny boy and began CPR and mouth-to-mouth resuscitation, skills he had just renewed at a child refresher CPR class the week before. On a day that seemed completely void of goodness, the dirt on which Patrick lay was a small blessing, because it had more give to it than asphalt. Had the parking lot been made of concrete, experts later said, Patrick would have died on the spot.

Beside herself with fear, Jennifer hovered over Bob and Patrick. Everything was happening so fast. After several rounds of CPR, she heard Patrick cry faintly. By then, the wail of an ambulance pierced the stunned silence and a team of paramedics rushed to take over. A helicopter landed in the middle of Palm Avenue, the main stretch through Imperial Beach, and Patrick was LifeFlighted to the Rady Children's Hospital in San Diego.

Bob and Jennifer sped to the hospital in his car. As they drove, darting through the streets, Jennifer gripped the headrest behind her, literally trying to keep from jumping out of her skin. Her mind had already skipped ahead to a future without Patrick. *I cannot live life without him!* she thought over and over again.

With a racing heart, she ran into the ER waiting room with Bob right beside her, but Patrick had already been wheeled into surgery. Paralyzed with fear but shaking nonetheless, Jennifer waited for some news of her son's condition. A nurse approached and informed her that her son was stable and the doctors had taken him to surgery to repair his scalp. They still weren't sure of the extent of his injuries.

"He's . . . *alive?*" she asked tentatively.

"Yes," the nurse replied.

Jennifer felt a wave of immense relief. She had been given a second chance. "He's alive! Thank God, he's alive!"

"Yes," the nurse responded quietly. "Is there anyone I should call?" she asked.

But there was nobody Jennifer could call to be with her. Her parents were away on vacation, and she had just ended a difficult relationship. The nurse, whose name tag said Aurea, stepped closer to Jennifer and enfolded her in her arms. With that one human touch, Jennifer broke down sobbing, crying tears of release and relief. *Her baby was alive.* That hug gave Jennifer the strength to face the grueling hours ahead.

Jennifer stayed at the hospital by Patrick's side for the next several days as teams of doctors and nurses walked in and out of his room. One day, she watched as two doctors gave Patrick a pinprick test, sticking needles into his legs. She didn't stop to comprehend why they were doing this particular test or why she should have been concerned when Patrick couldn't feel any of the needles. Only later, when they returned with solemn faces, did Jennifer understand the harsh reality: Patrick had suffered a C4/C5 incomplete spinal cord injury; all four of his limbs were affected, making him a quadriplegic.

Life, as Jennifer had always known it, fell apart on that day. She lived at the hospital for the next six weeks. She'd been fighting a losing financial battle and decided to give up the apartment she had placed a deposit on before the accident. She left the hospital only once just to put her things in a storage unit. She was now technically homeless.

As she returned down the hospital corridor toward Patrick's room in the ICU, she heard something. A beautiful something. It was the faint sound of Patrick laughing. One of those crazy baby laughs that just makes you smile. And it was at that moment that she knew that everything was going to be okay. Her baby was back: the silly, laughing, ever-happy Patrick that she had known. Since the accident, she had not heard him laugh, and was so afraid he never would. And now, as she rounded the corner to his room, she stored that beautiful sound deep within her. In that one moment, she felt overwhelming joy. Her baby would be all right.

Finally, after six weeks at Rady Children's Hospital, Patrick returned home. Yet despite the reality, Jennifer would not waste precious time wondering "what if" or "what could have been." She would do what she needed to do for her son—she would press on.

On Christmas Eve, 2004, ten-year-old Patrick and his seven-year-old sister, Samantha, were waiting in line to see Santa Claus at the mall. Jennifer stood by and listened carefully to what her children told Santa they wanted so that she could scurry off when they weren't around and play Santa's helper. But this time, money wouldn't be enough. When Santa asked Samantha what she wanted for Christmas, she asked him if he could make her brother walk again.

"Don't say that," Patrick said.

But Santa replied, "It's okay. She can ask for whatever she wants. I'll see what I can do."

Minutes later, as Jennifer and Samantha were wheeling Patrick through the mall, they passed two men in wheelchairs. Everyone nodded hello and then continued on their separate ways. It was only when Jennifer and her children were almost to their van that the two men came around the corner, requesting that the family stop and speak for a few moments. The men told Jennifer and her children about their organization, Fighting Chair Sports, a sports organization for people in wheelchairs.

"Have you heard about Project Walk?" one of the men asked.

Jennifer hadn't. Apparently, it was a spinal cord injury recovery center in nearby Carlsbad, California. Intrigued, Jennifer thanked the two men and researched Project Walk on the Internet when she got home. She was amazed to find out that many of their clients arrive in wheelchairs, only to walk out a few years later. Her heart began beating fast—*There was hope!* But then she felt despondent when she realized there was no way she'd ever be able to afford a program that cost about $30,000 for an average one-year treatment plan. She and Patrick had the motivation but not the money.

## July 2009

"Patrick Ivison! That's it, Ric. He's the one."

I had met Patrick a few times through Paws'itive Teams events, and as I sought to find someone for Ricochet's fund-raising, Patrick was the first person who came to mind.

Like Ricochet, Patrick was a surfer. Patrick would be graduating high school in three years, donning his cap and gown with the graduating class of 2012. I knew that he wanted a service dog to help him become more independent, but the cost to Patrick's family would be thousands of dollars. The determined teen also needed a great deal more for the suggested three years of therapy with Project Walk, which I had heard about from my neighbor who worked there.

A couple of weeks later, Carol, one of the trainers from Paws'itive Teams, called to invite me to the US Open of Surfing to watch Patrick surf at an expression session where several surfers with disabilities would catch some waves, inspiring the crowd with their enthusiasm and courage.

Patrick was an ambassador for Life Rolls On, an organization founded by Jesse Billauer, a surfer who had suffered a spinal cord injury himself and wanted others with disabilities to be able to experience the waves. The organization provided the support team to keep Patrick safe in the ocean during the expression session.

We arrived at the beach midmorning as the sun was breaking through the clouds to watch Patrick do the thing that made him happiest. The idea that Patrick could be out in those waves astounded me. I had a hard enough time managing the turbulent saltwater, and my disability wasn't anywhere near the degree of someone with a spinal cord injury. Learning that Patrick surfed caught my attention, but watching him surf made me believe that anything is possible if you put your mind to it.

I stood watching Patrick and his team of friends, family, and volunteers as they helped to carry him into the water and position him on his surfboard. I knew that he had done this many times, but it was impossible not to be afraid for him. I scanned the beach for his mother, Jennifer, but she didn't look nervous at all. She was shielding her eyes from the sun with a smile on her face.

I watched as the team launched Patrick into the motion of a big wave rushing toward shore. Tucked tight on his board, Patrick lay flat, balancing his body with the movements of the water. His smiling face said it all. The surf was his kingdom.

The volunteers set him up for a second and a third wave. Surfing seemed easier for him than I would've guessed, until on the fourth wave, he wiped out. The board careened sideways and dumped him into the water. I gasped. He was wearing a life jacket, but he wouldn't be able to turn himself upright. He couldn't swim. Of course there were volunteers positioned all around in the water, and in a split second, a boy with broad shoulders pulled Patrick up and into the air.

I thought the surfing session would be over then. Instead, Patrick whooped and laughed.

"Those were some great waves!" Patrick yelled, and the rest of the group patted him on the back and laughed with him. I was inspired by Patrick's confidence in his team. It truly was the ultimate show of trust. Patrick had to believe the volunteers would protect him and rescue him if he needed it. I tried to think if there was anyone in my life that I would trust so implicitly, but I knew there wasn't.

Standing on the shoreline, I realized that it wasn't so much work as it was camaraderie, team spirit, and a group of souls buffeted in the waves, doing what they loved. It looked like the team was going to be in the water for a while, so I wandered over to Jennifer, who I'd met when I'd first met Patrick. She was a pretty strawberry blonde with a smile as bright as her son's. I'd heard her say several times that their life went down a completely different path the instant Patrick was injured, but I'd never heard her complain about it. There was no doubt where the boy got his upbeat attitude and desire to embrace life.

"He's just amazing," I said to her. "Don't you get scared?"

She shrugged and explained, "I think surfing has let him know that there really isn't anything that he can't do." Then she smiled at me. "He wants to walk across the stage to get his high school diploma, and I know he can. We just have to find a way to pay for the years of therapy at Project Walk."

I nodded, an idea for Ricochet's fund-raiser starting to develop in my mind. When the team rolled Patrick up onto the shore, I smiled at him—it was hard not to—and said, "You looked great out there."

"Well, there was that one wipeout," he said. "I can hold my breath for a long time, but I prefer not to." Then he laughed.

"Have you always wanted to surf?" I asked.

"Yeah, but it's more spiritual than just surfing for me now." He paused for a moment. "I look back on the beach and I can see my empty chair." The words gave me chills. "I'm free out there."

I thought about Ricochet and all of the constraints I had put on her; how I had never really felt free from my own disability and, at times, from my own grief.

"You should try it sometime," Patrick urged.

"I've been out there enough to know it's not for me," I admitted, recalling how I struggled to emerge from the waves just a few days before. Ricochet was welcome to be the sole surfer in our family.

As I walked back to the car with Carol, I was inspired by Patrick and Jennifer's optimism in the face of extreme adversity.

"I enjoyed our adventure today," I told Carol. "Patrick's energy is so uplifting."

Carol's expression told me she agreed.

Opening the car door, I added, "Thanks for being a conduit between Patrick and Jennifer and me. If I can figure out how Ricochet's surfing can help Patrick, even if it's just in some small way, it'll mean so much to me. Things happen for a reason. When one door closes, another opens. It'll be interesting to see where this path leads."

Later that night, it came to me, and I couldn't wait to call Jennifer in the morning. When I got her on the phone, I shared my idea about how Ricochet could fund-raise for Patrick.

I suggested that we videotape the two—a boy and a dog together—on separate boards but riding in on the same wave. This video would then be used to promote Ricochet's fund-raiser for Patrick by showing what they had in common. It had also occurred to me that maybe I could even get some of the local news stations to cover it.

"Oh my gosh! That would be amazing," Jennifer said, and that was it. We were committed.

I figured the effort wouldn't generate a ton of cash, but I hoped there would be enough to pay for a few therapy sessions and a service dog. Every little bit would help Patrick get one step closer to his goal of independence.

"What do you think?" I asked Ricochet, as I plotted possibilities at my desk.

Ricochet replied with a wag of her tail, trusting me to make it happen. So I got to work setting up an exhibition surf session for August 20. Then, over the next few weeks, I contacted every potential corporate sponsor I could think of and sent out my first press release. I hoped that a couple of the local news stations would come to the session to help us raise awareness, but I wasn't holding my breath. Whatever happened, we'd still shoot our own video to promote the Web site, Help Patrick Walk, which Jennifer created to raise money for his therapy.

"You can do this, right, Ric?" I asked, but she didn't have an answer.

The next order of business was introducing Ricochet to Patrick. We'd just have to wait and hope and see.

The day before the event, I walked up the wheelchair ramp leading to Patrick's home.

"Good girl, Ricochet," I said to the dog by my side, who seemed to know just where she was going and what she was doing. Meanwhile, I wasn't so sure what to expect. But when a smiling Jennifer answered the door and ushered us in and I saw Patrick, I immediately knew I'd made the right choice for Ricochet's first fund-raising event.

Their golden retriever named Rusty bounced up playfully and Ricochet was momentarily distracted. But when a handsome and confident Patrick wheeled up to us and grinned a warm hello, I watched surprised as Ricochet ran directly to Patrick, waving her tail excitedly and then sitting gently beside him, even though Jennifer, Samantha, Rusty, and I were all there. It was as if she knew exactly who she was there to see. In time I would understand that Ricochet bonded instantly with everyone but seemed to always know what was needed most for whom, but at that moment I was still taking in the new scene. Jennifer smiled an easy smile, and the closeness between she and Patrick was palpable. We chatted about our upcoming venture for a half-hour or so, and as we said our good-byes, we all felt quite positive about what we could accomplish together.

When I checked my phone, I was pleasantly surprised to find several messages from the media. But as they continued to call, I felt a nervous pit growing in my stomach. The familiar thoughts of fear and negativity churned through my mind. More was riding now on Ricochet's ability to perform appropriately than before. Yet despite my fears and exhaustion from all of the planning, I felt more alive and excited than I had in years.

### August 20, 2009

As a gray dawn gave way to day, I was still as nervous as I'd been the night before. Ricochet had only surfed a few times. She didn't know Patrick that well. She might not even surf. The Purina Challenge could have been a fluke. What if she played with other dogs? Or what if she chased birds while the TV crews were filming?

"Ricochet, what have we done?" I asked, standing above her.

In response, she wiggled her body, wagged her tail, and looked up at me as if it was just the most wonderful idea in the world.

I loaded her into the car, and off we set for Del Mar Dog Beach. I was driving and thinking, preoccupied with my thoughts when I realized I'd missed the exit. No sooner had I turned back than the worries began once more and I missed the exit again! I wondered if my failure to navigate was some sort of message that I was making a huge mistake, but looking over at Ricochet's blissful expression, I pushed that thought away.

But finally, after I managed to collect my thoughts, focus, and get off at the right exit, we arrived at the beach. I let Ricochet run for a few minutes and then called her back while scanning the beach for birds. As the camera crews began arriving and setting up their equipment, I counted four different local stations. I felt the familiar nervous, sick feeling. Ricochet had never done this before. Even though she'd done well in the Purina Challenge, she was never the focus. I thought for the hundredth time about birds and all of the unknowns she was up against, all these people we didn't know. "Be positive. Just stay positive," I said to myself with zero conviction.

Patrick came onto the scene, pushed by his friend Zac. Commotion ensued, and the media people followed with microphones as he was wheeled down the beach. I watched from a distance. When he got closer, I heard him say, "There she is! Come on, Ricochet!" And with that, Ricochet made a beeline for Patrick, racing flat out across the sand.

I watched as she ran, ears back, bounding over the sand, her red coat blowing, and her agile, easy movements enviable. There were people all around, but again, like the evening before at his house, she knew who she was there to see. Patrick held open his arms to her as she came streaking to him at top speed through the salty sea air.

She was my dog and I knew her, but even I had to admit, it was an amazing and beautiful sight to watch. I turned and looked around me. Suddenly there was silence, except the pounding of the waves, and it seemed that, at that moment, everyone on the beach had stopped what they were doing and had simply paused to watch. Every head on the beach seemed to be turned in Ricochet's direction, moved by how excited this dog was to see Patrick. I thought she'd jump and dance around him, maybe flip a little sand up in his face, but when she reached him, she sat down respectfully by his side.

Even from a distance you could feel the emotional bond between the two of them—Patrick in his chair and Ricochet racing to greet him, gazing up into his eyes. I could actually feel Ricochet's focus on Patrick.

Still, I was surprised at Ricochet's enthusiasm. Their connection was electrifying, and although they had only met for a half-hour the night before, they blended so effortlessly, and knowingly, like pieces in a jigsaw puzzle in a life of its own.

True, he was an amazing person—the sort of boy everyone falls in love with and feels comfortable around immediately—but there hadn't been a lot of time for Ricochet to get to know him. Yet, perhaps, there had been more than enough time, for I had begun to realize that Ricochet saw things in people that I didn't see.

"Hello, Sunshine!" Patrick beamed.

I could almost hear Ricochet thinking, *Patrick! Are you ready to surf? Are you ready?*

They were communing like they'd been together a thousand times before, speaking to each other in a language that crossed species barriers and broke through incredulity. Just then, the commotion began again as Patrick's team lifted him into the water. I watched as he positioned himself on his custom board, giving him a way to hold on. The group helped him out past the breakwater and into the surf.

I walked out into the shallow water with Ricochet and a volunteer, and I felt a surge of pride as she hopped up gracefully and easily onto her blue board and balanced herself as the waves rolled and broke. But along with the surge of pride, that sense of nervousness rose up again.

Could she do it? Would she do it?

The scene before us was completely chaotic: helpers, handlers, media, and Patrick's support team were all out in the waves, shouting back and forth and jostling around. Ricochet was venturing out in the water with strangers away from me. There was a flurry of helpers and handlers for Ricochet and for Patrick in case he fell off. He was completely helpless out there in the waves and counted entirely on his team. But there, balancing on her board, wearing her pink rash guard and orange life vest, Ricochet seemed fine with everything that was going on. I stroked her to reassure her, but perhaps I was the one who needed reassurance.

"Ready, Ric?" I asked. She looked over at me.

"Are you ready to have some fun?" Her chocolate-brown eyes seemed to say yes.

Ricochet and Patrick were pushed farther out, their helpers wading waist-high in the breaking waves. Ricochet positioned herself on her board as Patrick's volunteers helped him through the waves on his board, and then pushed them both out into the water on their separate boards to catch their first wave.

"Here it comes!" someone yelled. "This one! *This one!*" The helpers moved Patrick and Ricochet into position to catch the wave. As the wave approached, the excitement on the beach intensified. I glanced to the shore at the people and news stations.

"You can do it, Ricochet. You can do it!" I shouted.

And then they were off, riding the same wave on their individual boards and gliding toward shore. Patrick rode, grinning the whole time, and as I watched, I remembered his words: "I look back on the beach and I can see my empty chair. I'm free out there."

I caught sight of Ricochet balancing on her own board, leaning into the wave, and then adjusting her weight. She surfed in on Patrick's right side, repeatedly turning her head in his direction. Her attention on him amazed me. She was watching him, checking up, keeping track of where he was and where he was going. As they both reached the shore at the same time, Ricochet leaped from her board and bounded back into the water, wagging her tail enthusiastically the whole time. I'd never seen her so eager and happy.

We walked out again and once more they surfed in. Usually after a couple of waves, Ricochet would refuse to go back in the water, planting herself like a toddler who crosses her arms and says "no," preferring to play on the beach instead. But this time, she kept eagerly running back in again, and again, and again. They rode a few more waves in and my spirits rose. Still, I just couldn't let go of the memory of Ricochet growing bored and quitting. This all seemed just too good to be true.

Ricochet constantly checked on Patrick, and Patrick focused straight ahead, grinning and laughing. Then Ricochet leaped off her board again, soaking wet and smiling, bouncing back into the waves, her tail waving back and forth. And then Ricochet did something beyond the scope of my imagination, but something that I would marvel over for the rest of my life.

At the end of a long ride, the two of them had coasted up onto the shore simultaneously. Ricochet hopped off her board, but instead of immediately turning around and jumping back through the waves like she had been doing, I watched as she jumped off her board and literally took a leap of faith onto Patrick's board. One of his helpers, probably nervous for Patrick and uncertain what Ricochet was doing, motioned gently for her to step off. I had no idea why Ricochet would do that, but something urged me to pay attention and to listen to what she was saying. All at once I knew without a doubt. I *felt* her message.

Right there, as clear as day, Ricochet was telling me she wanted to surf tandem with Patrick. It was something I never would have thought of on my own, but I was willing to try if the others were game.

"Patrick, she wants to surf with you," I said, not knowing where the words came from. How could I let a dog stand on a board with a boy who was quadriplegic?

"That'd be cool!" Patrick grinned.

"I can run home and get a bigger board," offered one of Patrick's friends.

It seemed everyone was willing to give this idea of Ricochet's a shot. It wasn't clear to me what I was feeling: Amazement? Shock? *Trust?* Maybe for the first time since Ricochet had come into my life, I was listening to what she had been trying to tell me all those long months when she'd resisted my training.

When the boy came back with the bigger board, I said to Patrick and his team, "I have no idea what to do. I've never done this before."

Ricochet had never done anything remotely like this before, and I had no expectations of her on this day beyond making a fund-raising video. And here was a boy with a disability and I was asking him and his mother and their assembled team to put their trust in a *dog*. He could flip over. Ricochet could unbalance him and he could drown out there. It was all so new. I had no idea how to position Ricochet on the board. *She* had no idea how to position herself with someone else on the board . . . or so I thought.

"All I can do is trust Ricochet to know what she's doing," I told them all.

As people hovered around us, I thought, *This is the dog who has let me down time and time again.* Now I was trusting her completely.

"Can you trust my dog?" I asked fourteen-year-old Patrick.

"Sure! Let's do it!" he answered without hesitation.

At that moment, I knew everyone there had to trust Ricochet.

Patrick's team lifted Patrick onto the board first. Then we let Ricochet hop on the board, and she positioned herself. She was unable to stand on the board the way she normally did when she surfed solo, with all four of her legs placed squarely on the surface. Patrick's outstretched legs took up the space, so she had to stand sideways, her legs between his, with one leg curled and with her paw resting over his back. I was apprehensive, but I simply had to believe that she would figure out by herself how to surf tandem with Patrick on one board. And she did.

Overriding my nervousness, I could feel the amazement of all of the people helping, together with the newscasters, at what was about to happen. I think more than a few people were holding their breath, afraid to believe that what we were attempting was possible, but ardently hoping it was. The team pushed Ricochet and Patrick out on the board together, turned them around through the rocking motion of the waves, and then in one incredible moment, Ricochet and Patrick were surfing together on the same board, riding a wave of hope that changed their lives forever.

The sounds of yelling and clapping from people in the water and on the shore rose to a crescendo louder than the breaking waves. There were so many different people and strangers, but little by little you could feel the bond growing as the blond boy and the red dog surfed tandem, uniting everyone, showing us what we had in common. The strangers I had met at the beginning now felt like one big family, sharing something that had never before happened. It was one of those brief moments, spaces of time, that seemed to exist outside of time, and just *is*. I could feel the purity of the moment.

When they coasted into shore amid the whooping cheers, chills tingled up my arm—and not from the cold. I looked at Ricochet, who was ready to do it again, and not only ready but eager and excited. The two teams, Ricochet's and Patrick's, came together as one and were trusting Ricochet. Again, they positioned them. And again, they caught a wave. As I watched Ricochet in her bright-orange jacket against the dark gray rolling waves, I saw a look on her face. It's a look I've never forgotten. She was staring so intently out into the ocean that I turned quickly, wondering if she had seen a bird, so intense was her look, but in the moment that I turned my head, I knew—I felt deep within me—that there was no bird. I don't know what she saw, only what *I* saw: that Ricochet was focused, intensely *focused*; she was alive and excited and not only doing something that she wanted, but something that had great meaning. It was a cosmic moment.

For the next several waves Ricochet and Patrick rode not on two separate boards, but on one. Ricochet was asking for someone to recognize what she had to say, standing guard behind Patrick as he fulfilled his dream to be free. It was as if she was always meant for this very moment. She was very clearly telling me what she wanted to do. It was as if this was her destiny. She had been reborn!

There was no doubt she felt completely comfortable, at home even, on that board behind Patrick. She was in her own way exactly as free as Patrick had described himself feeling. She may not have seen a wheelchair off in the distance, but she was looking at something that had finally set her free.

Patrick was nodding and grinning ear to ear, wider than ever, as Ricochet stood balancing between his legs. Patrick twitched and jerked as he rode the board because his legs were spasming, which shook Ricochet's body. I don't how she could possibly stay on, but she did, figuring it out all on her own. There she stood, her head just behind Patrick, watching, gauging their every movement, adjusting her weight just right, counterbalancing so Patrick wouldn't fall off, as if she'd been doing it for years. The rest of the world seemed to disappear as the light of her rebirth shone brilliantly even though the sky was gray. The universe pulsed with life, and everything became more alive.

It can take people a long time to learn to shift their weight and be in sync with someone else on the board. One surfer has to lean when the other surfer leans. If Ricochet shifted her weight the wrong way, the pair could've wiped out. And yet she knew instinctively how to counterbalance Patrick's movements. In fact, as I watched, a crashing wave knocked their board. They careened to the left, and just as soon as they did, Ricochet repositioned her weight. She saved them from wiping out!

The teamwork was amazing, especially since many of the helpers and handlers didn't know one another or hadn't worked together before. Of course, none of his helpers had ever surfed a person with a dog on board! Even so, everyone cared for Ricochet just like they did for Patrick. Standing in the ocean waves, I felt a warmth begin to spread through me as I watched Ricochet in awe. And as Ricochet stood, looking over Patrick's shoulder, ever vigilant, I knew then that nothing—no birds, no dogs, *nothing*—could distract this incredible creature from her newfound purpose. She was committed 100 percent. And she had chosen this all on her own. Ricochet's sacred work had officially begun.

I smiled at the awestruck expressions around me, as people nodded, cheered, and gave the thumbs-up or shaka signs. There was a collective feeling of euphoria on the beach that day. It may have originated with Ricochet and Patrick, but we could all feel it rippling outward, touching every person witnessing the two of them. I doubted if any one of the onlookers, supporters, or team members would ever forget these magical moments, as they seemed to have awakened something so incredibly profound in each of us.

No one on the beach that day would've guessed that this was an unmotivated dog who wouldn't do one thing I asked—that is, until she had finally convinced me to let her do what she was put on this earth to do. She was a different dog. I thought back to all those terrible months we fought—Ricochet resisting and me tearing my hair out—and somehow all that was wiped away as I finally understood what she wanted to do.

Ricochet and Patrick surfed about twenty waves together, and not once did she quit. I had the sense that Ricochet was doing much more than surfing. She was truly helping Patrick, giving of her energy. And when he fell off the board, which he did once, she was right there by his side. Not once did she need to be urged or even told what to do. She was bounding and happy.

For me the world had always been a negative and scary place, full of bad, and now here on the beach I felt an amazing energy that everyone was sharing. Ricochet was out there in the ocean on the back of Patrick's board. I knew her spirit was free. And I knew something else: Ricochet was finally able to show me her purpose. Her months of resistance had simply been her way of staying true to herself, not bending to fit someone else's expectations and desires. There was nothing else she wanted to do, and that was why she'd resisted anything that wasn't in line with her purpose. She was here for a reason, and now that I was listening to her, she was finally at peace.

In that one moment, I suddenly understood everything: all the frustrating days with her became crystal clear for me as I watched her surf with such empowerment and purpose, doing what she was born to do.

When I let go of my expectations, I created room in my heart for unconditional love and acceptance. Once I quieted my thoughts, and really listened to Ricochet, I finally understood her destiny, and it was something she chose herself. Her unique talent to be of service to others was finally allowed to break free of my fervent grasp and my expectations of what I wanted her to be. I knew with certainty that she was perfect the way she was. I accepted her greatness in the unique and novel way she presented it.

She was speaking and I was finally listening. I didn't need an animal communicator to tell me what she was saying, because Ricochet was speaking to my soul, and it was more powerful than if someone had given me a shot of adrenaline in the chest.

That day was perhaps my first glimmer of a feeling that would return to me again and again as Ricochet bonded with those who needed her: out there on that board with Patrick, with a whole family of people—whether related or not—trusting her, she was standing in a place of purity and goodness that few humans really ever touch.

When they finally finished, Patrick's friends and volunteers rolled him up into the sand and Ricochet bounded over to him, wagging her tail like a propeller. "Come on!" Patrick urged when she placed her head in his lap, and she jumped up onto him and into his arms, closing her eyes and rubbing her head against him.

Patrick wrapped his arms around her, both of them soaking wet and full of sand but high on surfing and life—a perfect picture of mutual love, respect, and trust. A reporter approached Patrick just then, full of questions about how it felt to surf with a dog. One part of the interview still sticks out in my mind:

"And were you ever scared?" the reporter asked.

"No, not really. There was a big trust thing going on. It's not the safest environment to begin with. But surfing is not about catching some perfect, epic wave," Patrick explained. "It's all about a spiritual connection. And trust. It's about being one with nature and the water . . . but to have that connection with a dog? *That* was mind-blowing! It was incredible, totally inspiring, a little surreal, and deeply spiritual. It's hard to put into words. Totally intense, and at the same time, peaceful and healing."

Ricochet was on his lap smiling proudly when Patrick said the next words.

"But it didn't seem like I was surfing with a dog. It seemed like I was surfing with a really good buddy, like a friend."

Some people stood by and filmed, others just watched, but all could feel that a small miracle had just transpired and perhaps transformed everyone who'd seen a boy and a dog, catching waves and opening hearts.

That evening, I went home exhausted but at the same time more energized and happy than I could ever remember. I collapsed onto the sofa between Rina and a happily tired-out Ricochet.

Beside me Rina thumped her tail and Ricochet looked up at me, satisfaction across her face. Her eyes looked into mine and I easily read her expression.

"I know, I know," I said. "You're just a free spirit. You don't want to be anyone other than who you are."

She continued to stare up at me, and for some reason, I nodded my head then while looking at her. I petted her head and gazed into her eyes. I had an odd feeling that she was thanking me for listening. She was finally happy. She had clearly told me what she wanted when she jumped from her board to Patrick's, hoping that someone would hear her. We could've missed the whole day. But for some reason, I was more aware and more open. I heard her and understood what she was asking. Still, I could've dismissed her. I could've pulled her from the board, afraid of what people would think, or afraid she could hurt Patrick. But I had listened to her and trusted her. Everyone trusted her. Ricochet was finally doing what she wanted to do. She was nineteen months old now, and she had been trying to tell me for so long what she wanted.

The sacredness of the day remained with me—the healing power of the ocean, together with the healing power of a dog, and how they had created a sacred space of purity that was filled not only with pure joy but with serenity and peace, enveloping all who watched. I knew that Patrick had felt it, too. And I knew that for each of us, Ricochet and me, there had been a rebirth; something had been released out there in the ocean waves and now something new was beginning. I felt a sense of overwhelming goodness. While I could feel it, at the same time, it was foreign to me. I didn't know what "good" was. I didn't even know how to respond to this incredible, overwhelming emotional high that I was feeling, for it was my first taste of pure goodness. The only way I could express it was through tears. Tears of complete and utter joy.

On the beach that day, I trusted fully in Ricochet and the divine higher power that was guiding her. Some may call it God or the Universe, but the name didn't matter to me. The fact is, I saw it and I felt it, and I was willing to trust it just as I had trusted Ricochet. From that point on, I surrendered my control to the incredibly powerful and positive energy surrounding me, and I could feel my own heart, open and alive, as I did.

Sometimes good things fall apart so better things can fall together.

# Chapter 9

# Goodness Always Prevails

*"Where there is light, there is shadow."*

—LAWRENCE ENGLISH

Jennifer was down to her last dollar for Patrick's therapy, scrambling to figure out how she would pay for his next visit, let alone anything beyond that. It was time to focus on fund-raising. I compiled a fund-raising video and sent an email to all of my contacts asking them to watch the video and donate to Patrick's cause. By joining Facebook, with a few clicks of a button, I watched as people began spreading the word of Patrick's goal to walk across the stage at his graduation, posting the links on their own Facebook pages, Web sites, and message boards. Just as when you throw one small stone into the water and it ripples outward, affecting the surface of the lake, so, too, does one good deed beget another. One friend knew someone who knew somebody else, and the story spread from one person to the next.

While the donations were not flooding in, the positive energy of the people supporting our cause was contagious to all, young and old alike. Everyone who saw the fund-raising video had beautiful things to say about Ricochet and Patrick, and I knew we were on the right path. My five-year-old niece, Andrea, was so inspired that she made her first-ever donation of fifty dollars. "Can we get him a doggie, Mom?" she asked after watching it. I savored the goodness that was coming from our efforts, even if it was not a steady stream of dollar signs.

Since Ricochet had done so well in the Purina contest, I entered her in a couple more surf dog contests that summer that benefited animal charities. Yet regardless of how she fared, participating would raise more awareness.

Our first competition was the Loews Coronado Bay Resort Surf Dog Contest. Sporting an orange "Sur-fur Girl" vest and matching lei, Ricochet found her spot in the sand with the Golden SurFURS, a local golden retriever meet-up group. She was one of the last dogs to surf, and by the time her turn rolled around, in true Ricochet style, she had to give a good chase to the nearby shorebirds first.

Thankfully, this event offered helpers in the water to assist the dogs, so I didn't have to worry about trying to position her into the deeper water and onto her board by myself. She didn't place in any of the heats and I wondered if her performance at the Purina contest was beginner's luck. As I chatted with the other participants, I learned that I'd need help handling Ricochet in the upcoming contests since neither event offered assistance.

I began my search for a water handler by contacting surf schools, Craigs-list, and friends, but it turned up nothing. *Where was a water helper when you needed one in a surfing mecca of the world?* I knew people were busy, and this was purely volunteer, but even so, with time running out, I needed to find someone. I didn't want my disability to hold Ricochet back from her purpose or hurt Patrick's fund-raiser.

With just weeks to go until the next contest, I got a call from my friend Sarah who had some good news to share. I didn't dare hope. Her friend Brian was willing to help Ricochet, and not only was he a surfer, but he recruited some friends to help, too.

On September 13, Ricochet entered the Helen Woodward Animal Center Surf Dog Surf-a-thon at Del Mar Dog Beach. There were close to a hundred dogs in the contest vying for the top spot in their heat, which would take them to the finals. It was crazy and chaotic with dogs in the water, dogs playing on the sand, and people milling about filming, watching, or waiting for their turn to surf.

My heart raced as Brian brought Ricochet out to take her first waves.

*Calm down, Judy, Ricochet knows what she's doing*, I told myself.

The sounds of dogs barking and people cheering ceased as I watched Ricochet doing what she loved. Suddenly I could only hear the waves flowing in, and as they curled around her, Ricochet was calm and completely in control of her board. She surfed many long rides, standing tall on the board, looking like a pro gliding in—sometimes facing forward, then turning around backward, then forward again. I winced when she almost collided with a big black Labrador on a yellow board, but she shifted her weight just in time and the board veered to safety. In the short time she'd been surfing, she'd improved so much. Apparently the judges agreed: she was the first-place winner in the large-dog category, second heat, which qualified her for the finals.

"You did it, Ric!" I cheered, as she sat on her board with a lei around her neck. But the excitement was short lived because Brian's friends had to leave before the finals.

*How would we pull off surfing with just one person helping Ricochet?*

Luckily, just before the finals started, Patrick's surf coach, Robbie, showed up to help. He'd heard that we might need a hand, and he volunteered out of the goodness of his heart.

The final competition was fast and furious as the dogs and their handlers rushed to get in as many waves as they could in twenty minutes. Dogs were scored on the length of the ride, the size of the wave, and any tricks they performed on the board, such as turning around or riding backward.

Ricochet and Buddy, a Jack Russell terrier, rode one of the last waves of the heat side by side, with their boards nearly touching the whole way. It was a race to the finish! Yet in the last seconds, Buddy edged ahead to take first place, with Ricochet coming in second place overall. Not a bad day's work for a competition with more than one hundred dogs! And since Buddy was an awesome surfer who typically won every contest, coming in second to him was a huge accomplishment and helped confirm that Ricochet was on a mission—and perhaps had been on one from birth. I was thrilled, not only because the event raised money for homeless animals at the Helen Woodward Animal Center, but also because Ricochet was able to surf to her full potential with Brian's and Robbie's help. Winning this contest gave us the momentum we needed—it meant more awareness, which meant more money and potential sponsors for Patrick.

Yet despite all of the positivity, a black cloud was looming. Someone in the surfing community had started a rumor insinuating that Robbie, our helper at the last event, was a professional surfer and that I had sought him out with the sole intention to help Ricochet win. Robbie's random act of kindness was being completely misconstrued by someone's warped view of a helping hand. While I knew some people could be spiteful, it was hard to understand how someone could be so negative about such a positive cause.

For my own peace of mind, I knew I had to ignore the rumors. Yet as hard as I tried, the deluge of drama was weighing on me. I felt like I had an albatross around my neck with the familiar sick feeling gnawing at my stomach. The energy and excitement I had over fund-raising was hampered by naysayers. I was being told by the person who started the rumor that other people agreed. I couldn't let Ricochet's goodness or mission be tainted by turmoil. While I knew there was some lesson to be learned, I couldn't find it.

I decided to contact the event officials and ask if they had any problems with Ricochet's win. They assured me that the contest had been a goodwill fund-raiser. Not only were they happy that Ricochet had taken second place, we hadn't broken any rules. Despite the backing from the officials, the negativity remained amplified in my head.

With the thoughts still ruminating, I received an email from a reporter at the Associated Press, who had been hoping to write a surf dog story for a while. She noticed the buzz building about Patrick and Ricochet and loved the angle that Ricochet was a service dog in the making and then became a "dropout." The Associated Press boasted a huge audience, and an article would spread the word of Patrick's fund-raiser on a much larger scale. I crossed my fingers when the reporter met us at the beach.

"Ricki and I have only surfed a couple times," Patrick told him. "It worked the first time, which kind of surprised me. I didn't expect it would go as well as it did."

"Patrick and Ricochet instantly connected," Jennifer agreed. "The first time they ever met, there was this instant bond. They clicked right away."

The reporter nodded, smiling as Ricochet looked up at Patrick, and Patrick stroked her head. "Ricochet will leap up right into his lap. I can tell Ricki loves to surf, and I *know* Patrick does. So when you put the two together, it's truly amazing," Jennifer said.

"She really knows how to balance," Patrick explained. "It's kind of crazy, but once when we were about to fall over, she just stepped on the other side of the board and evened us out."

The reporter wanted to round out the article by filming some live action at the next surfing event. We thought that if the contest officials agreed, perhaps we could even do a live demonstration with Patrick and Ricochet surfing together.

I contacted the Surf City Surf Dog event team, and they graciously agreed to team up with us to make Patrick an official beneficiary of the event; what's more, they gave us the green light to perform a tandem surfing demonstration for the media. Through our Surfin' for Paws-abilities program, any money raised would go directly to help fund Patrick's therapy and get him a service dog.

While this was wonderful news, I didn't have a chance to savor it. I heard there were more rumors brewing and even a plan of action in motion. Someone was contacting surf contest organizers, urging them to change the rules so that "only owners can be in the water with their dogs." I felt this suggestion was outrageous. I figured it was directed at Ricochet and me, and I couldn't believe someone would actually go to these lengths to keep us from our cause. I worried that if the rules changed, we'd be shut out of any competitions because I physically couldn't go into the deeper, rougher water.

Even though my disability isn't obvious to the naked eye, it's a ghost that's haunted me my entire life. While I've accepted my limitations as a normal part of my life, I didn't want Ricochet to be confined by my limitations. She'd finally found her purpose, and she was *doing good work*. And once again, just as things were looking up, it seemed that I was being told, "Sorry, Judy, good things don't happen to you."

The light that filtered into my world from Ricochet's triumphant surf with Patrick was dimming, snuffed out by one or two detractors. Something momentous was happening, but I couldn't enjoy it because my thoughts were consumed with negativity. Goodness abounded around me, but my mind kept going back to the badness. It was like I was standing in the most beautiful, sunny meadow and all I could see was one small, dark, menacing cloud hovering above.

Days later, Ricochet and I went to the beach to unwind with some friends. I was relaying the situation to Dave, a fellow surfer and a longtime member of Patrick's team of handlers. He graciously listened to me vent—probably longer than necessary—and then said gently, "Judy, goodness always prevails."

*Was he crazy? What world did Dave live in?* But he was so kind and sincere that I didn't want to burst his bubble of optimism. "You'll see, Judy," Dave said, as he looked out into the waves. "Ricochet's legacy won't be about winning contests. Ricochet's true legacy will be in how many lives she transforms."

I felt a tingle ripple down my arms. Dave had been involved with adaptive surfing all his life, and it had obviously taught him what really mattered. We were trying to change Patrick's life, not just win surfing competitions. I wanted to think we were making a difference, however small.

"Don't worry, Judy," he repeated louder. "Goodness *will* prevail."
I nodded to be polite, but I didn't believe him.

As the sun moved across the sky, casting a shadow on the beach, Dave came back to say good-bye. He said that, since he lived close to the next surfing event, he could help us if we needed him. *Boy, did I need him.* For the past decade, I had lived my life alone, closed off from people and afraid to reach out. But now Dave was reaching out to me, and even though it was difficult for me to accept help, I was ready to receive it for Patrick and Ricochet.

With all of the goodness that had washed over me quite literally in the waves the day that Ricochet and Patrick first surfed together, I wasn't going to let anyone keep Ricochet from surfing. I couldn't. What Ricochet was doing wasn't for me; it was for Patrick, and if she couldn't surf, Patrick might not get the money he needed for therapy. Then I thought of Ricochet, standing up for who she was, resisting for months, and I thought, *Don't give in.*

I accepted Dave's offer regardless of how it would be perceived by the one or two bullies who preferred to interfere in something they knew nothing about. I had found the first member of Ricochet's team—her first water handler who was to become a constant in Ricochet's life.

When I returned home, I received a phone call that lifted my spirits to incredible heights. I actually let out a squeal when I heard the news that would change Patrick and Jennifer's lives. Apparently, word of our fund-raiser had circulated and a charitable organization wanted to help. Things were looking up.

The day before the contest, I took Ricochet to the beach to let off some steam. She surfed a bit but kept jumping off her board, which was something she hadn't done in a long time. As the waves rolled in and out and the clouds drifted across the sky, I heard a strange sound. It was Ricochet whining.

"Ricochet, what is it?" I asked, looking into her eyes. She was limping. I examined her legs and they were fine, but when I looked on the underside of each paw, I found a pea-sized tear in her pad.

"Oh, Ricochet," I said, inspecting the wound, which was red, moist, and raw. "You poor thing."

She must have cut it on a shell when she was running, and my mind turned to what it knew best: *It figures this would happen. Something bad always happens.*

While the vet said the wound was minor, it was painful. He wrapped Ricochet's foot in a latex bootie and cautioned that we would have to wait to see if she'd be able to surf.

*What would I tell Patrick?* All of the media attention to help garner funds could unravel if we couldn't do the demo. But with the sand and saltwater, I didn't think Ricochet could surf without irritating her paw, and I couldn't imagine she'd *want* to surf.

I didn't dare call Jennifer and Patrick to tell them. I'd wait until the morning and see how Ricochet was feeling.

The next day Ricochet and I met them at the beach. Patrick took one look at Ricochet's latex boot. "We shouldn't surf," he said without any hesitation.

I was moved by his compassion. Instead of thinking of his own recovery and the money he and his mother needed for his therapy, he was only concerned for Ricochet's welfare. For weeks we had someone trying to prevent us from surfing due to their own agenda, and here was this boy who would selflessly give it up out of love for my dog.

"Let's see what she tells us later," I offered. "She may want to surf with you," I added, trying to sound hopeful.

Just then we saw a familiar face.

"Hey, Ricki!" Dave said as he walked toward us. Ricochet's tail wagged furiously and she moved in to lick his face as he crouched down to pat her. "What happened to your paw?"

"She had a run-in with a shell yesterday and the shell won; she cut her paw pad. We'll need to see if she's up to surfing," I explained.

"Hang in there, Ric," he said. "Those waves can get pretty rough even if you don't have a bum paw. But don't worry, Judy, I've got her back out there if she's able to surf."

Dave's reverence for the ocean was obvious, and his concern for Ricochet touched me deeply.

Knowing Ricochet was in good hands, I went to find Jennifer who was talking to Denise, a Paws'itive Teams assistant trainer. As I got closer, squinting through the sun, I noticed she was crying.

"Hey, Jennifer," I said, touching her arm while trying to contain my smile. "What's wrong?"

"Judy!" she exclaimed. "Nothing is wrong. In fact, everything is all right—so incredibly right!"

Jennifer's chest heaved, and although words were starting to come, she couldn't get them out. Suddenly she burst into hysterics—what she would later refer to as "ugly crying"—and she couldn't catch her breath. Then she told me the momentous news. Denise was able to coordinate the efforts of the Rose Foundation, a charitable organization that had become aware of Patrick's plight and his dream to walk at his graduation because of our fund-raiser.

Not only did they want to help, they wanted to contribute in a major way. They had most generously offered a grant that would cover approximately three years of Patrick's therapy!

With tears streaming down her face, Jennifer was finally able to articulate how this wonderful reality would impact their lives. "We didn't know where we would get the money to pay for therapy for next week. Now I don't have to worry for several years?" She jumped up and down, and then embraced me in the warmest hug I can remember. "I can't believe, it Judy!" she gushed. "This is so amazing! You are so amazing. We are so grateful to everyone."

The enormity of her relief and appreciation was palpable, and bringing joy of this magnitude to someone else was an incredible feeling.

"Patrick is going to get all the therapy he needs—*for three entire years!*" Jennifer was laughing and crying, her mouth agape. Patrick's dream to walk at his graduation was now a financial possibility.

She and I remained in shock, smiling, giggling uncontrollably, and at times snorting, shaking our heads at the generosity of this organization.

Still giddy, we laughed our way back to find Dave and Ricochet. When Dave saw our faces, he asked, "Who won the lottery?"

"You don't know how right you are!" we kidded and conveyed the wonderful turn of events. While we continued to bask in the glow of the news, Ricochet's heat was approaching.

"What do you say, Ricochet?" I asked. "Are you ready to surf?"

Dave grabbed the board and followed the rest of the team toward the water. Ricochet jumped up, her tail swishing back and forth. She was off in a flash. When we put the board down, she jumped right on with complete abandon.

"Well, I guess we have our answer," I said. "She wants to surf!"

It didn't matter how she placed in the contest, but we could still put on a good show for the media to help raise more funds. We still had Patrick's service dog to pay for. I watched as Dave set her up for each wave, whispering words of encouragement into her ear before each one. "Ready, Ricochet?"

Ricochet surfed every wave with focus and determination. I watched as she coasted into shore at least a half dozen times, never losing her focus. She was a bit subdued, but that was to be expected with her paw. She came in first in her heat, surfed in the finals, and then she and Patrick performed their demo in perfect harmony, just as they had the first day together. When the judges announced Ricochet as a winner, I turned to Patrick and asked him to go up and accept the award with her. No one was more deserving of the spotlight than this selfless soul. He and Ricochet reached the staging area to cheers, whistles, and clapping.

I stared at Ricochet, unable to really comprehend what she'd done with her injured foot. It was a lot to ask of her, and yet I felt she'd known her role in it all along . . . and she persevered. I couldn't believe how powerful one dog could be . . . when I just let her *be*. I felt more goodness encircling us, eclipsing the darkness and making our struggles seem worth it. I finally understood the lesson in the trial: When you finally allow yourself to let go and rise above the adversity, you can see virtue and hope on the horizon. Keep believing in yourself and what you know is right, no matter what.

The following week the Associated Press story was released to 1,800 newspapers, radio and TV stations, and Internet news sites. Soon Patrick and Ricochet were surfing together all over the virtual world, and Ricochet had a big, beautiful paw behind

The Purina Pro Plan Incredible Dog Challenge, 2009.

©KillerImage.com

Ricochet . . . free to be!

©Sit'nStayGlobal

Ricochet chasing ducks.

My original plan: Ricochet and Patrick surfing on their own boards, but on the same wave.

©Diane Edmonds

Ricochet's plan: surfing tandem on one board.

©Diane Edmonds

Ricochet and Patrick out in the surf.

©Robert Ochoa (Pawmazing)

Ricochet and Patrick.

©Robert Ochoa (Pawmazing)

Ricochet counter-balances the board to keep Patrick from falling off.

©Robert Ochoa (Pawmazing)

©Nikki Bowyer

Patrick walking across the stage at his high school graduation.

©Sean Callahan, SoCal Beaches TV

©Barbara McKown

Patrick, Jennifer, and Ricochet; the healing power of the ocean and the healing power of a dog.

Ricochet and Patrick after their first surf session.

Ricochet and Ian's first meeting.

©Barbara McKown

Mirror images of Ricochet and Ian.

©Robert Ochoa (Pawmazing)

©Robert Ochoa (Pawmazing)

Ian's Aunt Melissa's
THANK YOU in the sand.

Ricochet and Ian surfing.

©KillerImage.com

©Larry Brambles

Ian enjoying Ricochet's kisses.

©Barbara McKown

©KillerImage.com

Ricochet and her water handler Dave.

©Diane Edmon

Ricochet showing her gratitude to Dave.

all of it. I turned on my computer one day to discover that AOL featured the AP story with the top stories of the day. "Paralyzed Boy Is Surfing Star."

Jennifer called me, bubbling with excitement. "This is so unreal!" she exclaimed. "The amount of awareness this is raising is incredible!"

I could feel her joy and positive energy through the phone.

We continued fund-raising until the end of October. When our campaign was done, a group of us took Patrick and Jennifer out to dinner to officially present Patrick with the $10,000 Ricochet had raised and to celebrate the grant. Our crew included Carol, Denise, Charli, and Art, the executive director from Paws'itive Teams. Although the restaurant didn't allow dogs inside other than service dogs, the owner of the restaurant quickly invited Ricochet in when he heard she was outside. Also among us was Patrick's new service dog, Kona, a gorgeous yellow Labrador retriever/golden retriever mix that we funded with the donations.

I was thrilled that Ricochet could join us as we celebrated and replayed the amazing events of the past months, because she was the one who had done most of the work. When it was time for Patrick's picture with Kona, everyone wanted Ricochet in the photograph, too. Kona sat on one side of Patrick and Ricochet sat on the other side, and in between Patrick grinned out to the camera. Then, with Patrick proudly holding up his check, we took pictures of just Patrick and Ricochet. As the flashes flickered, Patrick turned to me and, with a nod toward Ricochet, said, "Kona is my service dog. But Ricochet is my *SURF*ice dog!"

I laughed, realizing how true it was. Ricochet leaped up and licked Patrick's cheek. I knew she understood.

Back at the table a brief while later, I turned to Jennifer and asked, "How are we ever going to top *this*?" I peeked under the tablecloth and saw Ricochet looking up at me. She was listening to everything we said.

"Here's to Ricochet!" Patrick said.

"And to Kona," I cheered.

Jennifer looked like she was ready to burst into tears. "I can't believe how much we raised! Ricochet gave Patrick the gift of independence and the gift of recovery, and you can't put a price tag on that. I can't thank you . . ."

I stopped her from going on. "I didn't do anything," I said with a smile.

"To Ricochet!" Patrick repeated.

*Yes,* I thought to myself, *to Ricochet—and to staying true to who you are.*

As we clinked glasses, I realized with a shudder how close Ricochet had come to having her mission thwarted. If I'd backed down from the rumors, or if the surf dog contest rules had been changed, none of this would be happening.

My little dog was still teaching me and, like her, I remained true to my heart and her mission. Most people have been bullied at some point in their lives, and some, unfortunately, buckle under the pressure, conforming to other people's standards. They lose sight of what makes them unique. Sometimes they even lose sight of who they are. Ricochet showed me how to honor and celebrate individuality no matter what anyone's expectations of you are or what obstacles they throw in front of you.

I realized that there will always be darkness in our lives—and that sometimes light actually attracts dark—but if we persevere, we will eventually find the beacon of light. Fortunately, I had found light: people like Dave, Patrick, and Jennifer, who were making dreams come true despite adversity. There's always darkness, but it's what you do with it that matters most. With that one difficult, yet valuable, lesson under my belt, I felt the good surrounding us again, blanketing us with powerful energy.

Feeling incredibly blessed by all that had transpired, I created another video called *From Service Dog to SURFice Dog*. I had always made videos of my dogs—mostly puppy training videos and some silly, goofy ones that I knew nobody but me would care about or watch. Now that I was on Facebook, I was able to post them to share with other dog-lovers. Since most of the people already knew Patrick's story, I wanted to share Ricochet's background before she met Patrick. In the video I revealed not only her strengths but also her perceived weaknesses, such as chasing after birds. I showed her birth and how she had been a puppy prodigy, but then I shared how distracted she became and how frustrated I was. I didn't sugarcoat anything. The footage was honest and real. Since I was surrounded by so much positive energy from the surf session, I'm sure the video captured that sentiment, but I had no expectations about whether anyone would even bother to watch it when I hit "upload."

When I logged on to my computer a few days later, I had to double-check the number: My video had reached 10,000 views in three days! I was stunned. In less than a week, the number climbed to 50,000 views. I couldn't believe my little homemade video was reaching so many people. Then it went completely viral. People sent comments from all over the world—Hong Kong, the United Kingdom, Argentina, and the Netherlands. Each person who watched the video found an individual message that touched them on many different levels, bringing them to tears while inspiring them to let go of their own expectations. The love Ricochet awakened when she first jumped on that board with Patrick was continuing, flowing ever outward, affecting lives far and wide.

But it was not only the dog-lovers who were sharing the video; it was parents and kids, therapists and life coaches, and even a group of biker guys who posted it on their motorcycle page! So many different walks of life were affected by Ricochet's message to stay true to yourself. It was such a simple mantra but not always easy.

She was like a spark that ignites and inspires others to focus on the can-do's in life. To teach people to let go of expectations, to accept others for who they are, to stay true to themselves, and to follow their hearts with the belief that anything is possible. She chose this unique way of reaching people through her surfing, but it was more than that; she was teaching life lessons.

When the leaders of "Pay It Forward Day," an initiative based on the novel of the same name, saw the video, they asked if Ricochet could be their ambassador. Of course I said yes, setting up a Paw It Forward movement on Ricochet's Web site, hoping to inspire many others to get active in their communities and "paw it forward" with their own unique talents.

As I powered up my computer each day, I was so uplifted by the positive messages that I almost didn't notice that the holidays were upon us. The most dreaded time of year for me. When my mother left the world on Christmas Eve, I discarded Christmas and all it represented. But this year, Ricochet was teaching me to turn my focus away from what I didn't have and focus instead on what I did have. I realized that I was blessed with good people in my life and that many people around the world had it far worse than I did.

On New Year's Eve, I turned on my computer, and once again, I couldn't believe my eyes. Before me was not five, but six zeros! Ricochet's video had hit the one million views mark! *One million?!* It was hard to fathom. Never in my life did I think Ricochet would make that much of an impact. In forty days, Ricochet's video had touched a million souls. It didn't seem possible, but there it was. I flinched involuntarily as I realized how close I'd come to finding her another home. Her life could have ended up very differently if I hadn't allowed her to be who she truly was. I wanted Ricochet to make a difference in one person's life as a service dog for a person with a disability, but Ricochet had other plans. She wanted to make a difference in the lives of millions. She took me on a completely different path than I'd set out on when I started Puppy Prodigies.

I knew then that I was only the driver; Ricochet was the navigator. For once in a very long time, I was actually hopeful as the new year dawned, knowing in my heart that Dave was right after all: Goodness *always* prevails.

## Three Years Later—Pawing It Forward

*In 2012 amid cheers, tears, whistles, and the deafening sound of applause, the announcer called out the name, "Patrick James Ivison" in the large school auditorium filled with graduating seniors, parents, siblings, and friends. Under normal conditions dogs would have been forbidden, but Ricochet was invited to this momentous event, where she lay on the floor by my feet. Then, as the cheering reached a crescendo, Patrick was wheeled to the stage. I knew how much work it had taken to get him here. Six hours of grueling therapy a week for the past three years, countless hours of stretching, and training at home. Yet each time he saw an improvement, however small, it encouraged him to work harder.*

*Now here onstage, in his white cap and gown, Patrick hoisted himself from his wheelchair with a look of strength and determination. Supported by a custom-built walker, and urged on by the trainer in front of him, each measured movement was his own as he stepped willfully across the stage. As his mother and sister looked on with pride, he reached for his diploma while standing on his own two feet.*

*The little blond-haired boy was suddenly grown up—the same boy whose sister had asked Santa if he could walk again had made his own dream come true with unwavering tenacity and a supportive group of family and friends—one of whom just happened to have fur. The crowd erupted into a standing ovation. Ricochet hopped up to her feet. I stood beside her, clapping and cheering, recalling that day in the water when Ricochet jumped on Patrick's board and their spirits merged, forever free.*

# Chapter 10

# Turning Tragedy to Triumph

*"It is often your deepest pain which empowers
you to grow to your highest self."*

—Karen Salmonsohn

The video was still going viral when the new year began. Since it had gotten so much exposure, I immediately turned the video into a platform from which Ricochet could spread her Paw It Forward message to help human and animal causes on a larger scale. I also added a small note at the end of the video asking for donations.

I found that people far and wide were not only willing to help, but *wanted* to help. They wanted to be part of something larger than themselves. Donations started coming in, so I knew I had to find a beneficiary. But who? With serendipity working once again, one morning I checked my email to find an article a friend had sent me titled "Ian Will Surf Again." It was the deeply tragic but ultimately uplifting and inspiring story of Ian McFarland.

On the night of July 2, 2008, Ian McFarland, along with his younger siblings, Lauren and Luke, and their parents, Stephanie and Tod, left their hometown of Carlsbad, California, en route to Boulder, Colorado, for a cousin's wedding. Ian had soccer assessments that day, so the family decided to drive through the night. The kids would sleep in the car on the way, and the family would arrive the next day. Stephanie's sister, Melissa Coleman, was also meeting them in Boulder, driving west from Tulsa, Oklahoma. The last time the sisters had seen each other was in May at their grandmother's funeral, and they were excited to spend more time together and with family. After the wedding, they planned to go camping in Colorado.

Melissa and Stephanie were two years apart and very close. They were used to talking on the phone every day, several times a day.

"I'm addicted to talking to you," Melissa joked to Stephanie because they spoke so often, each becoming worried if one was unable to reach the other.

Now Melissa worried about Stephanie, Tod, and the kids making the drive at night; she had a strange feeling a few days before they set out that something was not right.

Before going to sleep on July 2, Melissa called Stephanie, who was already en route, and the two sisters spoke briefly.

The next morning Melissa began calling to check on her sister and her family, but her calls weren't answered. Because she knew their route—full of mountainous passes and bad phone connections—she didn't initially worry. But as the day progressed, she began calling and calling more frantically. Something was wrong, yet she had no idea the McFarlands had been in an accident.

At 6:00 AM that morning, the McFarland family had stopped for gas and snacks. About forty-five minutes later, as they were driving up a bridge, they missed the curve. The driver lost control of the family's Ford Expedition on Interstate 70 about 150 miles south of Salt Lake City. The SUV veered off the road and into the median, then hit a reflector pole and continued down the median until it hit a wire mesh fence. There, it launched into the air, flipping end-over-end, falling off a bridge and onto the highway below where it came to a rest. The cement under the Ford Expedition was crushed.

Tod and Stephanie died on impact. Thankfully, the three children had been in children's seats but still sustained injuries; they were rushed to the Primary Children's Medical Center in Salt Lake City. Ian was five, Lauren was two, and little Luke was only a year old.

Melissa and her parents were already at the rehearsal dinner when the message came: There had been a terrible accident. But when they tried to return the call, they couldn't get through. They then decided to contact the police and ended up spending hours at the police department as officers called various hospitals and police stations, desperately trying to get some information on the family's whereabouts.

It was not until sometime after midnight that they were able to find out the tragic, unimaginable news—news that would forever change their lives. There had been an accident, and Stephanie and Tod had not survived. The three stood in stunned shock. Melissa's worst fear was unfolding. Her sister, her rock . . . was gone. But as the reality began to sink in, Melissa had one thought: She had to be with the kids. There was no question. Ever.

She walked away from her life in Tulsa, Oklahoma, without a second thought and didn't look back. She and her parents immediately tried to get a flight, her mind relentlessly thinking of the kids hurt and alone in the hospital without their parents, and that, combined with her sister's and Tod's death, was a pain deeper than she could bear. And yet she had to—for Stephanie's sake and for the sake of her sister's children. Not once did she waver in her decision. Not once was there ever a moment of "What shall I do?" She had no children herself; she had no attachments in Tulsa. She knew what she had to do. She just had to be there.

They arrived at the hospital desperate to get to the children. As they arrived, more details were emerging like bad dreams upon waking: The first reporters to the scene of the accident didn't think Ian had made it. Luke had been awake and screaming. The children were LifeFlighted to the hospital, and when rescue workers found Tod's ID badge to Scripps Green Hospital, they were able to contact his mother, who flew to Utah to be with the kids but had no way of contacting Melissa and her parents.

When they arrived, Ian was in a coma and having seizures. The doctors had put casts on his feet, and he had suffered a traumatic brain injury (TBI) called an axonal brain injury. There was no prognosis for him. That, for Melissa, became one of the hardest images to bear—seeing young Ian like that. She began praying to God for his survival. Lauren and Luke were badly bruised, but alive. The doctors urged the family to tell them right away that their parents were not alive. There were tears, shock, numbness .. . but ultimately the children were too young to understand what they were hearing. They thought Ian had not survived either.

The only thing that brought any remote comfort was holding on to these precious children. The doctors advised that it would be best to get them home and back to an environment that they knew, so Melissa, her sister, Christina, and her brother-in-law, Steve, left for Carlsbad, California, with Lauren and Luke—stuffing pillows up against the windows of the car so they couldn't see out. The freeway was now a very scary place for them. Melissa's parents and Tod's mom, Vi, stayed with Ian.

Once back in their own house, Lauren ran through the house crying, "Mommy? Daddy?" as Melissa stood by impotently, holding back tears. Scattered around the house were the to-do lists Stephanie had written before the trip; drawings and scriptures in Stephanie's handwriting. This time it was too much. Melissa crumbled.

But there wasn't time to crumble. The family had to care for the kids, and they knew Ian needed to come home. They began making preparations while Ian remained in a coma. After four weeks, he was flown to Rady Children's Hospital in San Diego, closer to their home, where he spent three months in acute rehabilitation. Just before being transferred, the doctors decided to place a shunt in his brain to alleviate some of the fluid buildup. There was still no real prognosis for him. He was still partially in a coma. But the next day, Melissa brought his brother and sister in to see him. . . . and that is when Ian started to wake up.

For the next three months, Tod's mom slept with Ian at the hospital. Melissa brought Lauren and Luke by for daily visits and she also met with doctors and attended therapies. The doctors wanted to put Ian in a convalescent center, but Melissa said, "No way." She'd made the tour of the center and knew many of those kids stayed there until they were eighteen.

Following four months in hospitals, Ian was finally discharged, but he was legally blind, attached to a feeding tube, and paralyzed on his left side as if he'd had a stroke.

The trauma to Ian's brain left him barely able to speak, and he was confined to a wheelchair. A real problem with TBI is that therapy through insurance is rarely enough, and Ian's therapy costs were astronomical.

As I read the article, I thought about the uncanny similarity to Patrick's situation, and I knew serendipity was at work again: Ian used to surf with his daddy. I knew that Ricochet would find a way to help Ian McFarland. There was also another similarity—this time to my own life—and I was feeling its poignancy deep within my soul. Like Ian, I had lost both of my parents. Although I had been much older than Ian at the time, one moment I had parents, and in the next moment, I was an orphan. Already I felt a bond beginning with this young boy whose life had dramatically changed in a blink.

I had no contact information but saw that the article had been written by the very same news station that had created a segment on Patrick and Ricochet. *Another synchronistic sign,* I thought. I contacted the news station: "Is there any way you could put me in touch with the family? Ricochet would like to try to raise funds for Ian," I inquired.

While the video was still making its rounds, I didn't know how much longer this wave would last. I felt the urgent need to jump on the opportunity *immediately* in case the views began to dwindle in the coming weeks.

The producer put me in touch with Max Moore, a classmate of Tod's, who'd created a page for Ian on the Web site CaringBridge.org. When Max heard about the accident, he asked simply, "How can I help?"

Max opened his home up to family members of the McFarlands, and they accepted his generosity. Working in medical research, with a specialty in brain injuries, Max knew that with TBI, Ian needed help immediately. Moving quickly was crucial, for the longer they waited, the less chance of recovery. It was urgent, Max said, that Ian should be treated to a course of rigorous therapy at once.

"If you're willing to let me work on this, I'm willing to help," Max told Melissa.

"Yes . . . anything to help."

It was Melissa who touched me on the deepest level because she left her life in Oklahoma and never looked back. She had one of the most caring hearts I'd ever seen. She would say there had never been any question.

But Melissa didn't have the deep pockets needed to provide the kind of therapy Ian needed—around $4,500 per week, in addition to leg braces at $3,500. She was just trying to survive. Funds were running low, and time was crucial.

"His therapy is in direct correlation to his outcome," Ian's doctor told Melissa and Max.

It just so happened, however, that Tod, Ian's dad, had worked as a physical therapist at Scripps Green Hospital, and there, his coworkers didn't have to think more than a moment to come to the decision to help start Ian back on the long road of reclaiming his life. The normal therapy course for a TBI patient was twelve sessions per year; with the help of Tod's friends, Ian received twenty sessions per week. I was in awe at Melissa's ability to manage three young children and such an overwhelming schedule of treatments.

Strangely (or not, as I would come to see with Ricochet's guiding paw), the first person Max met at the hospital while visiting Ian was Jennifer Kayler, Patrick Ivison's mom. Jennifer, who was training to be a nurse at the children's hospital, stopped what she was doing and sat down with Max and told him all the things he would need to do in order to raise funds, and all the people he needed to contact. She even wrote out an extensive list and emailed it to him, and, in hearing this, I could see the strange yet beautiful interconnectedness of all life.

Max knew he had to make Ian's experience of therapy a positive one somehow; he had to make it fun or Ian would quit. Young Ian would be training like an athlete, and that was hard on a child who was in pain and didn't understand why he had to work so hard and continue performing grueling tasks.

Max wondered if surfing might be a way to bring some of the fun back into Ian's life, but the idea was loaded with inherent problems. To begin with, Ian was still in a wheelchair and had little physical ability. There was the physical stress, but perhaps more than anything, there was the emotional pain. Surfing was what Ian had done with his dad. Tod was an avid fly fisherman, surfer, and rock climber who loved the outdoors, taking his family to the beach for picnics and dinners beside the crashing waves whenever he could. Tod had Ian on a surfboard by the time he could walk, and for Ian, those moments had been filled with love, not only the love of the ocean and surfing, but of that special time he spent together with his father, who shared his same sense of adventure. It was their bond together, their joy, their passion. They practically lived at the beach, surfing together whenever possible, and the beach and the ocean became a sacred place for them.

I sent Max a copy of Ricochet's video. With the way our image-driven society craved new stimuli, Ricochet might be old news tomorrow, so I knew we had to act quickly. I couldn't have known then how much influence Ricochet would have in the future. When I told Max we were interested in fund-raising for Ian, he was very eager for Ian to meet Ricochet. He said the surfing part could be great, but he was perhaps more interested in letting Ian be with a dog, because at this point Ian needed fun things in his life.

"Can you send me some pictures?" I asked. "I can make a fund-raising Web page for Ian on Ricochet's Web site."

Max did, and we transitioned into a new campaign that began fund-raising for Ian. But when Max told Melissa about Ricochet, she was understandably skeptical. One has to understand that Melissa and the children were in survival mode, just trying to get by day to day. Then one day she gets a call about a lady with a dog that . . . *surfs*.

"A dog?" Melissa said to Max. She really didn't know how she'd have the time or energy for one more thing. "Please, I don't have time for it."

But Max pushed her. Ian had always loved dogs. And he loved to surf. What could be more perfect? With little resistance left in her, Melissa agreed.

By then I realized the wave we were riding was bigger than I had ever imagined. When I first spoke with Max, I had no idea how long the video would remain popular, but since hitting its millionth view, it continued to climb, so I knew that Ricochet's impact was powerful and that she had the ability to touch lives far and wide. But it seemed she was destined to touch this one individual life in a very personal way.

We met first at Ian's house. It was January and too cold to surf. Melissa wheeled him out and down to the grass under the trees, while I walked Ricochet over to greet him for the first time. As if she knew exactly who she was there to see and what she was there to do, she walked right up to the little boy with the long brown bangs and licked his face. I had a moment of concern that he would be frightened, but my worry evaporated as I watched a smile crease his tender face. Each time she licked his face, I could tell by his expression that he loved it. So I said to him, "Blow softly on her nose." Every time he did, she responded with a lick. And Ian laughed.

I had no real expectations of their meeting—my main goal was only to get a good photo of Ian with Ricochet so that we might use that for fund-raising. His left side was still very weak, but he had regained his vision. He could toss the ball for Ricochet, which he did, and she pounced and brought it back. Sometimes she darted off to investigate life around the trees, and I wondered if she was perhaps giving him some time and space just "to be" so that our combined energies wouldn't overwhelm him.

"He's loving it," Melissa said. "He loved the neighbor's dog and always wanted a dog. I know he's always loved dogs, but look at *how* they're connecting," she remarked. "That's pretty beautiful and amazing."

They connected straightaway, and later on, when Ian would be interviewed by the press and asked about his connection with Ricochet and what it was like, he would say: "When I first met Ricochet, I was so excited. She ran to me and kissed me."

They were communicating on a deep level with no words exchanged between them. And yet they would not surf together until many months later. Ian was still afraid. The water was still too cold, and he didn't like getting water up his nose. There were perhaps the associations with his dad, but perhaps more notably, there were also the huge physical limitations. Just like Patrick, Ian needed a team of people to help him in the water, but unlike Patrick, he wasn't strong or big. He was little and fragile, and he hadn't learned to hold his breath if he went underwater for any length of time. It could traumatize him into never surfing again.

On Ian's sixth birthday, January 22, he and Ricochet met again at Cardiff Beach. Holding a birthday party at Cardiff was poignant, for each birthday or special occasion would find Stephanie and Tod celebrating with their children at that very beach, with Stephanie setting out a table with linen and candles. The beach was their special place. The beach was their true home.

On the day of Ian's party, Melissa set up picnic tables the way Stephanie once had and covered the tables with pizza and cake. There must have been about thirty people there—friends, family, and therapists. Ian was distracted by all the commotion, but when he saw Ricochet, he became excited, and when Ricochet saw him, she streaked across the sand, making a beeline directly to him and ignoring the people, the pigeons, and everything that wasn't Ian McFarland.

"It was amazing," Melissa said. "They'd only met once before, but they have a special connection."

"Hi, Ricochet," Ian said as she licked his face, and he threw his head back and smiled. "I wanna introduce Ricochet to my friends."

"You can do that," Melissa agreed.

"Ricochet is my new friend," Ian said, and I wondered if perhaps he said it with more confidence and pride than he had two weeks earlier.

Over the months that passed, Ricochet continued fund-raising for Ian, and I continued working the networking angle through media, Web sites, videos, and email contacts. I posted Ian's story on Facebook and Ricochet's Web site, and we raised $7,500 for his therapy. I got to know this extended family of Ian's, many of whom were not connected to him by blood but rather by love. It was not something I ever could have predicted in the dark days that followed my mother's death or my divorces and the many disappointments growing up. But I was willing to accept it and see where this new journey would take me. I knew there was a higher power at work. And as I stood there, I also realized there was a red dog waving her tail back and forth, wanting to do more good.

The third time we all met again was at the beach, so that we could present Ian with his check. He sat on a long surfboard with Ricochet by his side, and Melissa wrote THANK YOU! in big letters in the sand. Ricochet was exuberant around Ian, and yet she knew exactly how much stimulation he could take, perfectly content to sit or lie quietly by his side.

"Ricochet is my good buddy and my good friend," Ian said, looking around as he stroked Ricochet's soft coat.

A couple of months later, a documentary was being made about traumatic brain injuries, and the producer wanted Ian included in the film—preferably surfing with Ricochet. In the weeks leading up to this day, Max and Melissa tried to get Ian to go in the water lying on a surfboard, but he hadn't wanted to and he cried. He was filled with a fear of the ocean and a dislike of the water hitting his face—and, most likely, deep memories of his dad. Yet Melissa knew the water's healing effect on Ian because it had been in the water that he had first moved his leg after the accident.

"He moved his leg!" she exclaimed to Ian's physical therapist.

But they didn't believe her. She swore to them that he did, but when they still couldn't believe it, she took a video to show them, and one of his therapists came with her to the beach, that special place for Ian, to see for herself that he really did move his leg in the water.

Because the ocean was such a healing place for him, Melissa and Max knew the next step was to get him on a surfboard. They knew how much it had meant to him to be out in the ocean with his dad. But Ian knew that if he fell in the water, he wouldn't be able to get up like he used to. Plus, in the past, his father had always been there. Now he'd have to rely on someone else.

Nevertheless, on the morning he was to surf with Ricochet, for the first time since the accident, Ian woke up happy and *excited!* Gone was the fear and in its place was excitement and anticipation.

"I'm going to surf with Ricochet today!"

A crew of people met us at the beach—Melissa and Max, the documentary producer and his crew, Dave and his son Austin, and Prue Jeffries, a pro surfer—all ready to help with the important mission. When Ricochet saw Ian, she raced for him, licked his face as he loved, and then sat down beside him.

"When he woke up today," Melissa told me, "he said, 'I wanna go surfing! I'm gonna go surfing with Ricochet today.' I couldn't believe it. It was such a beautiful thing, a memory I'll always cherish and love. He loves the water—the ocean is his connection with his father—but he's been so afraid."

Melissa, Max, and Prue gathered around Ian. Dave and Austin helped get Ricochet up behind him on the board. Then came the first wave, which Ian and Ricochet rode in together. Then another. I think we all were a little tense, and we all let out a collective breath and began to relax. And then they fell. Ian's head submerged completely underwater, and Max told me afterward it had been a fleeting moment of supreme panic for him. But Ian's team reacted instantly, hauling him forth from the waves and, to everyone's amazement, as his head reemerged, Ian said, "Man, we wiped out," and then he laughed.

"Do you want to surf again?" Max asked anxiously.

"Yeah, I wanna go again."

Again the two—Ian lying down and Ricochet balanced adeptly behind him—surfed in on a wave. Ian looked as if he was focusing hard, but often a smile would break through his concentration. I looked at Ricochet's face, and it, too, was focused and intense. It was as if she was saying, "It's okay, I will guide you and everything is going to be okay."

And I thought to myself, *Yes, and all will be okay.* Maybe not in the way we ever expect, but somehow, some way, everything is going to be all right. Everyone present watched in awe as Ian rode in wave after wave with Ricochet. He was out there loving the water once again.

Ricochet was able to reach out to this boy in ways only a dog can . . . in ways only Ricochet can. Hearing Ian's laughter when they wiped out echoed through my heart. He talked about falling off the board more than he did about all of the perfect rides they made to shore.

When they came from the water, everyone was on a high. Ian's little sister Lauren ran up to him and gave him a congratulatory hug. It was so sweet to see these two young children embrace because of a fun experience they shared together.

"It was pure joy for everyone," Melissa said. "Just seeing Ian back in the water . . . and the excitement that Ian could surf again."

"I couldn't believe it when he wiped out!" Max exclaimed. "I really felt that was a breakthrough moment. I can't tell you how concerned I was—panicked is more like it—when his face hit the water. I'd talked him into surfing another wave, and the moment he wiped out I was terrified he'd never go back in the water again. And then to see him actually smiling after his spill . . . I can't tell you . . ." he trailed off.

"I was a little nervous, too," I admitted with a laugh.

"Ricochet made it exciting for him!" Max said. "Before he was very protective . . . he didn't want water in his face. But Ricochet brought out the kid in him. He doesn't want to surf with a forty-six-year-old man," Max said motioning to himself. "But the thrill of spending time with Ricochet taps into that child he'd lost. He doesn't always want to spend time with adults."

"Ricochet has a way of bringing out our childlike sides," I agreed.

"Ricochet inspires him to do it just for fun. There's no selfish reasons," Max chuckled. "I'll admit it, I want to surf. But Ricochet says, 'Come on, let's have fun.'"

*Yes,* I thought to myself. *How true. She has no expectations, she puts no pressure on anyone, and she accepts what is, no questions asked.*

It was innocent; it was pure. Yes, that was how Ricochet operated.

Ian and Ricochet sat in the sand, soaking wet and glowing with life, and Ian turned to Ricochet.

"Ricochet is my surf buddy."

Later I figured out that if Ricochet rode in the front of the board, Ian wouldn't get water in his face, so she now stands in front and he sits behind her, with his arms around her back legs. In this way, she takes the brunt of the waves for him.

After that day, Ricochet and Ian surfed together many more times, but they also spent a lot of time together on dry land. Ricochet would lick his face, and Ian, in return, would hug and pat her, making us all realize that a lot of therapy was transpiring outside the water as well.

As I thought about this, I also understood that maybe these experiences were therapeutic for me, too. After experiencing so much darkness, I continued to be surrounded by so much goodness. I was blessed to be in the presence of Melissa, such an amazing and selfless woman. She radiated such goodness that I felt like I was enveloped in a cocoon of safety and love.

"It's such a huge honor," Melissa told me. "Every single day is such an honor." She paused. "They call me 'Mom.' That is so beautiful; it's such a gift. And Ian calls me Happy . . . which I love because that was Stephanie's childhood nickname for me.

"And now when I think about how Ricochet has changed Ian's life," she continued, "I can't imagine our lives if Max hadn't talked me into letting Ian surf with a dog! My heart is filled with huge gratitude as I reflect on all that Ricochet has done to impact Ian's life, and his quality of life for years to come. Ian is fearless with Ricochet by his side."

I sat down beside Ricochet and Rina, who had joined us at this event, and I thought about the special boy we had come to know like family. I thought about our similar circumstances and how we'd both lost our parents. But I also thought about the families we now had—perhaps because of those very tragedies. And I realized that often our truest families are made up of people who may have once been strangers to us, but people who were now bound together through love and compassion. Life is one interconnected and continuous circle. Jennifer and Patrick . . . Melissa and Ian . . . they have opened their families to me, made me part of them, inviting me over for Thanksgiving and Christmas, because they know I'm alone. I am in one sense, but not in another.

Ian was very reflective. More than reflective . . . he was wise. Melissa told me that Ian had said, "I love surfing because it reminds me of my dad and the ocean is my place of peace."

I thought of his words as I watched him surfing with Ricochet, and I pondered all of the serendipitous events that had brought us to this moment. ESPN had come out and filmed one day, and now I thought about the questions the commentator had asked and Ian's wise-beyond-his-years responses:

"You used to surf, right?" the commentator asked.

"Yeah."

"How do you surf?"

"You have to trust the waves," Ian replied after a moment of reflection.

"How do you trust the waves?"

"Like you trust people," Ian answered.

"And now you're surfing again, right?"

"Yeah."

"Can you tell me about that?"

"Well, at first I was scared," Ian paused. "But Ricochet helped me not be scared anymore."

"What's that like?"

"I feel surprised because I don't expect her to jump on my back while we are surfing and then I feel happy because I know that she is there. I feel safer when Ricochet is there."

"You're not afraid anymore?"

"Sometimes I feel scared in the water because I don't like to go out really far, but Ricochet helps comfort me. My favorite thing about Ricochet is that she is a dog and one of my best friends. I have a poster of me and Ricochet in my room, and when I look at it, I feel strong and excited to see her again."

"How do you think you look?"

"Always smiling, always happy."

"Why?"

There was a long pause in which Ian never broke eye contact with the commentator. Instead he was looking intently at him, reflecting with tears welling up in his eyes. "It reminds me of surfing with my dad."

"Does that make you happy?"

"Yeah," he said, but this time he didn't hesitate.

# Chapter 11

# Everything Happens for a Reason

*"If you don't have a reason for your heart
to keep beating . . . it won't."*

—Dr. Mehmet Oz

A s Ricochet continued to ride the waves and fund-raise for many different causes, my life took an unexpected and terrifying turn. At the time, I was undergoing infusion therapy for common variable immune deficiency. The therapy for this autoimmune disorder involves using an IV to administer immunoglobulins, which are antibodies normally produced by red blood cells. While I was supposed to be treated with the infusions for the next several months, I started suffering from severe headaches, nausea, and high blood pressure, and I couldn't see how I would be able to continue.

One night in bed I felt the slightest bit of pressure in my chest. Since I was recording every possible side effect of the treatment, I called the doctor the following day to report it. Apparently it was enough to alarm him because he suggested I come in for an EKG the very next day. When the EKG came back abnormal, I was sent for an echocardiogram. I'd always known I had a mitral valve prolapse, a heart problem in which the valve that separates the upper and lower chambers of the left side of the heart doesn't close properly. But when the results of the echo came back, they indicated that my condition had become much worse. Yet never could I have expected the cardiologist's words: "You'll need a valve replacement in about a year or two."

I was shocked.

The cardiologist suggested I see a cardiac-thoracic surgeon. The surgeon performed an esophageal echocardiogram that revealed the valve was flailing and had severe regurgitation. He suggested robotic surgery in the next six months.

My mind went into overdrive, and I sought a second opinion. Bad news went to worse news. This time, the doctor recommended a cardiac catheterization, which involves passing a thin catheter tube into the side of the heart, usually from the groin or the arm, allowing him to take live images to monitor my heart. The procedure itself was daunting, let alone what it revealed. The images showed that I had *four* blocked arteries. Not only did I need a valve replacement, but I also needed a quadruple bypass, which couldn't be done robotically. And I needed it . . . *immediately*, even though I didn't have any symptoms. The doctor told me it was critical and highly recommended I schedule surgery within *two to three weeks*.

*Open-heart surgery. No!* I couldn't even think about it. *A doctor cracking open my chest on an operating table?* The thought was petrifying.

I felt like a walking time bomb. I was fifty-two; my mother had died of a heart attack at age fifty-four. It seemed like I was on the same exact crash course. The thought of developing heart disease just like she did had never occurred to me. Even though it's a hereditary condition, for some reason—perhaps denial—I hadn't added it to my list of worries. Now it topped my list. I had so much to process and absorb. My head felt like it was going to explode as I tried to wrap my brain around this new reality. I knew heart surgery was common, but it wasn't common for me. I was completely overwhelmed.

The stress of contemplating surgery within a year turned to extreme fear and panic of going under the knife in fourteen days. With the exception of the year both of my parents died, never had I felt such stress. Never before had I taken pills to relieve anxiety, but my doctor prescribed Xanax to help me. I needed something just to cope. Panicked thoughts consumed me and I couldn't fall asleep at night. I lay awake thinking about all of the possible complications of quadruple bypass surgery. *What if I didn't wake up from the anesthesia? Who would care for Ricochet and Rina while I was in the hospital? And what if I never came home?* If worry and fear were not enough, anger surged through me. I felt the bitter truth of John Lennon's words: "Life is what happens when you're busy making other plans." I was busy supporting Ricochet's work, and she was making a difference in so many lives. *Why this now?*

I couldn't figure out why something so bad would be happening when Ricochet was doing so much good. It just didn't seem fair. It was like the brakes were being put on a rapidly moving train on the road to goodwill.

Because I'd grown up thinking negatively, I could feel myself slipping back into negativity even when I tried to remain positive. I've always thought everything happens for a reason, from the seemingly inconsequential small coincidence to the monumental events of life. But I never figured out the reasons. And here I was again facing adversity, trying to understand why this was happening.

I finally decided on a surgeon in L.A. who had an impeccable reputation. Even so, my anxiety continued to mount. I made arrangements for Ricochet and Rina in case I didn't make it. I cried just thinking about it, but I had to be sure they were taken care of. I was at my breaking point trying to cope, and one of the only things that helped me was to focus on Ricochet and the causes she was helping—people and animals who, in many cases, were worse off than I was. I thought about all those Ricochet had helped and how they had made it through difficult circumstances. And for moments at a time, when I focused on others, my attention diverted away from myself and my fears, I'd be okay. But then the relentless reality of what I was about to endure would return, and I'd feel the anxiety cracking through my exterior shell just like the saw would be cracking through my sternum. The only surgery I could think of that could be worse was brain surgery.

On March 1, 2011, my heart stopped beating and a heart/lung machine pumped my blood for me during several hours of open-heart surgery. My brother had flown out the night before, and he was the last person I saw before they wheeled me into surgery. I told myself before going under to remember what Ricochet had taught me—to focus on what I could do. I would wake up from surgery, and when I did, I'd be able to blink. *Focus on that and not on what you can't do.*

Before going under, I spoke at length with the anesthesiologist. I explained that I had a tendency to wake up under anesthesia; that it had happened to me before, and I couldn't imagine the thought of waking up while the doctors were sawing open my chest, or while a machine pumped blood for me instead of my own heart. I closed my eyes tight each time the horrible thoughts came into my brain, trying to rid the vision. I also explained that due to degeneration in my neck from years of joint disease, I couldn't have pillows under my head. My neck had to be completely flat in the recovery room to avoid causing me severe neck pain. But when I came to from surgery, that's just what happened: I awoke with intense pain in my neck and back. I still had a breathing tube down my throat. And there was a pillow under my head.

In that place between waking and sleeping, sort of a twilight zone, it was difficult to tell what was real and what was imaginary. But it was real. *I was alive.* I could blink, but I couldn't keep my eyes open, nor could I speak to the two nurses fluttering about the ICU. There was a clock on the wall, and I wondered whether time had stopped. Every time I opened my eyes, I saw that the hands of the clock had not moved.

I heard every word the nurses were saying. They were talking about Dunkin' Donuts. The newscasters on the television were talking about Charlie Sheen. And still that clock didn't move. I was trying to get the nurses' attention. *Why won't they look my way?* I wondered. *Why won't they shut up about the doughnuts?* My hands were taped up and attached to tubes, but I tried to raise my arm anyway. That got their attention.

"You're fine," the nurse said, pushing my hand down. "You're fine."

I tried to motion for a pad and paper so I could ask her to remove the pillows from under my head, but her charades skills were sorely lacking.

"You're fine," she repeated. "*Shhh.* Don't try to speak."

One of the cardiac residents approached my bedside and explained that they couldn't take out my breathing tube because my throat had swelled. He further explained that taking it out might result in my throat swelling shut, and I wouldn't be able to breathe. In my anesthetized stupor, I panicked that they would have to do a tracheotomy.

I was desperate, waving my thumb and forefinger together like I was holding an imaginary pen and paper. They didn't get it. But I was frantic to know if I needed a tracheotomy. I was terrified, but the nurses couldn't understand anything I was asking.

I couldn't understand why they had no protocols in place to help intubated patients communicate—something as simple as picture cards or just a pad and pen by the bedside. Tears of pain and frustration were streaming down my cheeks when my brother got to the ICU. He knew at once what I wanted. He grabbed a pen and paper for me and removed the pillow from under my neck—taking charge and saving the day. He *knew* what I needed. Relief washed over me.

Later, I noticed that the clock on the wall was, in fact, operational. It had only seemed to stop moving during that interminable time in my semiconscious state. I had been neither completely awake nor completely asleep. I'd been in a sort of purgatory.

At one point, one of the residents told me that I was doing well, and I was so angered by her misreading of my situation that I pushed her away. Even though I'd just undergone open-heart surgery and had numerous tubes and IVs taped to me, not to mention a ten-inch incision down my chest, I'd somehow found the energy to push her! (Of course this resulted in being labeled as a "problem patient.") My brother laughed at my spunk—a heart patient in fragile condition pushing a cardiac resident—but he agreed that they lacked compassion.

Although the surgeon who performed my operation had an excellent reputation, it was mostly residents who looked in on me. I found their mannerisms anxiety-provoking. I suffered from extreme nausea and had to take Xanax to even communicate with the doctors.

The first time I looked in a full-length mirror, I was completely taken aback by the ten-inch incision that ran down the center of my chest. It was much longer than I'd expected. I remember seeing Barbara Walters on television after her open-heart surgery. Even with a V-neck sweater her incision wasn't at all noticeable. But mine was. My legs also had incisions along them where my veins were stripped for the bypass, and to this day they're still numb because they had to cut through nerves. Because of my arthritis, my bones were too soft and the doctors thought the normal wires would not work to hold my chest together, so they used plates instead.

While I was recuperating in the hospital, Ricochet and Rina stayed at my friend Jessica's house. I received daily reports on how they were doing, and, while Jessica said she could tell they missed me, she assured me that they were acclimated to their new surroundings and behaving normally.

My brother put his life on hold for a week to be with me, leaving his wife and young daughter back in Chicago. He brought his laptop with him and worked from my hospital room. I wasn't much of a companion, as I was still too loopy on medications to hold a normal conversation. I appreciated all of the sacrifices Bobby made on my behalf. Sometimes he'd run out to get me more sherbet, since it was the only thing I felt like eating. After the episode in the ICU, he stayed on top of the doctors and nurses, making sure they were paying enough attention to my needs and my requests.

His attentiveness made me wonder about people who had no one to advocate for them.

One of the people who came to see me during my hospital stay was Julie Carruthers, or Jo, as she prefers to be called. Jo is a beautiful, vibrant young woman whose life, like so many, took a different turn. One day while skiing, she fell on a ski run and had to be rushed to the hospital. The doctors told her she fractured her pelvis. However, that was not the difficult part; rather, it was what the doctors discovered when she had a CT scan. Jo had bone cancer. For a chance of survival, she had to have a hemipelvectomy or, in lay terms, she had to have her right leg amputated up to her pelvis and part of her hip. Despite her challenges, Jo has a beautiful spirit, and I'd been fortunate enough to be able to watch her surf with Ricochet. She held on to Ricochet's back and used her to balance in the way Jo once relied on her own two legs. It was freeing and beautiful to watch. Jo told me that being out in the water was the great "equalizer."

"I am free," she said. "I forget about my physical and emotional pain when I'm out there on the waves. To surf with Ricochet was absolutely magical. It was actually spiritual. I felt totally connected to her and could feel her love to serve someone who needed a little extra help. Her compassion resonated through me," she explained.

Jo had the love and compassion for me that so many of the doctors I consulted lacked. She had been through several painful surgeries for her cancer. She told me how scared she had been when she'd had her surgeries and she knew what it would be like for me. I was touched by her ability to feel another's pain. I was touched by her compassion. And I was touched by the words she said to me: "You look very tired but also, as is your character, you seem very determined to get better and carry on Ricochet's good work. I am so deeply proud of you, Judy."

Her words of encouragement inspired me to look at my situation differently. As I lay in bed, I began to question what truly mattered in life. I'd always been a somewhat anal person. I didn't like dirt on the driveway. Or Ricochet digging holes in my lawn. If a picture was crooked, I felt compelled to straighten it. I liked things in order—just so. But when my life hung in the balance, the last thing on my mind was whether the laundry was done or if the house was clean. While recovering, all I could think about were Ricochet and Rina. Their lives mattered; little else did.

As soon as I got out of the ICU, I was posting to Facebook, asking for donations to Ricochet's fund-raiser for the Reality Rally, which benefited Michelle's Place, a resource center for breast cancer. I couldn't type very well because I was weak and in pain, but putting my effort into helping others soothed my psyche and took my focus away from my own battered body.

And then the day came when I could return home. My brother drove me home and a close friend had lined up people to help me round the clock. I'd need people to do the shopping and cook meals, people to walk Rina and Ricochet, and people simply to help me get by. I couldn't wait to take a shower after being in the hospital, and I relished the small pleasures of the hot water against my skin and the clean scent of the soap. My brother was with me the first night I was home, and I realized then that, even though I didn't have the large family I'd always wanted, my brother was there for me, as was a solid support network of friends. For that I felt extremely grateful.

I was anxious to see Rina and Ricochet, but I was also worried they'd jump on me in their exuberance. This couldn't happen under *any* circumstances. I could easily get knocked down, and as fragile as I was, I could be badly injured, or the incision could rip open. Just to be safe, Jessica and I decided she should bring the dogs in one at a time to greet me. For added caution, we placed a baby gate across the bedroom doorway to keep their enthusiasm at bay. I'd stand on one side, and the dog would stand on the other.

Jessica brought in Ricochet first. I've always said that Rina is *my* dog whereas Ricochet belongs to everyone. Ricochet has never helped me the way she does the kids and people with whom she works, and it wasn't until after my surgery that, for the very first time, I got to experience what everyone else does with her . . . her soul-to-soul magic.

As excited as she was to see me, Ricochet walked in slowly. She kept her head lowered and came over to me, ever so gently. I saw at once she understood something was different, and I noticed, too, that she had absolutely no intention of jumping up on me. She acted nothing like a dog who hadn't seen her person in a week. Incredibly gentle, she sort of lowered her body as I was petting her. She just knew. She acted from her heart. I was fragile and she understood what I needed without being told. It was how she operated and I knew it—I'd watched it many times before—but still I was moved. I'd seen her interact with so many people, offering them exactly what they needed, but I'd never before experienced it for myself—until that day. And I never have since. Ricochet's interaction was intensely soft and loving, but at the same time, powerful and moving. She touched me deep within my soul, and we connected on a completely different level.

After my reunion with Ricochet, we let Rina in. She, too, was very concerned about me and very gentle. They both licked my hands over and over. They sniffed me, and with every whiff, they could discern strange scents: the smell of the hospital and the smell of surgery. The smell of a power saw, dried blood, and stitches. Lots of stitches. They wanted to know all about it and, by way of their noses, they could. But most of all, what they both knew was that something was really different and very wrong. I found their reactions fascinating, to see them trying to understand through their noses what had happened in those last five days.

As the days passed and people came and went, helping me with daily life, the dogs tried to adapt. Ricochet was more of a housedog, preferring to be inside, but Rina had always loved to be outside. I'd leave the door open from the time we awoke in the morning until the time I called her in at night. And there she would be, out enjoying the sunlight and outdoor breezes and scents, waiting for her daily treat from our neighbors and barking at their window if they were late. But now, while I lay inside recovering, I would find Rina popping inside frequently to check up on me. I was touched by her concern, and I'd intentionally drop things onto the floor so that Rina would feel there was indeed a reason to help.

Not letting them sleep with me was hard, as I needed to sleep on a power recliner that lifted me, like a crane, up and down to avoid putting pressure on my incisions.

One day, I wanted to hug Rina so much that I invited her up to sit beside me on the couch. "Up, Rina!" I coaxed.

Normally she would've leaped right up, but now she was hesitant. She walked in a large circle around me.

"Come on, Rina!"

She placed her front paws on the edge of the couch but still didn't jump up.

"What is it?" I asked her.

I really wanted her up beside me. She just wouldn't do it. Finally I stood up slowly. And it was then that she hopped up easily to the exact spot I'd patted and laid down. I sat back down beside her, and with that arrangement, she seemed content. Only then did I understand: My beautiful, kind Rina was telling me that I was too fragile. My once-in-a-lifetime-dog was trying to protect me. She'd been afraid to jump up while I sat there, and she waited until I stood. The nurses in ICU couldn't figure out what I wanted, but this dog understood what I needed in an instant. I leaned over and gave her the hug I'd been longing to give.

Two weeks after my surgery, there was an event at the hospital at which they were showcasing Ian's story. The sponsors asked that Ricochet be there. I realized the importance of her attendance at the event and knew we had to go. A good friend accompanied me to help handle Ricochet.

Then three weeks after surgery, I received word that *Guideposts* magazine wanted to do a story about Ricochet and Patrick. Despite still being very fragile, I wasn't going to stand in the way of Ricochet's mission. I was eager to take the focus off of me and put it on those whom Ricochet was helping.

Six weeks postsurgery, there was the Reality Rally, a road rally for breast cancer. Although it took considerable effort, I attended because Ricochet was a spokesdog for the event and my place was with her . . . and helping others. Throughout my recovery, I found that focusing on others helped me get through. When my team finished in tenth place, I knew I'd finally made it through to the other side of this long and painful ordeal. I have to say, I was pretty impressed with myself, but I was even more impressed with Ricochet. She was the top fund-raiser for the event, beating out all of the celebrity reality stars by far!

I was unable to drive for twelve weeks. People drove me and took the dogs for walks because I couldn't risk a tug on the leash jarring my chest. My friends all rallied around me to help in various ways, and I felt so thankful. Sometimes the amount of support overwhelmed me.

The months that followed my surgery and recovery were the busiest and most productive in Ricochet's quest to help others. Ricochet won several awards, including the American Humane Association's Hero Dog Award in the emerging hero category. Seven months post-op, Ricochet and I attended the star-studded gala event in Beverly Hills, complete with a walk down the red carpet and awards presented by celebrities. As I stood onstage to accept Ricochet's award from Joey Lawrence, I knew I'd conquered many obstacles in my life to get to this place.

When the cardiologist first told me I needed open-heart surgery, I considered it a very bad thing. I questioned why it was interfering with the good that Ricochet was doing. Even though I knew everything happens for a reason, I couldn't understand it, and I didn't know why. But, after I persevered through to the other side of my recovery, I knew this truth so completely. Now when I say, "Everything happens for a reason," I no longer just believe it; I *know* it.

At the time I felt that the surgery was barbaric, but I was thankful because I realized the surgery saved my life. What this life-threatening experience taught me was invaluable—for afterward, not only did I know, unequivocally, that everything happens for a reason, but I now saw clearly *why*. If my rheumatologist hadn't been so thorough, I probably would've died without warning. But it wasn't my time to die because Ricochet wasn't finished fulfilling her destiny. Many people still needed her help, and she needed me to continue facilitating her journey, wherever it would lead. There was still much more to be done.

# Chapter 12

# Divine Intervention: Protected by Angels

*"I've seen and met angels wearing the disguise of ordinary people living ordinary lives."*

—TRACY CHAPMAN

Ricochet and I continued our work, many times helping people whose lives had changed completely, often in a split second. Yet one Sunday in 2011, the same thing nearly happened to Ricochet. A group of friends and I had planned to meet at Huntington Beach with our dogs for a casual surfing day, including Dave, who lived nearby. I loaded Rina and Ricochet up into the car, thinking we'd play and hang out on the beach for a bit, and that Ricochet and the other dogs could catch some waves.

When we arrived, the parking lot was crammed full of cars. Ahead of us were ten or fifteen cars waiting alongside of Pacific Coast Highway to get into the lot. I pulled up behind the last car and saw Dave standing on the sidewalk.

"It's about a half-hour wait. Do you want me to take Ricochet and Rina down to the beach while you wait?"

I knew Rina wouldn't leave me. Ever since I dropped her off for advanced training, she wouldn't willingly go with someone else if I wasn't going as well.

"Rina won't go without me," I said. "Ricochet probably won't either. But you can try."

I handed him Ricochet's collar and leash, and as I did, I had a momentary thought, the feeling of knowing you should do something, but then you shrug it off. *I should give him the harness instead.* But the thought passed on, slipping from my mind. I was surprised when Ricochet leaped enthusiastically from the car to follow Dave down to the beach, which was quite a distance from where we were. I guessed she was tired of being in the car from the ninety-minute drive it took us to get there.

Once on the beach, Dave took off Ricochet's leash so she could romp with the other dogs. But in the next instant, to my dismay, she was running through the grass on the side of the road. She had turned and run back up the long ramp leading to the sidewalk. Dave scrambled after her and was able to catch up, clipping her leash back on.

"She came looking for you!" he called, motioning toward Rina and me. "I'm not taking her leash off this time!" he yelled as he walked back down to the beach with her.

But that wasn't enough to stop a determined Ricochet from trying to find her missing mom and sister. Although I didn't realize it at that moment, Ricochet slipped out of her collar, then bolted back up the ramp, past the bluffs, past the sidewalk, and straight into four lanes of fifty-five-mile-an-hour traffic.

My friend Bill, who was also waiting in the line of cars just ahead of mine, had gotten out to chat with me through the car window. And it was only then, in one terrifying moment, that we saw Ricochet running into four lanes of cars. The car closest to the sidewalk beeped and slammed on its brakes, but Ricochet kept running, zigzagging with no destination in mind, just knowing she had to find Rina and me.

And then I watched in horror as Ricochet's life flashed before my eyes. She darted in front of a white Yukon SUV in the next lane and I realized there was not one thing I could do. I was about to watch my dog get hit and killed. As the tire of the SUV reached her, Ricochet's neck crooked backward, and her eyes widened with fear as she faced the giant white monster that was about to crush her. My screams competed with the sounds of metal machines barreling down the highway. The passenger of the car screamed, too.

*"Oh my God! It's a dog!"*

Then, in that split second, Ricochet ducked her shoulder. She dodged the huge vehicle by mere inches while the SUV simultaneously slammed on the brakes. And it came to a screeching halt . . . instead of Ricochet's life.

But then Ricochet disappeared behind another car, as I frantically opened my door to get out. Bill was already out and running into the highway, holding his hands up to stop traffic, but confused and frightened, Ricochet kept running from all the cars coming her way; her reflex was to flee the monsters and run to find me.

By the time I got out of my car, Bill was holding Ricochet in the middle of the road. Everything had happened in a few fleeting seconds, but it felt like an eternity. I called out her name, and the fear in her eyes turned to relief when she saw me. Bill opened his arms, and Ricochet ran to me. I clutched her tighter than I ever had before.

Back at my car, I opened the car door and Ricochet jumped inside. I sat down in the driver's seat to catch my breath. Startled by a beep from the car behind me, I looked up and saw that the cars were moving toward the parking lot. During the ten minutes it took to finally get a space, I was able to calm myself. Of course I was still shaken, and I certainly didn't feel like playing. I couldn't imagine that Ricochet would feel like surfing after what she'd just been through. However, since we'd waited so long, I decided to take the dogs down to the beach anyway and meet our friends.

As we headed for the sand, I agonized over what Ricochet must have been feeling in her desperate search to find me. The image of her coming so close to getting hit played over in my head. I knew I should've given Dave the harness instead of the flat collar, and even though I knew it wasn't anyone's fault, I couldn't shake the guilt.

Yet on another level, I sensed something else at work. Although it wouldn't fully dawn on me until I returned home and more pieces of this miraculous day were revealed, I began to feel the significance of what had happened—or hadn't happened. It was more than the fact that Ricochet had come inches from being hit and, at the last moment, had been spared. There was absolutely no earthly way she should've avoided being hit by that car and crushed beneath the tires. And yet I'd watched with my own eyes. It was then that I began to understand a higher power had everything under control. I found solace in knowing there were guardian angels at work, stopping the car and giving Ricochet the quick reflexes she needed to dodge the SUV.

I now saw that it was her submissiveness—another trait I hadn't appreciated about her because she was often bullied by other dogs—that had actually helped save her. And I felt at once grateful that she was always true to herself. In this case, she used her submissive body language to escape death. This was another lesson for me in acceptance.

That evening, I posted about the incident on Ricochet's Facebook page, sharing my belief that guardian angels were protecting her. Of course, the post received many comments due to its nature.

Sometimes it takes time to process an event like that. It was such a horrible image for me, yet there was a sense of serenity . . . of just how powerful divine intervention can be. Both Dave and I later agreed that Ricochet's work here on earth wasn't finished yet, and that's why her guardian angels stepped in and saved her life.

The following afternoon, there was a post on Ricochet's page from someone named Teri, which read:

> *We were there—Ricochet ran in front of the car next to us and almost into our tire. But she zigged and zagged and went behind our car. I did not know who the little dog was at the time—but she looked so scared. I prayed she would be ok and so happy to know she is!*

I commented on the post, asking Teri to email me. Because my memory was thwarted by the trauma, I wasn't able to process everything, and I wanted to hear exactly what Teri had witnessed. We exchanged several emails before I realized that Teri was a *passenger* in the white SUV that almost hit Ricochet. I couldn't believe it when I read her words describing what happened:

> There was a large vehicle, dark in color, driving in the lane closest to the beach, and slightly ahead of us in the lane near the center divide. They laid on their horn and slammed on the brakes. Out of the corner of my eye I saw a dog; she was running in front of the car next to us. She was just at their bumper, but didn't get hit, but was very close to the vehicle. We moved a little ahead of the

car next to us now, because they slammed on their brakes. At that moment, I saw her running, and it looked like she was going to go right under our front tire. If she escaped the front tire, then the back tire would hit her for sure. It appeared that she was going to go under our car. I closed my eyes. I was waiting for impact. I braced for a thump, but, *Thank God. No thump.* What a wonderful silence.

Goose bumps popped out on my arms and a lump formed in my throat when I read her words, but there was more: Teri and her husband, Danny, had made other plans on that Sunday when, at the last minute, their plans fell through. They discussed the options of where to go with their two golden retrievers, Maggie and Molly. Huntington Beach Dog Beach was fourth or fifth on their list. During their discussion, Ricochet's SURFice dog video popped into Teri's mind seemingly out of nowhere. She told Danny, "I want you to watch this." As they watched the video, tears formed in their eyes. Still, they could not have known at the time that their path would cross with the dog in the video in the most frightening way.

When Teri got home Sunday evening, she still didn't know that the dog who'd been loose on the highway was Ricochet. When she signed on to Facebook and saw my post in her newsfeed about Ricochet's near tragic plight with a car, she couldn't believe it. The reality of what had happened began to sink in, and she realized with incredulity that the little dog who almost got hit was the same dog in the video: Ricochet.

Teri had only joined Ricochet's Facebook page a week before, so she hadn't engaged in conversations yet. After reading and responding to Teri's posts, an instant bond formed between us. We both were witness to what could have been a horrible tragedy.

She wrote to me that, at that moment, she realized the many decisions she and Danny made that day had placed them on a path that would cross Ricochet's path, and she knew there were other forces at work. In one of her emails, Teri said:

> As we exited the parking lot, my husband turned right onto Pacific Coast Highway. To go directly home, we should have turned left. My husband said he just felt like driving south on PCH for a while. It was very crowded, and after a block or so, he changed lanes from the right to the left lane, heading south. We had traveled only a short distance when I saw and heard the car in the next lane slam on their brakes and saw the blur of dog fur running directly in front of the car.

Teri realized she was meant to be there at that moment, looking out the window, and her husband was meant to be driving the car. Angels had been at work.

Another connection came into play as well. The way Teri first navigated to Ricochet's page was through the Facebook page Dog Bless You, an organization that posted Ricochet's Facebook page on theirs and also awarded a $5,000 grant to Ricochet's work, which she used to help twenty different rescue groups. And yet another synchronistic sign: Bill, the man who was in the car in front of me—the man who ran after Ricochet—was the person whose dog had to drop out of the Purina contest, which enabled Ricochet to begin her surfing journey. This twist of fate exemplified the mysterious and beautiful way we are all connected, causing me to wonder, *Were guardian angels already preparing for their future convergence on Pacific Coast Highway even back then?*

Ricochet was very near hitting the $100,000 mark in her fund-raising. I'd been watching in anticipation and awaiting this milestone, along with many of her Facebook fans. Back in the early days when I was trying to train her to be a service dog and she'd given up, I never would've believed she'd make such an impact. But on July 24, the night after she was almost hit by the SUV, Ricochet achieved this momentous milestone.

We had hoped to reach this goal by August 20, the two-year anniversary of the first time she surfed with Patrick and became a SURFice dog. Her one-hundred-thousandth dollar was raised for the New Jersey SPCA in honor of an abused dog who'd almost lost his life—and his name was Patrick. She began with a boy named Patrick, raising her very first dollar, and she raised her one-hundred-thousandth dollar for a dog named Patrick. The circle of life. Throw one stone of good intentions into the vast ocean of life, and you never know how many lives that one stone will touch . . . and change for the better.

Perhaps Ricochet's experience can serve as proof to anyone who doubts there is goodness in the world—to anyone who questions fate, guardian angels, interconnectedness, synchronicity, animal angels, or the Rainbow Bridge, and to those who bear witness to the horrors of war, animal abuse, and a myriad of other negative things that fill our TV screens, radios, and social media—that there is so much more goodness than there is evil.

All of us are on journeys, and we're guided along the way. Sometimes our guides are signs, like synchronicities that often seem like coincidences; sometimes our messengers are human; and sometimes the animal messengers show us the way most clearly. No matter who or what guides us, it is always when we open our hearts and listen that we are better able to hear and hopefully understand the message.

When I look around me and see all of the goodness, I realize it didn't all happen by chance. Each individual journey is connected to the larger whole. When we are following our life's purpose—our destiny—events fall more easily and gently into place. I am struck by the many synchronistic events surrounding Ricochet: How Jennifer later became a nurse, turning her adversity into action by working at the children's hospital where young Patrick spent so much time. How Max and Jennifer met in that same hospital and how she helped him. How Melissa left her life to care for her sister's children: "My life was available," she said. And how Tod worked as a physical therapist, and when he died, his coworkers rallied to give Ian the therapy he needed.

I have no doubt that every single person and animal who played a part on this journey was perfectly chosen and guided. The outcome of that day at Huntington Beach would have been tragically different if all of these synchronicities hadn't occurred the way they did. Ricochet, Bill, Teri, and Danny were guided by their guardian angels that day. They all kept Ricochet from harm. Because of them, a potential tragedy turned into an incredibly powerful realization: that a higher power was guiding this divine intervention on our path.

Both Ricochet and I survived life-threatening events. We needed each other—the way we all need each other—to serve the purpose we were both on this earth to fulfill. Neither one of us had completed our purpose.

# Chapter 13

# Empowerment: Finding a Voice in a Language Left Unspoken

*"Dogs do speak, but only to those who know how to listen."*

—ORHAN PAMUK

"Y ou want to take West where?" asked Lauren Chavez.
"To the beach. To see a dog named Ricochet," West's grandma replied.

"Mom, I'm sorry, but that's crazy. By yourself with the two kids at the beach? West will have a meltdown for sure. He'll probably take off and chase after a bird, and you'll never find him. You know how he gets."

West's mom, Lauren, often found herself having such conversations. Checklists and routines were the norm. Spontaneity was not. A day at the beach required planning and preparations.

Eight-year-old West was born in February 2006, after two excruciating days of labor and an emergency C-section. Lauren had lost a lot of blood, and when she finally gazed at her newborn son, she was in awe of his preciousness, but she also felt intuitively that something was wrong.

When the anesthesia wore off and she visited with West longer, something still seemed wrong to her. When the lights were on, her baby wouldn't open his eyes. She told relatives that if they wanted to see his eyes, they'd need to turn off the lights. To her, he seemed lifeless, like he wasn't ready for the world. Yet he had been diagnosed with severe jaundice, and it was no doubt taking its toll on his tiny system.

After being released from the hospital, a nurse came to the house every day to monitor his condition. Within a week, the nurse felt he was strong enough to be released to his parents' full-time care.

"You can relax now, Lauren. There's nothing to worry about," her mom assured her.

But as a new mom, Lauren couldn't stop worrying. She knew in her heart that something was wrong. West was a happy baby most of the time. And so incredibly cute. He walked and crawled on time but didn't babble or talk at all.

Most alarming, when Lauren tried to cuddle him, he'd scream, recoiling from affection unlike other babies. Even when he teethed, he didn't want to be comforted by his mother. Once when she attempted to cuddle him, he head-butted her so hard that he bruised her lip. When someone asked why her lip was black and blue, she was ashamed to admit what had happened.

She knew this wasn't normal behavior for a one-year-old. Oftentimes, she'd find him standing by a window staring blankly outside. This could go on for quite some time if she didn't redirect him. If he got angry, he threw toys at the nearest person. Even if he hurt them, he didn't show any of the age-appropriate signs of empathy. But he was still very young, and Lauren hoped he'd outgrow his quirks. Nevertheless, she had a suspicion that her son had autism and shared it with the other moms at the playground. They assured her with a laugh that they didn't agree. "He doesn't have autism. He doesn't flap his arms or walk on his toes."

One day West injured his hand. As his inconsolable shrieks pierced through the ER, a doctor asked Lauren to talk to her son, calm him down, and explain what they needed to do. Lauren looked at him like he was crazy.

"You mean you *can't* reason with him?" the doctor asked.

"No," she said. "Can *you* reason with other kids this age?"

"Absolutely yes," he answered.

Another red flag. Lauren shared her concerns with family members who told her she was making too much of it. She heard statements like "Boys take longer to do things," and "My son didn't talk, either; you should read to him more often. Then he'll start talking." So Lauren bought more books and tried to engage her son.

"West, get the ball! Get the ball for Mommy."

West stared flatly at her as if she had twenty heads. He didn't seem to understand what the ball was or who *Mom* was either. He didn't even point at things.

As time passed, his differences became more evident. At the playground, he didn't play like the other kids, preferring to pour sand on their heads instead of into the sandbox. If they took his toys, even his favorite one, he didn't care—he'd just walk away.

Lauren kept repeating, "I think he has autism."

This time, the other moms didn't refute her comment, and their silence spoke volumes. Perhaps they felt something was amiss, too, but didn't want to voice it out loud.

When West was fourteen months old, Lauren took him to the doctor, who assured her that he was fine: "Boys talk later," she said. The doctor pulled out a tongue depressor for West. He grabbed it. "See?" she offered. "Look at that. He grabbed it. Kids with autism don't do that."

Lauren wanted to believe that the doctor was right. She hoped with all her heart that West would outgrow these behaviors, and she rationalized that maybe she was making too much of them. Then she asked her Grandma Ginny, who had raised two kids of her own, if she thought something was wrong with West.

"Yes, Lauren, I do," she admitted. "I think something is very wrong."

Lauren and West's dad, Steve, brought West to a psychologist for a full evaluation, which included a speech exam. Some of their friends' children were in speech therapy, so they assumed the recommendation would be speech therapy a few times a week. They had no idea that West's speech was the last thing that would concern the doctor.

"We are not recommending speech therapy at this time."

"What do you mean?" Lauren gasped.

"We're not recommending speech therapy because his cognition is the problem. Ms. Chavez, he has the cognitive level of a six-month-old."

*Six months?!* Lauren was floored. Her son was twenty months old!

"What happens now?" Lauren stammered in shock. "How bad is it?"

The therapist handed her a pamphlet with the word "AUTISM" in big bold letters across the top.

"My son has autism?"

"He's exhibiting the traits of being on the autistic spectrum."

*What does that even mean?* Lauren thought. *English, please.*
"That's not what I'm asking you. Does he have autism?"

"We can't diagnose him, but he's at risk."

The therapist recommended intensive intervention on a daily basis for the foreseeable future. With her fears confirmed, Lauren marched back to her pediatrician who gave her a referral. She wasted no time in scheduling an appointment.

After a fifteen-minute exam, the neurologist turned to Lauren and Steve, and said, very matter-of-factly, in the same monotone voice one might use when giving directions, "Your son has autism."

"You think he has it?" Lauren asked.

"No," she said, "I *know* he has autism."

Even though Lauren knew it, too, she still couldn't process it. As she struggled to wrap her mind around the diagnosis, the neurologist delivered more bad news. West's case was not only severe, but it was compounded by a motor speech disorder called apraxia, in which the brain has difficulty coordinating the muscle movements necessary to say most words.

"Will he ever talk?" Lauren asked.

"Not likely," was the doctor's response.

Lauren, Steve, Reese, and West drove home—their family forever changed, their hopes for a bright future bleak. Steve and Lauren's shared dreams for West were shattered. *He may never speak.* And time was not on their side. The neurologist warned that they had a small window of time to make a connection with West. If he wasn't speaking by the time he was four, he likely never would. They risked losing their son to autism before they even knew him.

Lauren retreated into West's bedroom and lay on the floor. In the shelter of the room, surrounded by Legos, blocks, and toys he may never learn to play with, she found the reality of the situation all too much to bear. With the door closed, she broke down crying for the first time since West's birth. Then, looking at the baby pictures of West and Reese—seeing their eyes, their smiles, and their potential—she found her resolve. West and Reese needed her to be strong.

*Okay,* she thought, *that's the only time you're going to cry about this autism thing. Pull yourself together and get a handle on it. Do what you need to do.*

She knew that West had been born for a reason. Faced with this crisis, she didn't question where God was or wonder why he left her. She knew that God was there that day perhaps more than any other time in her life. In fact, she was sure that he himself picked her up and carried her out of the room.

But then the hardest road began. Daily occupational and behavioral therapy were extremely frustrating for West. When he was two years old—a month after Ricochet was born—things got drastically worse. West's "terrible twos" manifested in angry, violent, and aggressive outbursts. One night he grabbed a heavy toy and smacked his father in the face with it. Still reeling from the shock, the next day the family took a walk while a therapist was working with West. When they returned home, the therapist was outside with all of her things packed up.

"I'm sorry," she began. "I really like West, but he's the most aggressive child I've ever worked with."

*Ever?* Lauren thought. *He's only two!*

"I simply can't work with him until you get his aggression under control," she said.

The doctors recommended medication, even though they had never prescribed it for someone so young. But West's case was the most extreme they'd ever seen. Lauren and Steve resisted; medication would be their last resort. Yet soon they couldn't afford to ignore the problem. In a rage, West whipped a light hand weight at his sister's head. Luckily, she wasn't hurt. But what if something had happened or lay ahead? They had to protect Reese—and protect West from himself and the grip of autism.

"If you don't do this, you're going to lose your son," the doctor urged.

With no other options, they reluctantly agreed. And then they waited . . . and watched. They'd know within six weeks if the medicine worked. And yet, after a mere four days, West's aggression subsided. No more hitting. No more kicking. It was like a new West. The *real* West. For a brief span of wondrous time, Lauren almost let herself believe that West might start talking, that the medicine might magically revive something inside his brain. It didn't. But even so, they had their sweet son back. Now they could begin his therapy in earnest on a physical level and give him the love he so desperately needed on an emotional level.

While I was busy introducing Ricochet and her littermates to beams, planks, and moving obstacles, West's therapists were trying to introduce those types of things to him, too. Part of his therapy meant pulling him out of his comfort zone and putting him on things that moved—platforms and swings. But West despised it. He craved control. He hated his legs being off the ground for even a second and would scream and throw himself on the floor, refusing any part in the much-needed work.

At three years old, he was still not talking, but he could make certain sounds. With much struggle and repetition, one day he said the word "Bye." It was a glimmer of hope, but the critical fourth year was approaching, and time was running out.

West's school suggested placing him in a very low-functioning class, which Lauren asked to visit. When she entered the room, she knew instantly it was not the right place for him. The kids didn't react to people the way West did; they were on a much lower level cognitively. She begged the principal to evaluate him.

"On paper he is like that, but that's not who he is as a person," Lauren pleaded. "Please at least meet him before you put him in that class."

Upon meeting West, the teacher noticed his spark and agreed that he needed a different class. They placed him in a higher-functioning class, but he didn't fit there either. While he could communicate thirty words through sign language, he refused to potty train and dumped his fruit on the floor every day.

"I've taught here for twenty years, and he's the first one who's ever broken me," the director said. "When West doesn't want to do something, he won't do it. He just shuts down."

Sadly, West didn't quite fit in either world—and he was retreating further into his own. He cried every day for two years but was unable to tell his parents why. Then, right around his fourth birthday, West found his voice. As he struggled to force his mouth to make each sound, it looked painful to Lauren.

"Why does he look like he's in pain?" she asked.

The therapist assured her that West was not in pain, but that he would struggle to form each word because of the apraxia.

At five years old, he had the vocabulary of a three-year-old, and if people didn't know him, they had trouble understanding him. Because of this, West didn't have many friends. He spent a lot of time alone in his room, which he preferred. He didn't like going outside. When Lauren would open the door to the yard, he'd get anxious.

"I don't want to leave. I don't want to go," he'd cry.

Unless West knew exactly what would happen, he didn't want to take any risks. The outside world was too overwhelming for him. He needed complete control of his environment or he would simply shut down.

Hoping for some positive stimulation, Lauren's mother took West and Reese to story time at the library where kids could read to a therapy dog. West sat on the other side of the room, afraid and unsure. A few weeks later, Lauren's mom saw Ricochet's SURFice dog video on the Internet and decided to take the kids to meet her.

"That's crazy, Mom. First we have dogs who read—now a *surfing dog?*"

But her mother was undeterred; she was determined to take Reese and West to the beach to meet Ricochet.

"You're going to take two kids to the beach by yourself?"

Lauren listed a litany of reasons why it was a bad idea: *West might have a meltdown. What if he runs away?* Ever since he was little, he loved to chase birds. He would see a bird and take off. She recalled the horror of watching West once fall down some concrete steps while tracking a bird, and how she and her brother had to chase after him in the park one day for a good quarter of a mile. He just kept going after the birds. But birds or no birds, her mom took the kids to meet Ricochet.

As Ricochet and I stood in the sand, Nana Cindy approached with Reese and West in tow. I was struck by Reese's natural beauty set off by her sense of style with her horn-rimmed glasses and a crocheted pink cap.

"Say hello to Miss Judy," Nana Cindy said.

West was a bit reserved, but as soon as he saw Ricochet, his confidence perked up. "Nana, it's Wicochet!" he pointed, darting over to her. "Hi, Wicochet," he said.

While the beach was busy with people milling all around, West stayed for quite a while, patting and talking to Ricochet. She looked into his eyes, her eyes crinkling, and then lay back to enjoy a rub as he stroked her belly. It was pure relaxation for both of them.

Hours later, their grandma returned home with two sun-kissed, grinning children wearing matching pink Paw It Forward wristbands. West, with an unfamiliar glint in his eye, ran up to his mother, eager to show off the photo on his grandma's cell phone.

"Look, Mom, look!" West exclaimed, jumping up and down.

Peering at the screen, Lauren saw a picture of West and Reese sitting beside this dog named Ricochet. What struck her the most was that her son was not a full arm's length away from the dog like he typically would be. He was sitting cross-legged right next to her in the sand, leaning in and looking relaxed, with an easy, happy smile. The face reflected back at her wasn't West's typical look of trepidation that he wore around other dogs.

"When we go again?" West asked Lauren.

The boy who was so afraid of dogs and never wanted to leave his house was suddenly interested in something beyond the confines of his room and routines. He wanted to see Ricochet again! Reese was just as enamored. She told all of her friends at school that she and her brother had met the surf dog named Ricochet.

When the kids were naughty, Lauren discovered she could use Ricochet as the bad cop: "We're gonna tell Ricochet," she'd warn, and the problem behavior would stop immediately. If West was getting frustrated or a meltdown was imminent, Lauren would play a video of Ricochet, and West would calm down enough for her to talk him through the problem. Some kids had security blankets to comfort them; West now had Ricochet.

With Ricochet becoming a furry surrogate member of their family, Lauren wanted to meet her in person, so she took Reese and West to another charity event. Lauren approached me to say hello, and I was struck by her warm smile. She was a mirror image of Reese.

"Hi, West, how are you, buddy?" I asked.

But West's attention was elsewhere. He was off to say hello, his face lighting up along with his voice. His reaction was typical—I was used to playing second fiddle to Ricochet.

"Wicochet!" he beamed.

Ricochet trotted straight to him and sat down, gratefully accepting his pats and hugs. His affection for her was obvious. Shaking her head and smiling as she watched her son, Lauren told us how much Ricochet meant to West and how he was now opening up because of her. Before they left, we exchanged email addresses.

When West got home, he was so excited by his time with Ricochet that he went to fetch his boogie board, which had been collecting dust in the garage. "Take a picture of me surfing. Send it to Wicochet!" This from the boy who wouldn't dip his leg in water and who despised wobbly surfaces.

Elated, Lauren snapped a photo of West's therapist steadying the boogie board with West standing proudly on top. Here was her son, in the water, balancing on a jiggling boogie board, with a snorkel mask obstructing his face. *Because of Ricochet.*

After that, West asked if he could try taking swim lessons—"for Wicochet."

Ricochet was pulling West out of his world and into hers.

Several months later, in May 2013, I received an email from a producer at ESPN who wanted to film a segment about Ricochet's one-of-a-kind SURFice dog work. I remembered how West's face lit up when the two met and how his mother told me she had eased his fears. I emailed Lauren to see if she'd be open to having West surf with Ricochet for the piece.

Intrigued, Lauren agreed, but she didn't want to tell West because she didn't want him to get too excited. It was hard for him to understand time and space. He didn't grasp "when" and "where." Also, the cameras would worry him. He hated people taking his picture, and video recordings were out of the question. Lauren had no idea what to expect. As the day approached, Lauren's concerns ran the gamut: *They'll need to put a microphone on him. There will be strangers there. Will he be overwhelmed? West has never surfed before. He's the only one in the group who will be doing it for the first time.*

The night before, Lauren and Steve helped West try on his new wetsuit. His excitement was contagious.

"I'm gonna surf with Wicochet!"

Steve, an avid surfer, had always wanted West to surf. They had gone boogie boarding once, but a wave knocked West off the board, and he went under for a second. He never went in the ocean again.

"He's gonna surf with a dog but not with me?" Steve half-joked, but with the progress his son was making, he was looking forward to the experience. He expected Ricochet to be a brawny, 100-pound dog. When he first saw her, he was surprised at her small stature. "*That's* the dog?"

West was nervous when they arrived at the beach, but Lauren told me that she knew as soon as he saw Ricochet that everything would be okay.

"Ricochet is so intuitive; she knows what West needs. As soon as they see each other, West will relax. She knows exactly how to work with him and has a calming spirit. She waits for him to see what he needs; she never pushes him too far. I trust that it will take care of itself."

And it did.

West ran to pat her. "Wicochet!"

Knowing West's fear of water, one of the volunteer water helpers named Patti walked to the shore with him to build a sandcastle. West's head was down; he didn't speak a word, but he crouched to help build it. As he dug his hands into the gritty sand, the water streamed in, dousing his feet and legs. He didn't seem to mind. He was busy helping Patti make walls to protect their castle from harm. West was good at building walls, at protecting his environment. But today, the tide was turning and the ocean's unrelenting waves were slowly seeping in, crumbling his walls faster than he could make them.

As the castle slowly melted away, I called out to West, "Ready to surf with Ricochet?"

"Weady!" West chimed.

Dave, Patti, and Deb, another volunteer, chatted with West as they walked out into the breakers, which was chest high for West. Yet he didn't hesitate. Giving words of encouragement, they helped him onto the board where he lay stomach down, the board rocking and swaying, the cold waves slapping his face.

Ricochet and Dave were now behind West—out of his line of sight—and his parents and sister stood hundreds of feet away from him on dry land. West was now completely out of control, completely out of his element, yet his smile was wide.

"Ready, Ricochet?" Dave asked, spying an upcoming wave. "Ready, West? One, two, three!" Dave pushed the board into the cresting wave.

West held on. And in a flash, he did something that most people who are new to surfing don't do as they struggle to keep their grip—he turned his head to gauge Ricochet's reaction. Then, and only then, when West saw that Ricochet was happy, did he smile a smile that shone brighter than the sky. The boy who craved control, and was afraid of water and dogs, was now gliding, his arms fully outstretched into the sky, with a huge grin—as he coasted into shore with Ricochet.

When Reese saw his face, she clapped wildly. "Yes! You did it, West!"

Cupping her hands to her mouth, Lauren laughed and then exhaled a huge sigh of relief. "Good job, West!"

His dad chimed in with whistles and cheers.

West's screams of excitement could be heard across the beach. I couldn't help but smile as I watched them, Ricochet and West— their souls connected—both with a penchant for birds, both who shut down when the expectations of others became too much to bear, both born with sensitivities just beyond most others' under-standing. They were communing together in a special place in time, embracing the feeling of spontaneity and the love between two beings.

When they reached the shore, West hopped off the board to make sure that Ricochet was safe. Then he skipped through the water, kicking up spray, and ran to share his accomplishment with his family.

"I did it! One, two, free!" He held up three fingers, signifying his three rides with Ricochet.

His fears had dissolved, evaporating into the waves beyond. The family hugged, embracing the moment in a huddle of electrifying energy and radiant smiles.

Lauren turned to me. "To see him surfing is beyond anything I could ever imagine. He's completely out of control; there's a *dog* in control. It's so outside of his comfort zone, but it's obvious he loved it. Ricochet took him to a new place. She found that middle ground."

As Lauren watched West race into the waves for another ride, she continued, "Today he was the most lit up I've ever seen in his life."

I had to believe her. Everyone, from the cameraman to Dave, Deb, Patti, and a host of other volunteers, said the same thing: "West is pure joy; he just comes alive in the water." Ricochet brought out his true essence that autism had kept hidden for so long.

When we were done with the surf session, the videographer went to West's house to do more filming. West was hamming it up, showing him all of his toys and his room. Lauren was amazed at the transformation.

"Here's the kid with such a severe diagnosis, who couldn't speak, and now he's talking—*on camera*—with a videographer!" she explained. "He's completely changed because of Ricochet."

In June, we met West again for a surf session with a few families. West hadn't been in the water since the last time he was with Ricochet. This time, he didn't just lay on the board. With Ricochet positioned in the front, West used her body to steady himself as he stood up on the board and coasted in. With Ricochet's help, West was now standing on his own two feet, both literally and figuratively.

Bounding back in the water with a splash, West took charge, signaling to Dave, Deb, and Patti. "Hey guys! Hey guys! This time I want to kneel, okay?"

We all laughed that the boy who didn't speak was now telling the handlers what to do as he directed the surfing session! He was taking over Dave's job!

I watched him kneeling on the board as he held on to Ricochet, gliding into shore with spray shooting around them. As he coasted in, he approached Patti, who was ready to give him a high-five. Swatting her hand as he passed her, he shouted with excitement.

"You got the high-five?" I asked, impressed at West's ability to let go on the board—in more ways than one. With his trusted companion by his side, West had become a new person—his real self.

In September, ESPN returned to film more footage, and West was once again excited to surf with Ricochet. The filming was taking longer than expected, and West had to wait. And wait. A delay was not in the game plan, and everyone held their collective breath for his turn, hoping he wouldn't have a meltdown. Yet just knowing that Ricochet was there and taking in her calming presence, West waited patiently.

As he stood patting her in the shallow water, he watched with great self-control as a soldier, an Iraqi veteran, arrived at the beach for his first-ever surf with Ricochet. Like West, the soldier was working with Ricochet to overcome his own fears and anxieties caused by post-traumatic stress. While West's compulsions had plagued him since birth, this soldier's fears were born on the battlefield.

As the soldier donned his wetsuit and eyed the waves, he introduced himself to West and asked him if he had any advice for surfing with Ricochet.

"Just have fun!" West chimed, which was music to my ears, coming from a young boy who struggled to have fun in the conventional world, but who was finally free out there in the surf.

The soldier nodded and smiled at West, who was splashing through the waves, waiting for his next ride with no fears or inhibitions. He probably would never have guessed that, for West, moments like these were rare, that autism had robbed him of most of the carefree moments of his childhood.

When Dave launched the board, the soldier swayed and bobbled for only a second, but his years of physical training showed as he sprang up with ease and grace.

Seeing his newfound friend coast in, holding on to Ricochet, West jumped up and down, cheering with unbridled glee. "You did it!" he screamed. "Woo-hoo!"

There were thumbs-up all around as the man, in turn, handed Ricochet's leash to West.

"Alright, West," he said, "let me see you do it."

These two strangers—a thirty-one-year-old army sergeant and an eight-year-old—were becoming buddies in the surf, continuing to cheer each other on and helping to fetch the board when Ricochet jumped off. The boy whose brain was born autistic and the soldier whose brain was changed by war—both imprisoned by their fears—were reaching out to help each other in the water. It was a beautiful moment, the kind that gladdens your heart and compels you to stop and savor it, like a fleeting sunset, when two separate colors, each with its own unique vibrancy, come together to meld into something so spectacular that it seeps into your very soul.

Dave looked on amazed. "Judy, in the eleven years I've been doing adaptive surfing, I've never seen the participants become volunteers like these two are doing for each other."

I nodded. Both of them struggled to connect with people every day, but out here in the ocean with Ricochet, it was coming naturally.

Back on the beach, Lauren found me as she was readying to leave. "Meeting Ricochet has truly altered the course of West's life," she said. "Ricochet has empowered him to try things he never would have before. Now I know it's not impossible—that it's not so bleak."

I couldn't find the words to answer her.

"I had hopes for West, but I never thought he'd be capable of doing things like this. I was scared to put him out there; I was afraid he would get hurt or be judged. But he's so much stronger than I ever knew, and I credit that to Ricochet."

Lauren reached out to hug me, and my throat caught as I felt her arms around me, the warm, thankful embrace of a mother who wanted what every mother wants—for her son to be okay, to find his unique place in the world, and to grow up safe, happy, and loved. While I knew that she was thanking me, I was grateful to her because, in that moment in time, I felt the deepest kind of love. I was the lucky one. I was blessed to know this special boy, to experience his love for my dog, and his caring for another being.

But I wasn't the only one impressed with West. Dave, Deb, and Patti also noticed how helpful he was and how he waited so patiently during the filming, so several weeks later, Dave suggested treating him to a private surfing day with just his sister. Not only would this be a special day for West, but for Reese, too, since she was always the patient big sister, tagging along to therapy and doctors' appointments without complaint.

When we reached the beach, the waves were a tad rough. Reese, who had never surfed before, was understandably a bit nervous. Reese wanted West to surf first. However, West was insistent that Reese go first. It was a typical sibling standoff.

Deb, the consummate peacemaker, explained to West that if he surfed with his friend Ricochet first, they would help show Reese how it was done. Of course he agreed—Deb had uttered the magic word: "Ricochet." The younger brother could now teach his older sister something he was good at. Despite the rougher chop, West once again stood up behind Ricochet and surfed the wave all the way to the beach.

"Now it's your turn," West said, helping to bring the board over. West happily and expertly gave her the lowdown: "You need to make sure you hold on; don't worry, Wicochet will be there to help you."

West's instructions paid off. When Dave gave Reese a push, she popped right up behind Ricochet, her smile just as wide as her brother's.

"Good job, Weese!" West yelled, clapping for his sister as Patti handed out a high-five.

When she reached the shore, West ran to help grab the board, and they both laughed, a brother and sister, sharing a normal day at the beach—the kind of a day that had been few and far between for them.

"Can I push her?" West asked.

We were touched that he was so interested in being a part of his sister's experience and how empowered he felt to reach out to help.

"Sure you can!" I said, as Deb and Dave did their best to position Reese on the board, allowing West to assist them.

"Weady, Wicochet?" West asked, parroting the instructions that were usually Dave's domain. "Go!"

The three of them released the board in unison with Dave giving Reese and Ricochet the final push in. Still nearly chest-high in the water, West jumped up and down as his eyes followed them coasting into the beach.

When we were all dried off and enjoying a snack, we thanked West for all of his help. It was clear to me that he and Ricochet had communicated in a language left unspoken and that West would be following in her paw steps in his quest to help others.

Looking around the picnic table at the six of us, he said, "You're welcome. As long as I never lose my job as the surfer. . . ."

We all chuckled.

"Don't worry, West, you will always be the surfer!" Lauren assured him.

And he would be. Surfing was now a part of his soul.

# Chapter 14

# Empathy, Intuition, and Communicating from the Heart

*"Everyone is gifted but most people never open their package."*

The more I observed Ricochet's unspoken communication, the more enlightened I became. I believe animals are messengers, on this earth to teach us lessons; they are constantly communicating with us, we just have to listen. Sometimes, it's very subtle, like the raise of an eyebrow or the flick of an ear. Other times it's more obvious, like a tilt of the head or a happy tail wag. And when we open our hearts and accept what our companion animals have to share on a soul level, we gain a greater sense of their empathy and intuition.

Research shows that dogs can show empathy to their families, and I've seen firsthand that they can show empathy to each other as well. For example, whenever Rina joined us during one of Ricochet's surf sessions, she would stay with me at the shoreline, whining until Ricochet coasted in to meet us. Perhaps she was concerned that Ricochet was so far away from us.

But one day we took our places along the shore, watching Dave push Ricochet into a wave. As she rode the wave to shore, the wave suddenly dissipated, leaving Ricochet out in the water, waiting patiently for Dave to retrieve her. However, from Rina's perspective, it must have appeared that Ricochet was "stranded" in the waves. Her empathetic instincts overruled her land-loving nature, and Rina bolted and started swimming out toward Ricochet.

Rina doesn't even like jumping over waves when she's playing, so to see her going out to "save" Ricochet was a testament to the power of canine empathy. When Ricochet saw Rina swimming out to her, *she* became concerned about Rina. Ricochet jumped off her board to "save" Rina, the two dogs paddling steadfastly, trying to save each other. It was incredibly touching to see the concern that they had for one another.

Not only did my dogs show empathy to each other, Ricochet shows empathy to complete strangers—marked by an acute sensitivity to their emotions, instantly connecting with them in a profound manner. I can't explain what goes on energetically during the interaction, but she gives each individual exactly what he or she requires, even if the person isn't aware of his or her own needs.

One day, when Ricochet and I were at Doheny State Beach with the Best Day Foundation, we met a boy, probably no more than ten years old, with Down syndrome. He sat on the beach with his shovel, talking to Ricochet, who sat right beside him. He decided that he wanted to bury her with sand, so he dug his shovel into the sand and began scooping and pouring shovelfuls of sand all over her—from her head to her paws. A couple of photographers wanted to capture the moment, so I dropped her leash to give them more space and walked about four feet away.

Just then, I noticed a flock of shorebirds about six feet away from us and, of course, Ricochet noticed them, too. Even though they must have looked tempting, there she sat, patiently, without me holding her leash, silently letting the boy dump sand all over her. She remained in the moment with that boy and nothing else mattered to her but being with him. I know she was connecting on a soul level and giving him exactly what he needed.

Dogs have been surfing for many years, and although Ricochet can instinctively adapt her surfing style based on each individual's disability, it's not the act of surfing that makes the interactions so life changing. It's the powerful heart-to-heart connections she makes that have touched the lives of many, including Sabine, a woman who was born with very short arms due to her mother's use of the prescribed drug thalidomide; Hunter, a young boy born with spina bifida; and Jake, who has a rare neurodegenerative disease causing severe disability. All of these people have very different challenges, yet Ricochet is consistently able to reach them on a deep level. The more she connects, the stronger her gift becomes.

For these reasons, people gravitate toward Ricochet and feel safe in her presence. When we're at the beach for one of her surfing sessions, she is typically exhausted afterward. But her lack of energy isn't from the physical demands of the surf; it's from absorbing other people's energy and giving them hers while they pet and interact with her. Sometimes I can actually see the transference of energy.

I can typically tell how a person is feeling based on Ricochet's behavior. She often takes on their emotions, and I notice it manifesting by her body language. Ricochet is like a mirror to the people with whom she interacts, reflecting back their feelings with a sense of confidence. As such, she can help people go inward to find a place of peace while, at the same time, moving outward through their greatest fears.

For instance, my friend Nedra is a Reiki practitioner. One of her clients was a four-year-old boy named Connor who suffered from infantile spasms so severely that he was enduring several hundred spasms each day. In 2012, Connor's hospice doctor said he wouldn't live to see his fourth birthday because of the severity and frequency of his seizures. At that time, he could not see, laugh, or smile. In desperation, his mother turned to alternative medicine and began seeing some small, positive changes.

Nedra believed that Connor had suffered so much pain and fear in his physical body from the chaos of the seizures that he had somehow "checked out" and was no longer present. Nedra suggested that a meeting with Ricochet might help. She wanted to see if Ricochet could communicate with Connor on a heart level and thus elicit a reaction. At this point in his treatment, Connor could see again, but he didn't make eye contact with his mother. He'd just stare into space.

As soon as Nedra invited us in, Ricochet's behavior became spastic. She couldn't settle down and had no focus. We were sitting on the floor next to Connor, who was in a child seat. After about fifteen minutes of talking with Connor's mother, I asked her if she was nervous. She told me she was and said she didn't really know much about dogs. From her comment and her demeanor, it appeared to me that she was apprehensive about having a creature she knew nothing about interacting with her son. But she was desperate to help him and was willing to try anything. I felt that Ricochet's unsettled behavior was a result of the combined emotions she was mirroring from mother and son. Then Connor's mom took a deep breath, and Nedra placed Connor's foot on Ricochet and helped him pet her. At that point, Ricochet began to settle down.

When Ricochet settled, a sense of calm enveloped the room. Suddenly, Connor turned toward his mom, who was sitting next to him, and I watched as they locked eyes for about fifteen minutes. Connor was actually engaging his mom, and she was talking softly to him as he cooed. It was the first time he had ever done that with *anyone*. It was a huge breakthrough that started Connor on a new path to healing.

Today, Connor is four and a half and progressing with his recovery through various alternative treatments. He interacts, engages, and enjoys a better quality of life. He knows who his mother is and he is aware of how much she loves and believes in him.

I don't know exactly what happened during Ricochet's interaction with Connor, but it was obvious to me that she was not only mirroring his emotions but also his mother's. Yet somehow she was able to ground Connor long enough to give his mom what she so desperately wanted—a connection with her son. It was a beautiful moment that I will always treasure. It also stands as a testament to just how powerful Ricochet is as an empath, making herself a vehicle for transformation.

Ricochet has always been a good communicator. She's always made it very clear what she was trying to convey—from coming in the house and nudging my arm when the neighbors have leftover

West giving Ricochet a hug.

©KillerImage.com

Ricochet and West's congratulatory pawshake.

West looking back to make sure Ricochet is having fun.

©KillerImage.com

©Heather M. Moana

©Robert Ochoa (Pawmazing)

West holding onto Ricochet in his first attempt to stand up on the board.

Ricochet and Randy.

Randy and Ricochet saluting.

Ricochet giving Randy some puppy love.

©DL Photos

Randy using Ricochet for balance.

©DL Photos

Randy and West.

©Amy Mejia

Ricochet helping Gina stand up.

©DL Photos

chicken to putting her head on my thigh so that I can open the door for her to see the critters in the field behind our house. But the behavior she uses the most is stopping and planting. She uses planting to tell me when she's done surfing for the day or when she doesn't want to go back into a warehouse-type building because the acoustics hurt her ears. She also uses planting as a way to communicate a person's physical or emotional distress.

An experience with West best epitomized her communication and energy exchange, and its ability to transform. Lauren mentioned that West was terrified of boating since his last experience. According to Lauren, the family had gone on a boat with their Labrador retriever, who sat contentedly as the wind whipped his fur. West, however, was completely inconsolable, scared that his dog would fall over the edge and be gobbled up by sea lions. West screamed and cried, and if anyone tried to talk to him, he'd push them and launch into a total breakdown, becoming rigid and controlling. Not only was boating out of the question for West, but he would get anxious and upset simply by seeing the boat docked in his great grandma Gigi's backyard.

One day, I had to be in Orange County where Lauren's grandmother lives, so I asked Lauren if she'd like us to try to help West overcome his fear. As I don't think that anything "just" happens, this particular day was Lauren's birthday.

When I arrived at Grandma Gigi's house with Ricochet and Rina, Lauren told me that West was already acting out in the car ride over because he didn't want to get near the boat. Even so, West greeted his beloved Ricochet, bending down to give her a big hug. Yet as we walked out the back door to go outside, Ricochet stopped and planted herself, and I could tell by her body language that she was mirroring West's fears and anxiety.

West was nervous, saying something about sharks being in the water, but knowing West's strong desire to help others, I asked him to take Ricochet's leash, and he was happy to do so. I had double-leashed Ricochet, which allowed West to feel like he was in control, when in reality, I was also holding a second leash. West grabbed the leash to help me, and both he and Ricochet started moving forward. Then, as we approached the steps leading down to the dock, I asked West to help me get Ricochet into the boat.

"No, I don't want to do that," he said. He wouldn't even take a single step onto the dock.

"Let's just take one step forward," I coaxed. "A step at a time."

And that's what we did. West, Ricochet, and I worked our way down the dock, and then Ricochet jumped into the boat excitedly.

I was able to encourage West to get into the boat by having him help Rina, who is not as agile as Ricochet is on unsteady surfaces. Once we were on the boat, West was nervous, continuing to talk about sharks and how he felt scared. He handed me Ricochet's leash several times and got off of the boat, but I continued to tell him that I needed help with Ricochet so he climbed right back on every time. I could sense his conflict between being afraid and wanting to help. But after a while, Ricochet's presence calmed West down. Normally by this point in an outing, Lauren said he'd be fighting, kicking, and screaming; yet this day he was scared but more willing to take the risk.

Then West lay back against Lauren's chest and closed his eyes. He asked us all to be quiet so he could sleep. For many kids with autism, excessive noise makes for too much stimulation, and sometimes it's overwhelming when too many people are talking at once. By quieting our voices, West could feel the sense of calm emanating from Ricochet. I think West knew on a subconscious level that he needed to concentrate on feeling Ricochet's energy.

As we all sat quietly, it was like a switch had flipped in West. Lauren's dad unexpectedly untied the ropes of the boat from the dock, and West didn't flinch. Fortunately, the boat is electric, so Lauren's dad turned it on quietly, and again, no response from West. He just lay against Lauren. Normally even putting the key in the ignition would cause West to become frantic, triggering a full-blown meltdown. Before we knew it, we were pulling away from the dock. Some kind of incredible communication was happening between Ricochet and West on a heart level. With grins on our faces, we all remained quiet and shared looks of amazement with one another.

Within a few minutes, West was so at ease that he opened his eyes, got off of Lauren's lap, and actually drove the boat with a huge smile on his face, as Ricochet sat by his side at the helm. As he steered the boat back, he became our tour director: "Ladies and gentleman, on your right you'll see a paddle boarder . . ."

With Ricochet's calming energy, West's experience of boating had completely changed from terrorizing to tame.

"This isn't so bad," he said as he looked around. "This is actually fun."

When the boat ride was over, Lauren was overjoyed and relieved. Ricochet had helped her son achieve one more milestone and found another way their family could spend leisure time together. "This was the best birthday gift I could have gotten," Lauren said.

While Ricochet has always been able to make deep connections with many different types of people, she displayed an extraordinary sense of intuition when working with the members of our military in the Paws'itive Teams Canine Inspired Community Reintegration (CICR) program, which helps active-duty military with post-traumatic stress (PTS), traumatic brain injuries, and other physical injuries.

For six weeks, two hours at a time, Ricochet and I would work with a service member, helping to reduce his or her anxiety and other symptoms of PTS. We'd also provide valuable experience handling a dog, since many of the military members hoped to get their own service dog in the future. Because the volunteer dogs were therapy dogs rather than service dogs, local businesses gave us special permission and allowed the dogs to accompany us to places that would normally evoke anxiety in the service members, such as big-box discount stores, hardware stores, and a number of other places.

As I read through some literature before our first session, my heart went out to these soldiers. PTS is a mental health condition that is triggered by a terrifying event that results in psychological trauma. It's considered an invisible disability. People with PTS experience depression, severe anxiety, hypervigilance, numbing, avoidance, uncontrollable thoughts, fear of public places, and panic attacks; as a result, they often end up living very secluded lives.

I was disheartened to learn that more people were joining the ranks: roughly 20 percent of the 2 million veterans who served in Iraq and Afghanistan struggle with combat PTS. While many of their physical injuries could be healed, their psyches were wounded, and they found themselves looking at many things in life as potential threats.

On many occasions when working with the CICR program, Ricochet was able to sense subtle changes in people's physiological, psychological, and emotional well-being—even if those changes weren't obvious to the people experiencing them. When they were feeling stressed, beginning to have a panic attack, anxiety response, increased pain, or other compromising symptoms, she instinctively alerted them by planting, which interrupted their response and helped them to refocus on her and work through the problem.

As keen as Ricochet's sensibility was, I was at first worried that she wouldn't be able to continue her work with the military. The first time she entered a room of service members, she responded with uncertainty and apprehension—completely counter to her typical behavior.

Gregarious and people-oriented, Ricochet didn't want to leave my side to go a couple of yards away when the service member held her leash. She was becoming anxious, looking to me for direction and reassurance. And then I realized that she was standing in a room with adults who were haunted by terrorizing experiences, whose trust was completely shattered. *They didn't trust anyone—not even themselves.* Being highly empathetic, Ricochet took in their emotions tenfold. She felt their stress, anxiety, and fear.

A soft and sensitive dog, Ricochet was used to seeing the world through eyes of pure love and innocence, and in all of her SURFice dog work, she had been surrounded by complete trust—trust created through an instant bond with Patrick upon their initial introduction, trust between all of the water helpers who exuded a sense of confidence, and trust with the kids she surfed with who embodied pure innocence. Yet with the military members, Ricochet was unsure of herself and her new environment. She was mirroring their distress.

During our first six-week session, Ricochet became even more anxious than she'd previously been about pop noises like gunshots or fireworks, perhaps because the service members had issues with these types of noises themselves. One day, when we returned home from a session, I noticed a FedEx package at the end of the driveway.

Rina's favorite thing in the whole world was retrieving packages from delivery drivers. Knowing Rina would be excited, I opened the door and she bolted to fetch the box, carrying it up the driveway with a determined look and wagging tail. When I opened the packaging, some of the bubble wrap fell to the ground, and Rina stepped on it. *Snap, snap, snap!* Ricochet's ears flicked back, her eyes grew intensely focused, and she had a look of confusion.

*Why weren't Rina or I running from the noise?*

"It's okay, Ricochet. It's just bubble wrap," I said, watching her slink quietly under my desk to hide. After that, she would react with fear even when benign things popped, if I clapped, or if I simply said the word "pop."

It was heartbreaking to watch her become so sensitive when she heard a common noise. While to me it was just bubble wrap, to her it represented something so horrible . . . something I couldn't see . . . something I couldn't feel, any more than the partners, parents, siblings, and children of service members could see or feel it.

I couldn't even begin to imagine what those men and women were going through for the weeks, months, and years at war, then returning to lives tormented by memories. We'll never be able to relate to the horrors they'll live with for the rest of their lives . . . but I think Ricochet did. She just knew.

After our first six-week session, I took her to a Reiki session with my friend Nedra, which helped her find her balance. I also made sure she got quiet time to decompress after each session, including time to run and play to burn off energy so she could stay grounded. By the time we started our next session, she taught herself to balance (just as she did on a surfboard). She could now empathize with the service members' emotions and physical pain without taking them on as her own.

One day when the CICR class was doing agility training, the marine she was working with was having a lot of pain in her neck and back from an auto accident earlier that week. Once a marine, always a marine, and Maria said she wanted to press on. But Ricochet had other ideas. All throughout the activity, Ricochet just kept stopping in her tracks. I figured she was alerting to her pain. And much to my surprise, a few days later, I got an email saying that, unbeknownst to her, Maria had actually fractured her spine the day of the accident. Ricochet—without the benefit of an x-ray or a doctor's note—knew that Maria shouldn't have been partaking in those physical activities!

On another occasion, we were working with a marine named Ely, who we'd just met. After about an hour, we went outside for a bathroom break for the dogs. We were walking across the parking lot to get to the toilet area, and Ricochet planted twice. Watching this, I thought Ricochet had stopped because Ely was anxious about interacting with the other participants.

However, when we were inside, Ely shared with me that he put two and two together and believed Ricochet had stopped because there was a black truck parked in the direction we were headed. Black trucks are triggers for him. This time she was alerting him *before* he had an anxiety attack.

Regardless of whether Ricochet has worked with someone for six weeks or six minutes, her empathy, intuition, and communication are acutely the same. In time, I would come to understand that Ricochet's intuitive gifts were constantly evolving and that she would continue to teach me what she's capable of. And, true to our journey, serendipity would intervene again, aligning our path with one service member who was in need of a heart-to-heart connection of his own.

# Chapter 15

# Service and Self-Sacrifice

*"The best way to find yourself is to lose yourself in the service of others."*

—G<small>ANDHI</small>

### Baghdad, Iraq, April 5, 2005

As the Humvee's tires crunched over the sunbaked grit at Camp Liberty, the oppressive air was heavy with the stench of smoke and sewage. Today's convoy security duty was a routine mission—escort a patrol through Baghdad. But routine or not, every day was a deadly game of Russian roulette. One wrong move and anyone—solider or civilian—could be blown to bits by what looked like a bag of trash on the side of the road. The biggest tactical problem with this war was that it wasn't soldiers fighting face-to-face—it was guerilla warfare, where the enemy planted their bombs and then hid. The only person you could trust in the desert was the one sitting next to you.

The unit had barely made its way outside of the gate when a deafening roar rocked the ground and the blue sky turned black in a plume of ash and smoke. Sergeant Randall Dexter was sent reeling in a tornado of debris, the back of his head smashing into the metal partition of the cab. Even with a concussion, and through the soot and the screams, he sprang into action as his training had prepared him. Although he'd seen some horrific things in his years as a medic, he wasn't prepared for the carnage he'd see, hear, and feel for the next forty minutes—images that would haunt him for the rest of his tour and beyond. A civilian Iraqi car had been jolted by the bomb, careening and crashing head-on into a tree. As he assessed the damage, he saw that the driver and the passenger were riddled with glass shards. Their car was a mangled mass of twisted metal, and blood and brains were everywhere. Unfortunately, despite his best efforts, a life would be lost on his watch.

It was just another day on the battlefield, but it would forever alter Sergeant Dexter's life. Something within him had shifted. In his bunk that night, he couldn't shut out the images. He couldn't stop the thoughts. "If only . . . " His efforts weren't enough to save the driver. He tossed and turned, sweat pouring off his forehead, his heart pounding out of his chest.

"You okay, man?" his bunkmate asked.

Randy said yes, but the answer was no. Although he had been on active duty for two years, the war inside Sergeant Dexter's head had just begun, and would only intensify with each successive horror he witnessed.

Once home from his second deployment to Iraq, in June 2008, Sergeant Dexter's life spiraled out of control. Even though he was safe on American soil, he remained in hypervigilant mode; he couldn't turn it off. The horrors of war had shattered his concept of power and his sense of control, and he no longer felt secure. With his battle buddies still in Iraq and dispersed to other bases, his life was upended, along with the routines that provided some semblance of order.

Every time he fell asleep, he'd have horrific nightmares that made him scared to sleep. So he wouldn't sleep, or he'd get so drunk that he would pass out. Going out in public with crowds caused agonizing panic attacks, so he isolated himself, avoiding anything that might trigger his anxiety—and his triggers were many: loud noises, a car backfiring, the smell of trash, or a drawer slamming. If his baby dropped a toy on the floor or a balloon popped, he would jump out of his skin, agitated, his entire body ready to go to war again.

The man who signed up to protect and serve, who was brave enough to risk his life for his country, was now too anxiety-ridden to go to the store to buy his baby daughter some diapers. It was no way to live. He mourned the person he was before he left for Iraq and his life, which had changed so drastically. He had done his time, yet the war at home dragged on.

Racked with guilt over not having done enough to save a man's life; the stigma of not being strong enough to handle the horrors that other soldiers endured; and the shame of not being the husband, father, and man he wanted to be, thoughts of suicide enticed him. Using his rifle seemed an easier way out of this hell that was worse than his time in Iraq. Unlike Iraq, there was no foreseeable way out of this tour.

### San Diego, 2013

"Come on, Ricochet, we're going to meet a new friend today," I said.

Ricochet sprang up, hopping into the car with enthusiasm. She obviously knew it was a workday. Normally, she was like me, content to be a homebody, relaxing in the sun by the porch, but if I told her we were going to work, she was up and out. Today I was just as excited as Ricochet was for our next assignment.

We'd be meeting with Carol Davis, the service dog program director of Paws'itive Teams CICR program to find out which service member we'd be matched with.

According to the paperwork, we'd be working with a man named Randall "Randy" Dexter, a staff sergeant in the US Army. I knew that he was someone's son, brother, uncle, or husband; that he was more than just a name on a piece of paper that happened to be teamed up with Ricochet. But the rules of the program stipulated that for privacy purposes, we didn't receive any details about the person with whom we were matched. Our role wasn't to ask questions about the participant's past or pry into the person's problems, but simply to be there with our dogs to help. I knew that Randy must've experienced some type of trauma, and for that, I felt a familiar kinship. Panic attacks and nightmares had plagued me since my attack, but in no way could my experience ever compare to anything Randy might've faced on the battlefield.

When the door opened and the participants filed in, Ricochet bolted up and headed straight toward a broad-shouldered man with black hair. His perfect military posture softened as he leaned down to pet her.

"Hey, pup," he said, rubbing the scruff of her neck.

As he stood up, I noticed his name tag: "Randy Dexter."

*How did Ricochet know that was him?* Or the better question: *Why was I surprised? Of course she knew!* She always knew. Although she couldn't read words, she could read people's souls. She knew she was there to help Randy.

When I walked toward him and we shook hands, he told me in a reserved voice that this class conflicted with a surf therapy class that also met on Thursdays.

"Oh, you like to surf?" I asked, smiling.

"Yes, I do," he answered, still stroking Ricochet's head.

"Well, I think you found the perfect partner then," I laughed, pulling out my phone to show him pictures of Ricochet surfing. We took turns swapping family photos. He showed me pictures of his son, his two-year-old daughter, and his wife, Becky, who was pregnant. As we exchanged photos, Ricochet had hopped up and was now sitting happily on his lap.

"I think it's safe to say Ricochet likes you," I smiled. "She didn't even wait for an invitation!"

With the introductions over, we all headed to the training area for some icebreaker exercises. My job was to stand back and allow Randy to get comfortable with handling Ricochet. When I saw the setup—an obstacle course and a short relay race—I wasn't worried. This was like a bigger version of Ricochet's puppy play yard.

They completed the course with ease and then we wrapped up the session with each service member sharing an interesting fact about each dog. Randy revealed that Ricochet was a surfing dog and that fate must have placed them together because they both liked to surf. The recreation therapist who matched them chimed in to say that she had no idea that Randy liked to surf. Once again, it seemed that synchronicity had put him on the same path as Ricochet's—and since nothing in life was random, there must have been a reason or a divine order as to why we were matched. I didn't know yet what our purpose beyond the program was but I'd find out in time. Interestingly, Randy hadn't wanted to take this class, and I'd balked at the idea initially because the class met early in the morning and I'm not a morning person. Yet I reminded myself that six weeks of early rising was the least I could do for the service members who'd sacrificed so much for us.

The *Oxford English Dictionary* defines *self-sacrifice* as "the giving up of one's own interests, happiness, and desires, for the sake of duty or the welfare of others." I can't think of anyone who embodies selfless service and sacrifices more than the men and women who serve our country. They put themselves in harm's way every day, willing to sacrifice their lives for the sake of helping others. They leave their families behind and often come back different people. Some never come back. They make the ultimate sacrifice, as do their families.

"Becky, it was pretty cool," Randy told his wife once their daughter was down for the night. "This dog actually surfs."

With that, Becky pulled out her phone and began searching to find some of Ricochet's videos and her Facebook page. Becky hadn't seen this kind of spark—or any spark—in her husband for many months. She was used to his extreme highs and lows, but mainly the lows. Most days, she felt like she was living with someone she didn't even know. It was as if Randy had two separate personalities: the PTS person and the person she fell in love with. She could always tell when he was in the grip of the PTS demon because she could see the rage in his eyes. But tonight it wasn't rage or the familiar look of defeat: it was a sparkle of hope, a glimmer of the Randy she had fallen in love with before PTS reared its ugly head.

The demon snuck up gradually with the nightly pattern of Randy coming home from work and cracking a beer because he was anxious; then the soft-eyed man turned into the demon—yelling, screaming, swearing, and punching walls. The next morning he'd wake up as if nothing had happened. But tonight it was different. There was a hint of the old Randy.

They sat on the bed, like a normal couple, watching Ricochet surf, enjoying a pleasant conversation—something they hadn't done in a long time. Tonight he wasn't too numb to connect or too distant to talk. When their eyes grew heavy, Randy said it was time to try to get some sleep. *Try* was the operative word.

"Good night, Becky," he said and kissed her forehead. But instead of rolling over and turning out the lights, he left for the living room. He'd been sleeping on the couch for months, ever since the night he woke up to see Becky sitting upright across from him, her eyes frozen in terror. The look of fear in her eyes was something he never wanted to see again—and it was all because of PTS. In the throes of a horrible nightmare, he'd lashed out, kicking and hitting. He didn't remember a thing—especially not elbowing her in the face. But the damage had already been done. Until his nightmares were under control, it was safer for them to sleep separately.

For the next few weeks, our group met for our two-hour sessions at parks, dog-friendly restaurants, and other local places. Since isolation is a big part of PTS, the goal of each training session was to get the participants to interact with each other, the dogs, and the general public in nonthreatening environments, with the ultimate goal of helping the service members feel less anxious in large public places like superstores. It was a process, getting them to learn how to manage a dog in a public setting, but more important, getting them to trust themselves, other people, and the world again.

On one of our first excursions, we met at Balboa Park for a scavenger hunt. Ricochet bounded over and jumped up on Randy. With both paws on his chest, she greeted him with a full-frontal doggie hug. Randy's expression immediately brightened as he rubbed her head vigorously.

"Hey, Ricochet," he said. "How ya doing?"

His voice had perked up; simply by seeing Ricochet, he'd received a jolt of energy.

Once again, my job was to stay in the background in case they needed me—which they didn't. As I watched them together, working side by side to complete each checkpoint, their chemistry was obvious. If you had passed them in the park, you'd probably smile. And you, just like me, would never guess the depths of Randy's despair—that it could take just one trigger to find him holed up in a dark room, crying for days on end, or that it may have taken every ounce of energy for him just to find the courage to leave his house on an ordinary day like today. By outward appearances, Randy was calm, but inward a silent storm raged. But today none of that mattered. Today Randy wasn't trapped in the past or worried about the future; he didn't need to talk or explain; he was simply enjoying the present moment with Ricochet, freely accepting her nonjudgmental interaction, unconditional love, and companionship.

As the next few weeks progressed, Ricochet and Randy's bond continued to grow, and his respect and care for her showed me that he would do well with a service dog some time in the future. He was even able to manage her when she saw a squirrel at Balboa Park, handling her distraction like he'd been working with her forever.

During one class, the participants and the volunteers went to a restaurant where we sat outside for breakfast. I'd taught Ricochet how to salute, and Randy was getting a kick out of showing everyone her trick. At one point, he mentioned something very casually about PTS, and I shared with Randy that I, too, had panic attacks in the past. That no lock or alarm ever made me feel truly safe and that until I got Rina, a "good night's sleep" was anything but.

"I know just what you mean," he admitted, meeting my eyes for just a second before getting back to his breakfast. It was a silent knowing that we were part of the same club, albeit my membership dues weren't nearly as high as his. There was no drama, no explanations needed, or questions asked. Randy was still reserved with me, which was to be expected—it's a hallmark of PTS. Just then, I noticed Randy was folding a napkin over several pieces of bacon and a portion of his eggs, saving it for Ricochet, who was looking up at him from under the table.

"I do believe you're spoiling her," I joked.

"Well, she takes care of me, and I take care of her."

And take care of him she did. During one of the next classes, Randy mentioned that he had undergone sinus surgery earlier in the week, but he said nothing more about it. During this session, the service members were competing in a fun relay race, in which they would lead the dogs around cones to the other side of the room and back. While all of the other dogs set off trotting, Ricochet took a few tentative steps and then stopped cold.

Randy looked perplexed, as Ricochet had always cooperated fully. I motioned for him to say "touch" so that she would walk a few steps to his outstretched hand. She touched, but then once again, she took a few steps forward and then planted. By this time, most of the other dogs were making their way back, but Ricochet stood there calmly looking up at Randy.

Since I knew she had alerted other service members to pain with her behavior, including Maria, I asked Randy if he was in pain. Only then did he admit that he was, but had been trained to push through it. Randy wasn't going to say anything about his discomfort, so Ricochet did the communicating for him, telling us that he shouldn't have been participating in the relay race. Randy was noticeably impressed by her abilities, and I hoped his confidence in her would help him during their final task: their trip to the superstore.

When the day finally arrived, we met in the parking lot of the store, and I could sense Randy's anxiousness immediately. In all of our other outings, Ricochet's presence had been enough to quell his anxiety, but today his nerves were evident. Previously, he had been very talkative, but this time he was very quiet. He was a bit jumpy, his face tense, and his shoulders tight.

"My wife made Ricochet some bacon," he offered, pulling a bag out of his jacket. "She said that she thinks she's not really a dog but an angel in a dog suit."

I was touched. This woman who didn't even know me or Ricochet, who was eight months pregnant, woke up early to make my dog some bacon. *What a sweet sentiment!* Ricochet thought so, too, devouring the salty treat in a few enthusiastic gulps.

"How are you feeling?" I asked.

Randy said that his head was pounding, which was common with brain injuries and anxiety, but true to his nature, he said that he could deal with it. His biggest concern was walking by the displays in the middle of the store, because he couldn't see around them, and it would be difficult not to react to people popping out of nowhere.

"Well, if you need to get out of there or if you need to take a break, you can always leave," I offered. Yet knowing the army mindset, I guessed that he would see leaving the store as a failure. He'd want to finish the mission.

"Okay," he agreed. "I say we go for it. Let's get this done."

"Remember, you have Ricochet," I assured him. "She'll help you through it."

He bent down and patted Ricochet, who was sitting on his feet and looking up at him.

As the electronic doors whooshed apart, he headed in with Ricochet on a short leash in front. She was his buffer, creating more personal space for him if people started crowding him in.

We made our way through the store, and all of a sudden, Ricochet planted herself as Randy tried to walk down the housewares aisle, looking up and into his eyes as if she had something to tell him. Since we knew how Ricochet alerted, it was up to us to decode what she was trying to say. Scanning the aisle, I noticed quite a few people and told Randy that she was alerting him that the aisle ahead was crowded. We meandered through the store, even passing the center displays that Randy was dreading so much. Sure enough, several more times when there was something Randy might perceive as a threat, such as a cluster of people, Ricochet would alert by stopping and planting. After several instances of her doing this, Randy understood that it wasn't a fluke; that this was how she would alert him to a perceived threat or oncoming anxiety attack.

"Wow, Judy, she just knows," he said, shaking his head. "By stopping she's telling me, 'It's not a good time to go down there. Wait and then regroup. Move when you're ready.'" This type of pausing gave Randy the opportunity to stop and reassess his surroundings because Ricochet was picking up on something.

Randy crouched down and patted Ricochet, rewarding her with a dog treat that Becky had packed. "Good job, Ricochet!"

She looked up at him, her tail wagging wildly.

Once outside in the open air, I congratulated Randy and Ricochet on their accomplishment. They had mastered their mission. Randy exhaled with relief, and I suggested he take Ricochet to the back of the parking lot so they could both run around and release some nervous energy. I explained that, just like people, dogs need to decompress after a stressful activity.

When I caught up with them, I told Randy I was curious how he felt when Ricochet planted because I wasn't sure if that was the best way of alerting. I asked him if he had a service dog, would he want the dog to *keep* him from doing something like Ricochet does when she plants, or would his goal be for the dog to *get* him to do something. Randy's response was revealing: He explained that soldiers are warriors, trained to persevere through pain—to do anything to get the job done. Since his tendency was to push through, he really needed someone to tell him to stop.

Yet again, Ricochet knew *exactly* what he needed.

After their shopping success, we all went to a burger place to have lunch and celebrate each service member completing the program. While there was little pomp and circumstance, there was an abundance of pride for the men and women and their dogs because deep relationships had been formed.

When it was my turn to speak to the group, I tried to keep it short. "It has been an honor for me to work with you, and we trust you completely with our dogs. You have given us the greatest gift by loving and caring for them."

As they handed Randy his certificate, I was moved beyond words: "Because of these six weeks with Ricochet, I'm ready to conquer this. She gave me the confidence and the strength I was lacking for so long. From now on, I will kick this PTS in the ass like I was trained to fight in war. That's the soldier in me. Because of Ricochet, I'm now on a mission."

That night I messaged Randy's wife on Facebook to thank her for the bacon. Her response made me feel grateful for the opportunity to help such deserving people:

> Before Randy met Ricochet, we were at a really low point; there was talk of divorce. But now we have a chance. When Randy gets home from being with Ricochet, he is so relaxed and open. If I have any issues or situations, that is my time to ask him.
>
> Even after just two weeks, I could see a change in him. He's not nearly as tense or as stressed out as he was. It's nice to be able to share things with him again. He now feels like he has hope for the future—that if he can get a service dog, he will have more independence. I can never thank Ricochet enough for what she's done.

But unfortunately, as with many journeys, sometimes you take two steps forward and one step back, and Randy was about to face a hurdle. The following week after the class was over, Becky texted me early one morning: *Is there any way Randy can see Ricochet? He had a really bad night.*

I was conflicted. This program was relatively new to all of us. I wanted to help, of course, but I didn't want to jeopardize the program or get anyone in trouble—the military has rules and protocols, and I wasn't sure if I was allowed to see Randy outside of the group setting. Perplexed, I called Carol and asked her.

"Just go, Judy," she urged without a second's hesitation. "Just do it. Sometimes you have to do what you have to do to help someone in need."

When Ricochet and I pulled up to the parking lot of a nearby church, immediately I could see that Randy was upset—his face was tense and he was definitely on edge. Ricochet ran up and gave him her standard full-body hug. We said our hellos to Becky and Randy's daughter, and then Randy briefly mentioned what happened. Apparently, one of Randy's retired military friends who recently moved to the area experienced a bad flashback the night before. He had gotten into a fight and was hospitalized. Randy had accompanied him to the hospital. Seeing his injuries and hearing his experience were enough to rattle Randy, triggering old memories and making him question the progress he'd made so far.

As Becky strolled through the parking lot keeping their daughter occupied, Randy, Ricochet, and I sat on the ground. He told me how immensely Ricochet had helped him, and he admitted that he wished he could go through the program again—that he didn't think he was ready to face the outside world. And then he began opening up.

"I used to love going out and people watching. Now I can't even be around large crowds because I just don't feel safe," he explained. "When I have a flashback or experience a trigger, my entire body reacts. It's just like I'm back in Iraq. My heart races like crazy," he said. "It got to the point where I couldn't sleep or go out unless I had a drink or two. Or three," he admitted.

As Randy spoke, Becky came and sat down, keeping a close eye on their daughter as she explored the nearby surroundings.

"And there's the stigma, too," he revealed. "I have PTS, but someone else who went to Iraq and saw the same things I did doesn't have it. You feel like you are looked down upon. Your job is to take care of other people, but you can't even take care of yourself."

Listening to him talk, Becky told Randy that she was grateful that he was finally opening up—that she understood for the very first time what PTS was and what he'd been going through.

It dawned on me then that Randy had been carrying his burden entirely alone—that he'd never even spoken to his wife about his past or his PTS. While I was understandably in the dark, as I'd only recently met him, Becky knew little more than I did. She could only watch and wonder what was going on, helpless to offer any support. Physically he was with her, but emotionally, he was a world away. Unfortunately, this kind of isolation is very common, and it is the number-one reason why so many military marriages end in divorce. Randy and Becky were living apart, isolated like two separate islands, and it took a cinnamon-coated dog with deep brown eyes to act as a bridge to help bring them back together. While Becky couldn't erase Randy's trauma, at least now she could begin to understand it. It was a new chapter for them.

As their little girl came running over, laughing with pure glee, I thought back to my own childhood. My father had loved me as much as he could, but his drug-fueled behavior created chaos. And while my mother was married on paper, she had raised us alone.

I hoped that Ricochet had helped to break what could have been a devastating cycle for this family—that Randy's children wouldn't have to live in fear or with shameful secrets the way I had. Now that the demons were out of the shadows, whatever happened in their future, they could face it together.

We stood up to leave and Randy confided that he really wanted to make a difference for other struggling soldiers. "PTS is just like someone who is struggling with alcoholism or depression," he said. "We are not bad people; we've been through a lot, and once we are educated and learn how to deal with it, we'll be great assets again."

"You can borrow Ricochet wherever and whenever you need her," I promised. "I mean it, Randy." And I did.

Before we said our good-byes, we talked about how important it was to raise awareness about PTS and to provide support to other military families. Randy had an idea to create a video of his story and how Ricochet helped him. Even though he wasn't totally comfortable speaking publicly, he thought it would be a good idea if it could help another service person. Not only would we raise awareness with the video, we could provide education and other resources on Ricochet's Web site and Facebook page. I thought it was a wonderful undertaking and an optimistic sign for Randy, because I knew from past experience that through helping others, you can find a way to help heal yourself.

That night I got a text from Becky: *OMG! I don't know what magic spells you and Ricochet put on Randy, but when we left the parking lot, he was my husband again, not the depressed soldier he has been or the broken man I've seen cry for days straight. Thank you so much.*

I was glad to see that Ricochet was making a tangible difference, and I hoped our video would help more people like Randy who were struggling alone in silence.

The parking lot was crowded the day we met at the superstore to start filming the video, with Ricochet leading the way to highlight how she helped Randy navigate the aisles. She planted a few times upon entering the store so that Randy could regroup, and then she walked a few steps in front of him, checking the aisles for anything Randy might perceive as a threat before he reached them, her head turning from right to left as if she were watching a tennis match. Randy felt more comfortable knowing Ricochet would alert him if there was something that could cause anxiety in an aisle. Things went as usual until we reached the back of the store, at which point Ricochet suddenly stopped. She wouldn't budge. She was much more deliberate in her alerting behavior than usual.

"Try prompting her with the Touch cue, Randy," I suggested, thinking that when Randy said *touch*, Ricochet would move forward and touch his hand with her nose, at which point he could get her moving again.

But when he uttered the cue, it seemed as if it fell on deaf ears. Ricochet didn't budge. She had firmly planted herself, but why? The back of the store was empty. Why would she alert us when there weren't any people around? Randy continued prompting her, and she still wouldn't listen. I was getting irritated. Truth be told, I was a little stressed that her resistance was being caught on camera.

I stepped a few yards ahead, and that's when I saw it—what Ricochet already knew was there. Directly over my head was large metal scaffolding above a two-tiered bicycle display with a heavy metal beam that swung from the end of it. Surely Randy would have experienced a reaction to this trigger. I remembered him telling me that he'd hit his head on the metal in the Humvee in Iraq. Yet how did Ricochet know that? Had she truly taken in his experiences, his memories, his trauma? Even if she hadn't, how could she possibly know about the metal beam, two full aisles away, which was beyond her scope of vision?

"You always have to trust the dog," I said aloud, still not fully believing what had just transpired. In service-dog training, we call this "intelligent disobedience," when the animal refuses to do a requested task for the welfare or safety of the person they are helping; for example, when a guide dog leads a person with a visual disability, and the dog stops and won't cross the street because he sees something that could be problematic. Even though the person gives the cue to cross the street, the dog "disobeys" to keep the person safe. That's what Ricochet did, but without any formal training to do it.

As humans, we forget. Even with all that Ricochet had shown me about intuition and how important it is to listen to our animals, even I forgot—yet again. She was doing the best job she could to tell us, "There is something there, and I cannot let him go."

If Randy had come upon the display suddenly, Ricochet knew he would have a reaction—maybe even a flashback. But I didn't listen, just like all of those months when I didn't listen to her when she was a puppy. Being on this journey with Ricochet was an ongoing learning process, and she taught me something new all the time. I had learned to listen, but at the time, I was preoccupied with the filming and had gotten sidetracked.

"Always trust the dog," I repeated.

Ricochet was trying to tell us something very important, but what she displayed was far more than just intelligence—it was true intuition, an absolute ability to sense what others couldn't see. Or maybe it was something even more, something we still haven't learned that dogs are capable of.

When Randy saw the metal contraption, his jaw dropped.

"Judy, that's just crazy," he said, shaking his head in disbelief. "The fact that Ricochet planted a couple of aisles before that metal frame proves she knows *exactly* what's going on," he remarked as he bent down to pat her. "She knew that if I were to walk by that beam without knowing it was there, I would have jumped for sure; I would've been totally freaked out. She knows that would've caused me anxiety. She totally had my back. You had my back, didn't you, Ricochet?" he asked.

We continued walking through the aisles, still amazed by Ricochet's sensibilities. Since Randy had the luxury of having Ricochet with him, he decided to stop and look at sunglasses. We walked to the sunglass department, and he said to Ricochet, "Watch my back." This was a trained task we taught her where she sat next to him, but facing the other direction, watching his back, seeing what was behind him as he looked forward and tried on the glasses. With her scouting what was behind him, Randy was able to peruse the merchandise in a way he couldn't without Ricochet with him. When she'd stand up or nudge closer to him, it was her way of telling him that someone was approaching. To know that someone had his back was a huge stress reliever for Randy.

As we moved toward the registers to pay for the sunglasses, it was extremely crowded in the lobby area with lines of people that were growing longer. I could see Randy becoming tenser, looking around and eyeing the doors. And if his behavior wasn't enough, I could tell he wanted to get out by the way Ricochet was acting. She was on high alert. In the checkout aisle, she paid close attention to the slightest movement, ready to warn Randy of a perceived threat. She stood a few steps ahead of him, providing him with a buffer so he had his own space.

Just as I was about to remind him that he could leave if he needed to, Ricochet turned back and lay down right at his feet so that it would be hard for anyone to pass by. By laying on the floor instead of taking her usual stance, she was ensuring he had his personal space while telling him to stop and take a breath. And, in fact, she was right. By the time he had paid for his item, the crowd in the lobby had dissipated. The three of us left the store, Randy and I still amazed by Ricochet's intuition.

"Ricochet can read me and know what I'm feeling even before I do," Randy said. "She gives me a sense of protection, letting me know, 'Hey, I've got your back.' Now I'm not blindsided," he explained. "When she stops and alerts, she's my battle buddy. I had battle buddies in Iraq who had my back. Now *she* has my back, letting me know if there's trouble down the road. She's my extra set of eyes."

The next weekend, Ricochet and Randy morphed from battle buddies to surf buddies, finally meeting up for a day of surfing. An ESPN film crew was at the beach filming a segment on Ricochet, and when Randy arrived on the scene, Dave, Patti, and I were on the beach with West and his family.

As Randy donned his wetsuit, he said hello to West and then broke the ice by asking him for some advice on surfing with Ricochet.

"Just have fun!" West beamed, handing Randy the leash.

Randy walked out beyond the breakers with Dave, who chatted warmly and gave him the typical safety instructions.

"You ready, Ricochet?" Dave asked.

She dug in, ready for the next wave.

As Dave launched the board, Randy wobbled for just a second, and then he popped up, holding on to the handle of Ricochet's life jacket, his smile wide as he coasted all the way in to shore. While Ricochet provided a point of balance on the front of the board, Randy was in control of his course, steering the board as it veered side to side in a trajectory of salty spray. When he reached the shore, his smile was glowing. West was equally as excited for his new friend, jumping up and down and cheering.

"To pop up that easily with her was amazing!" Randy said, walking toward me. "Seeing her in her element is something that I will never forget. It was not only a spiritual connection but a way for me to get closer to her because that was what *she* loves to do. We're always doing things I need to do, so this was her turn."

The quiet, reserved person I had met twelve weeks earlier was night and day from the confident, fun-loving person standing before me.

"But what made it so special wasn't just that I was surfing with a dog; I was surfing with my friend," he said as he bent down to pat her wet fur.

He turned to bring the board to West. "Alright, West, let me see you do it," he encouraged, giving West a high-five.

As I watched Randy and West interacting along the shore, I realized how more alike they were than different, this eight-year-old and this soldier. We all struggle, some of us with more difficult challenges than others, and often in silence. At one time, both Randy and West were held hostage by uncontrollable rage, and neither could find the words to speak about their inner turmoil. Both battled an invisible enemy—and a label—that many people didn't understand. And while scientists and specialists didn't always know what would help, Ricochet always did. No matter the day or the emotion, she intuitively and empathetically knew what each of them needed, and she gave it unconditionally.

Both Randy and West had risen above the stigma of a misunderstood diagnosis. By persevering through their fears—and possibly because of them—they had both emerged as stronger people, possessing and reflecting back to others a depth of understanding and compassion that most people would never understand. But Ricochet always understood. She knew their deep capacity to feel and to care for others from the moment she met them. In her own unique way, she had tapped their hidden wellspring of emotions, which was now trickling out to others.

Randy and Ricochet surfed several more waves together, with Randy using Ricochet to balance himself—as she had balanced his emotions all those weeks together. As I watched them teetering and tottering, but never falling, I thought about the thousands of other soldiers in Iraq, Afghanistan, and other places—about how they were thrust into many foreign, harsh, and unnatural environments and how difficult it must be to endure. Yet out here, Randy was immersed in the abundance of the ocean and the rhythms of nature. Perhaps in some subtle way, by hearing the crash of the waves instead of the crack of gunfire, and the whistle of the wind instead of the whistle of mortars, it might help wash away some of the painful memories with enough time and distance.

As I witnessed the incredible bond Randy and Ricochet shared—the mutual respect and her keen sensibilities toward him, I had an overwhelming realization: Randy needed Ricochet more than I did. It could be six months or longer before he was matched with a service dog.

I gazed over at Ricochet, and I realized that even though she wasn't an appropriate service dog for a person with a physical disability, she would have made a great match for someone able-bodied with PTS due to her intuitive alerting.

I felt a surge of guilt for not handing over her leash to Randy right then and there. How could I keep this dog from him when she was helping him so much? Yes, I loved Ricochet with all my heart, but I always knew she was not my dog—she belonged to everyone. Randy sacrificed himself for our country. Shouldn't I make the sacrifice and let her go?

It seemed selfish of me to keep her when Randy needed her more. But then my rational side reminded my emotional side that Ricochet was six years old. It wouldn't be fair to place her with Randy because her work career would be shorter than a newly placed service dog's. Randy needed a service dog who could provide as many working years as possible.

Despite this realization, I was still conflicted over the decision when the day came to film more footage of Randy being interviewed for our newly titled "PTS Battle Buddies" initiative.

"Ricochet saved my life," he began as the camera rolled. "Before I met her, I was suicidal . . ."

As if on cue, Ricochet walked over to him and put her paws on his lap, but then she began licking his face rapidly. Unlike Rina, Ricochet was not the type of dog who licked very much.

"Randy," I asked, "are you more nervous than usual doing this?"

He admitted that he was feeling very anxious. Despite his calm demeanor, by watching Ricochet's behavior, I could tell that he was stressed. She was trying to calm him down in the only way she knew how. She was redirecting his attention so he could stop for a breath and remember to take his time. He exhaled and then started again.

"When I left for Iraq, it was after 9/11 so I knew what I was getting into. Even so, I had all the hope in the world. But day after day of never knowing who you can trust . . . it starts to get to you. You lose hope. At least I did."

As he spoke, I choked up with pride over his bravery in coming to terms with something he had hidden for so long.

"The nightmares started the day of the explosion. That night in bed, I couldn't stop replaying my actions in my head. *Did I do enough that day to save him? Did that man die because of something I did or didn't do?*

"But now I know there was nothing I could have done to save him. I did everything I could have," he paused. "Even if he was in America, he still would have died. But the worst part about PTS is that I've inflicted pain on the people I love the most—that is something I would never intend to do," he explained.

"From the moment I met her, I felt Ricochet understood what I was going through. I didn't feel pressure to express my experiences to her like so many other therapists requested of me. I didn't have to talk. I was able to live in the moment with her and not worry about yesterday or be anxious about tomorrow. Ricochet knew me right from the start. She was instantly in tune with me, and to know that I could have that bond in my lowest of lows gave me hope for the next day."

With the camera still rolling, I asked Randy to describe how Ricochet alerts. As he started to explain, I couldn't help but blurt out that when I noticed their strong bond and the way she alerted him to potential triggers, I felt compelled to give Ricochet to him to be his service dog.

A big grin lit up his face. "I know *I* thought about it!" he admitted. "At one point, I told my wife that I selfishly wanted to keep Ricochet as my service dog."

*Had he really been thinking what I'd been thinking?*

"But then I told Becky that being my service dog is not Ricochet's mission. I firmly believe that Ricochet was put on this earth to help millions of people. She's not meant to be with just one person. To me, it was divine intervention that I met Ricochet when I did. Ricochet was put here on this earth to do great things. And she has. It makes me laugh that some people might have labeled Ricochet to say that she wasn't cut out to be a service dog," he explained. "She just wasn't meant to be a certain kind of service dog. For me, she's going above and beyond in the things she helps me with."

And with that, Ricochet rolled over on the floor to get a much-deserved tummy rub.

"I want to say to other service members who are struggling, there is life to be lived again. It will never be the same as it was, but it can be enjoyable again. Whether you find peace through surfing, through hiking, or a dog, you can find joy again; you can and you will find that place."

The very day that we posted the Battle Buddies video on Facebook, Randy's phone rang. It was one of his best friends, an army buddy he'd known for years. He'd seen the post and admitted to Randy that he had recently tried to commit suicide. He was going through the same things Randy had and, for the same reasons as Randy, he never felt comfortable talking to anyone about it.

He and Randy talked for three hours on the phone, during which time his friend was able to get his feelings out and begin the healing process. If we hadn't posted our video, this soldier would never have contacted Randy.

Randy was right—it was divine intervention. He had paid it forward by saving a soldier. A veteran like Randy with PTS dies by suicide every sixty-five minutes. Randy may not have been able to save the man in Iraq, but he had saved someone at home and countless others who would see our video and visit our PTS Battle Buddy Web page (www.SurfDogRicochet.com). They would find a reason to keep fighting.

With Ricochet as the impetus, Randy had begun a transformation—from being holed up in a dark room alone to playing with his toddler in the living room, from sleeping on the couch to back in his bed. He would have good days and bad days, but now he wouldn't have to battle it alone. While Randy had been on American soil for five years, Ricochet, his battle buddy, had finally led him back home—body, heart, *and* soul. Randy always possessed honor and courage, but Ricochet gave him what he needed most: freedom.

And fortunately, Randy could now pass that gift on with a new service dog to help him. Ricochet held a fund-raiser on her Facebook page to raise $10,000 to pay for a service dog for Randy, which would give him the ability to be more independent.

What's more, one of our long-term Battle Buddies goals was to offer surf experiences to wounded warriors, veterans with PTS, and military families. But synchronicity intervened once again, and the initiative presented itself sooner than planned.

As fate would have it, one day while Ricochet and I were at a Best Day Event for kids with special needs, we met an adorable nine-year-old girl named Gina who had autism. Ricochet doesn't usually surf at these events. Instead, she interacts with the kids on the sand, accompanies them through the obstacle course, or rides with them on a kayak. But on this day, one of the organizers spontaneously asked if Ricochet could surf with Gina. So, of course, I said yes.

Gina rode the first wave while lying down with Ricochet behind her. But then, on the next wave, she stood up on the board to the amazement of all the water helpers. Ricochet had given her the confidence to try something she had never done before.

I posted photos on Ricochet's Facebook page later that day, and one of the comments in particular caught my attention—it was typed from about 7,500 miles away. It read: "I'm Gina's dad in Afghanistan. Thank you for surfing with Gina. *Bradley Gill*."

My throat caught as I thought about this father so far away from his little girl—missing the first day of school, the holidays, and just the ordinary moments of life. I responded as I knew Ricochet would by making a promise that when Brad returned home from his deployment, Ricochet would surf with Gina again just for him.

After eleven long months, Brad returned home, and the day finally came for him to see his daughter surf with Ricochet. Since it was December, the water in San Diego was cold, and Gina needed a wetsuit. Ricochet held a fund-raiser on Facebook to purchase a wetsuit and booties, and donations started coming in. A few days in, I received an email from a marine. "How much do you need?" he asked. He told me he'd pay the difference, no matter how much, to give back to one of his brothers. And so, with his donation, we were able to cover the cost of a new pink wetsuit and booties for Gina so that she could surf for her dad.

It was a beautiful sunny day in December—New Year's Eve, in fact. I couldn't think of a better way to celebrate than by Ricochet surfing with the kids, adults, and military members she had surfed with this past year, including Randy, who brought his young daughter along.

I had sent out a press release a few days before to raise more awareness about PTS and autism, and when I got to the beach, some news trucks were waiting. As the morning wore on, seven different local news stations arrived, ready to film Brad's momentous homecoming event. He and his wife, Gail, stood on the beach, video camera in hand, as the water helpers—Dave, Austin, Ryan, and Grant—took Gina and Ricochet out on the surfboard.

Patti, Deb, and Devyn, another water helper, waited in the shallower water to catch Gina if she needed help. A big smile was plastered on Brad's face as his daughter climbed onto the surfboard and lay down with Ricochet in front of her. As Dave pitched them on the wave, the surfboard careened, and I was sure they were going to wipe out. But they didn't. As the board glided through the water, Gina got up on one knee, and then the other, and finally popped up into a standing position.

Cheers erupted behind the surfing duo from the volunteers in the water, and high-fives were exchanged on the beach between Gina's parents and others who came to watch. Even the film crews seemed to choke up as they watched the proud dad. Glancing over at Brad, I caught him wiping away a tear.

Gina and Ricochet rode several more waves, with her gaining more confidence with each successive ride. As Gina started walking back to the beach with Grant, he held out his hand and pointed to her dad. Gina took off in a quick sprint, running into the waiting arms of her daddy. The father and daughter hugged, and then Brad gave Gina a proud kiss on her head as seven news crews rushed to them to get their reaction.

There was something about that moment between father and daughter that touched me deeply. Brad's pride was palpable. Not having any children of my own, I don't know what it's like to feel that type of pride. Of course, I often feel proud of Rina and Ricochet, but I'd never experienced that kind of relationship with my own father, and it warmed my heart to witness the exchange between the pair. Bringing joy to a father and daughter who'd been worlds away for so long felt amazing.

Brad spoke into the microphones in front of him. "It makes me feel proud. This is a child who's afraid to ride a bike without training wheels but has no problem going out in this cold water and hopping on a surfboard with Ricochet. It's really special for me today because it's the first time I've gotten to see Gina surf with Ricochet, and it was amazing. I can't think of any place I'd rather be than watching this."

When a reporter asked Gina's mom what she thought this surf session did for Gina, she replied, "It's building her confidence enormously. She has a lot of trouble with everything else in life. Socializing and school. Things can be really hard for her. She's kind of a loner. It's hard for her to make friends."

One of the reporters handed Gina a microphone and asked her the same question. She smiled and said, "Ricochet helps me have courage."

Courage, just like her dad.

Gina wasn't the only confident one on the beach that day. Randy's three-year-old daughter Selena watched with delight, running around the beach with her friend Rina. She, too, wanted to surf with Ricochet like her dad and the big kids, but she didn't have a wetsuit.

Grant improvised with an approach he used at Best Day events that wouldn't require Selena to get wet. He instructed Randy to sit on the board with his legs around Selena, who stood with her arms outstretched above, holding hands with Grant, who ran alongside them into shore. It was teamwork if I ever saw it, and everyone on the beach clapped as they glided in. Selena giggled all the while, making happy memories with her dad.

Brad looked on as Randy and his daughter jumped up from the board. The two soldiers—once landlocked in the desert—were enjoying a carefree day at the beach. And both of their daughters had received the best gift: their dads were home where they belonged.

When a news reporter walked up to Randy with a microphone in hand, he asked him what stood out most about the day. Without hesitation Randy eagerly replied, "To see the joy in people's faces, whether it's vets who have gone through similar things or these kids, it puts a whole new perspective on how great life can be. PTS makes it very difficult to go out, but now that I've met Ricochet, I get to enjoy the things I used to love. Being able to do things like this and enjoying them is something I really can't put into words; just how grateful and blessed I truly am. To me, Ricochet's an angel."

# Chapter 16

# Sacred Journey

*"The meaning of life is to find your gift.*
*The purpose of life is to give it away."*

—Pablo Picasso

Every year on August 20, the anniversary of the day when Ricochet and Patrick first surfed together, we have a celebratory surf session with Patrick. In 2013, however, instead of going surfing, we were invited to attend a San Diego Padres baseball game, which was scheduled just a few days later.

After watching an ESPN segment of Ricochet, a Padres representative invited Ricochet, Patrick, and Ian to throw out the first ceremonial pitches. The representative graciously gave me one hundred tickets to the game. Of course, I invited all of the people with whom Ricochet had surfed, as well as their siblings and parents. I also invited all of the wonderful water helpers and volunteers and the people who'd taken care of Rina whenever Ricochet and I were away—in short, anyone who had helped make Ricochet's work possible.

As the Padres fans streamed in to PETCO Park, Randy and Becky arrived, with their children in tow, winding their way through the walkways. Being at such a crowded venue this evening was a big step for Randy. He was pushing the stroller, using it as a buffer between himself and the throngs of people. Becky noticed that he was gripping the handle especially tight as he always did when he was nervous.

"Are you okay, Randy?" she asked.

"I will be once I meet up with Ricochet," he said, as they scouted for their seats.

As Randy and Becky made their way through the crowds, Patti was walking in. She noticed Maria, the marine who she had met one day on the beach. Knowing that Maria didn't like crowds, and seeing that she was looking a bit uncomfortable, Patti motioned to her. "Come with me," she offered. "We'll find the seats together."

One by one, all of the guests arrived, decked out in baseball attire, excited to see the people they'd come to know so well in the ocean doing something completely different around a baseball diamond.

Looking handsome and confident, Patrick was home for a break from college, where he was studying film. He sat tall in his wheelchair, flanked by his sister, Samantha, and his mom, Jennifer. Ian sat next to Patrick with his sister Lauren and brother Luke. He was much taller and broader, looking as if he'd grown up quite a lot since the last time I'd seen him.

Both Patrick and Ian were wearing matching Padres jerseys and giant grins across their faces, as they posed with Ricochet in the infield. Ricochet sat dutifully beside them, sporting a royal blue Padres shirt around her shoulders that draped down her back.

The crowd had their attention on the jumbo screen above the stands which commenced with footage of the stories of Ian and Patrick's lives, their families' struggles, and how surfing with Ricochet helped them in their recovery.

The plan was for both Ian and Patrick to throw a ceremonial pitch, and then Ricochet would run to home plate in a symbolic gesture of "striking out" violence in honor of Chris Lane, an Australian baseball player that had been killed earlier in the week. As we stood on the field, the Padres catcher, René Rivera, squatted down to prepare for Patrick's pitch. But just then Ricochet sauntered slowly, yet purposely, over to Rivera and nuzzled him. He smiled and gave her a loving pat. And there she remained, by his side.

The few people who noticed may have understood the significance of Ricochet's gesture: Chris Lane had been the catcher for his Australian college team. I wondered if Ricochet had somehow known it, too. She sat next to the catcher, who was crouched and ready, and then Ian and Patrick threw their pitches.

As the announcer yelled, "Play ball," I realized, as synchronicity would have it on this anniversary outing, that the Padres were playing the Chicago Cubs, my old home team. I realized how far I'd come since my Chicago roots.

In the early days of this journey with Ricochet, I struggled to find a name to describe what was happening because I knew it was not ordinary—it was much too powerful and full of overwhelming goodness, grace, and purity to even be of my day-to-day existence. I felt like I was experiencing a spiritual awakening of my soul.

I finally realized that I couldn't come up with a name for it because it wasn't mine to name. Everyone calls it something different: God, the Universe, Spirit, love, a higher power, and a myriad of other descriptions. Rather than naming it, I've left it blank and open-ended for your interpretation, based on your own beliefs or whatever aspects of my journey resonate the deepest with you.

The closest parallel I can offer to explain what I've experienced is found in the work of author Joseph Campbell. Campbell calls it the hero's journey, a sacred call to action for your soul to pursue what makes it happy, or your bliss. If you follow your bliss, doors will open where they were closed before, and you will be met with synchronicities, signs, mentors, and muses to guide you along your path.

Unfortunately, we often refuse the call or, perhaps more accurately, we don't hear the call at all because of the noise in our day-to-day lives. For those who listen and are bold enough to embark on the journey, it will be fraught with challenges. When faced with the challenge, some people will turn back. But for those with the courage and perseverance to face their adversity, they will step forth into an awakened new life. They will emerge from the darkness and into the light, transforming their ordinary existence into an extraordinary one. Their old ways of living will no longer serve them, and they will be empowered to use their true gifts to better the world by reaching out in true connection to others. This is where Ricochet helped to lead me.

When tragedy strikes, most of us are understandably too enveloped in our feelings of grief, depression, and anger to see the opportunity. That was the case for me when I closed myself off after suffering so much loss. Yet when life seems the most challenging, we can tap a power within ourselves greater than we ever imagined. For some, grief can consume; for others, it can catalyze. Consider Ian's aunt Melissa. When her best friend and sister died tragically, she answered a higher calling to take care of her niece and nephews as her own. While her heart will always ache for her sister, she has brought joy to her own life and enriched the lives of Ian, Lauren, and Luke.

None of us are immune to suffering, and unfortunately, some of us must endure more than others. But for the most resilient, many times the bad things in life are like stepping-stones upon which each of us, on our individual journeys, must walk. Each difficult event helps us to gain more strength, more wisdom, and perhaps most of all, more compassion and understanding, so that we might be better able to empathize with others' pain and, in turn, assist them in times of need.

As a child, I wanted to help people. Even then my soul was on its journey. Yet as I grew, I was trapped by overwhelming fears, negative thinking, and locks to keep the world out. I now understand that the most trying times in our lives can lead us to our purpose.

I have no doubt that all of us, both humans and animals, have a purpose in this world that is uniquely our own. Some may be like Ricochet, here to teach life lessons to a worldwide classroom. And others may be like Rina, on this planet to help just one human. But they are both equally sacred.

We all have our distinct brilliance and part to play, like a kaleidoscope of colors that meld and change with each additional color. Being different is what makes us special. We should take our passion and run with it like Ricochet does when she chases birds. In fact, even though Ricochet is laser-focused when she surfs, there are many times when she's surfed into shore and then jumped off the board and run down the beach after a bird. Nobody cares. In fact, we celebrate and embrace her one-of-a-kind spirit.

Embracing our true spirit is essential because fulfilling our purpose depends on our willingness to stay true to ourselves and to act from the heart, free of agendas. And while it sounds like a simple formula, it eludes many of us. Many people go through life without really living it. They are in turmoil or pain, and succumb to depression, drug abuse, or even suicidal thoughts. They are more negative than positive. I was one of those people. I could've remained stuck. I could've numbed my fears with alcohol or drugs like my father had before me, blaming nature or nurture for my lot in life. But, fortunately, I was nurtured by nature when I met Rina and Ricochet. They opened my eyes and heart to the infinite power of acceptance without expectations.

Many of us struggle to be something we are not in an effort to fulfill the expectations of others. We all have aspirations for ourselves and our loved ones. Goals. Should be's. Could be's. But conforming to someone else's ideas at the expense of our own will usually lead us off course. No one else can tell us what we're here to do.

As Campbell explains, if we go into the forest on a trail that's already been cleared, it's the one true sign we're not on our own path. If you follow someone else's entry, you're on someone else's path. To discover who we really are, we need to find our own path. When we do what we love and what comes naturally, we are usually more aligned with our true purpose.

After accepting Ricochet for who she was, I was gifted with the most magnificent outcome. I learned that letting go of control frees your spirit and opens a new pathway to living. Ricochet helped me understand just how powerful the splendor of surrender is.

I realized that even though I always tried to control my life, in reality, control is just an illusion. We really have absolutely no control. It seemed like such a simple concept, yet it was a foreign proposition to me. Letting go of control meant I had to face my fears and flow with the tide, not against it—going beyond the limits of my comfort zone.

Surrendering is not being complacent or lazy; it's about being at peace with wherever life leads. When our notion of control is shattered, when things don't go the way we planned, the typical reaction is to get upset or feel frustrated. For example, suppose you are sailing along on a carefully charted route and then the wind picks up and knocks you off course. You can either get upset, flailing your arms and fighting the current, or you can realize that you are exactly where you are meant to be in the moment. Sometimes the current of life carries us forward in strange and mysterious ways. Surrendering means letting the current take you and realizing that the winds of change may actually lead you somewhere better.

I now remind myself that if something doesn't work out a certain way, then it wasn't meant to be. The most wonderful paradox has been that by giving up control, my life has become much more fulfilling.

Despite the pain and losses in my life—or perhaps because of them— I finally understand why I had to lose so many of the people I loved and had to endure the many hardships I did. Even though I would've chosen something different, like having the children I always wanted, I wouldn't have been able to assist Ricochet in the way that she needs to fulfill her unique destiny. In Melissa's words, my life wouldn't be "available" to the extent it is now. I believe I've found my bliss. I've discovered my purpose, and I am content with my life and how I got here, because I know I am exactly where I'm supposed to be.

All I had to do was put all my trust in a higher power, and once I did that, everything became more peaceful. My heart, which had been closed for so many years, became open. Once I stopped trying to make something happen and allowed life to just present opportunities to me, things began to occur in serendipitous and synchronistic ways—from Ricochet being born with a patch of white fur on her chest, to Patrick and Ian, who came into our lives as surfers, to Rina and I moving from Chicago to San Diego where surfing is a lifestyle, to the angels that saved both my and Ricochet's life, to the name "Rina" being a synchronistic guidepost in our lives.

It was Rina who awakened my passion for service-dog training, and I don't think it was a coincidence that the first apartment I rented when I moved to California to study service-dog training was owned by a woman named Rina. Years later, Ricochet was asked to be part of a short film written by a fifteen-year-old girl who lost her battle with mitochondrial disease. Her last wish to her mother before she died was to make sure her film was made. The girl's name? Rina! The film was called *Rina's Magic Bracelet*, and my Rina was a constant source of comfort to Rina's parents on set, offering a physical sense of their Rina, who I believe was with us spiritually the whole time. So many serendipitous events like this in my life have confirmed my belief that our lives are predestined, part of a divine plan, with people—and animals—coming into it for specific reasons.

Ricochet came into my life because we needed each other. Neither one of us could've traveled this journey without the other one. And, equally, nothing could've occurred if it hadn't arisen from a place of trust.

The crack of a bat roused me from my thoughts. I looked out at the field to see several players in blue uniforms tearing around the bases. Just then, a startling "boom" of the cannon signaled a Padres' home run.

Ricochet's eyes darted around frantically, and she began to shake, her fear trembling up to my hands as I patted her. I was concerned that Randy might also react to the noise, with the loud *bangs* an all-too-vivid reminder of Iraq. And yet it was Randy who surprised me: he extended his hand for Ricochet's leash.

"Here, Judy, I'll take care of her," he offered.

I turned to him and let go of the leash.

"Hey, girl, it's okay," he said softly, stroking her fur.

As I watched Ricochet fix her eyes on Randy instead of searching for the cause of the frightening noise, I realized that I was witnessing something momentous in one seemingly small gesture—by reaching out to take care of Ricochet, their roles had been reversed. Ricochet always had Randy's back, but tonight he had hers. I smiled as I watched him hand her a piece of his bratwurst, which she happily gobbled. His concern for her was overshadowing his own anxieties. It was another step toward healing.

Once more I saw the interconnectedness of life: how love and kindness can cross species, and how humanity can assert itself outward from one soul to another, from person to person to pet and back again . . . all these people who were here tonight, at different ages and at different stages of their own individual journeys, were also inextricably bound to mine and Ricochet's.

Even though I wasn't meant to have the family I'd always envisioned, I realized that I did have a family—a really large and loving one. The life I have surrounds me with people who share their benevolence and compassion when they come out to help us. The people like Dave, and all of the other volunteers who help

Ricochet in the ocean, are connected through the heart. These are the real unsung heroes, for without them, Ricochet couldn't do her work. It's amazing to me that they take time out of their weekends and holidays to surf with a dog. They could be out with their families or friends, but instead they are out in the waves, filled with love and kindness, exchanging high-fives and making the kids feel so special.

When I stand among the volunteers, I feel the passion they have for the ocean and for helping others. I feel their selflessness and willingness—a universal love of what they are doing. But it's so much more than that: it's stepping outside of selfish boundaries and reaching out to others in need. Out there in the water, it seems like creating happiness is the only thing that matters. We all bask in the pure joy that fills our souls. When individuals come together for a common selfless intention—without agendas—they achieve a greater good, often without being conscious of their far-reaching effects. Pure joy of this magnitude isn't possible unless your intentions come from a place of authenticity.

People credit me with being the driving force behind Ricochet's work, but it's not me. Ricochet has the power. I made one good decision: letting Ricochet be herself. When I allowed her to be who she truly was, she showed me she was here to be of service through her own unique talents. That was the door that began opening all the others.

Ricochet sees the world through the eyes of unconditional love, innocence, purity, and acceptance. And because she operates from a place of purity, untainted by the woes of the world or the fears and negativity that humans can hold on to, she has the transformational power to help heal others simply through her presence and creative expression.

She continues to teach me profound lessons, not just from our spiritual kinship, but from the people I continue to meet because of her. I'm often asked, "What are you going to do next?" But by living this lifestyle based on surrendering control, I don't have a long-term plan. I wait for whatever is meant to be to manifest. Messages come to me in different forms. Often it will happen by an email coming across my desk or a post on Ricochet's Facebook page. Sometimes it's directed by random thoughts or gut feelings, and often it's just paying attention to Ricochet's intuitive-based behavior. These seemingly random connections often turn into the next steps on our journey, and everything falls into place.

Ricochet has taught me to believe, with unflinching certainty, that although the world can be a dangerous place, it's also full of goodness, and good things will always happen; it's not a matter of *if* but *when*.

While I never expected to be where I am today, I am grateful that I was chosen to be Ricochet's guardian so that she can touch the many people who need her help. She's taught me that even if the horizon isn't crystal clear, you should still step forth into the mystery and vastness of life. Before where I may have seen fog or haze, I now see infinite possibilities.

Still reflecting on how far I'd come since my Chicago days, I felt someone tap me as the baseball game came to a close. It was Dave, who once again spoke his quiet, understated wisdom.

"Wow, Judy," he said, surveying the crowd around us. "I never knew we helped this many people."

I didn't answer him right away because a lump was wedged in my throat. I looked around at the faces of the former strangers who had become my family.

"I guess we *have* made a difference," I replied.

And just like Clarence, the guardian angel in the movie *It's a Wonderful Life*, Dave was showing me how many lives we had touched. I knew then that we had been a force for good.

I looked over at Ricochet, who was now sitting calmly on Randy's lap, and I smiled at my dog—the "square peg in a round hole."

The dog who defied labeling.

The dog who took me outside of my box and transformed lives while staying true to herself.

Yes, it *had* been a wonderful life. I didn't know where our journey was headed, but I did know that Ricochet would tell me, and I had promised to get her there.

Just as the moon's pull creates the tides that make the waves, Ricochet's messages remain, and her spirit will always live on, not only in the waves, but in the hearts and souls of the people she touches.

# Chapter 17

# The Perfect Wave

*"You can't control the waves but you can learn to surf."*

JON KABAT-ZINN

As we were throwing out the first pitch at the Padres game, 2,500 miles away, in Apopka, Florida, the Acosta family was sitting down to dinner. While joining hands to bless the food, Clinton Acosta said the prayer: "Our Father in Heaven, thank you for this food we are about to eat; may it bless our bodies, and especially continue to help Caleb in his healing. In Jesus's name we pray, Amen." He looked across the table at his oldest son, who was just about to begin a six-week course of chemotherapy. He would give anything to trade places with him. When the treatments were over and his son had beaten the odds, his family would celebrate and put these trying months behind them.

The last few weeks had been a blur—the worst kind of blur—beginning just after Caleb blew out fifteen candles in June. When the school year ended, he was beyond excited for summer to begin and spent it like most teens: playing Wii and Xbox with his two younger brothers, working as a counselor at his church's day camp, and riding his motorcycle. When he mentioned to his mom, Cathy, that he was having headaches, she didn't think much of it. After all, migraines ran in her family, and her son was not immune.

Yet one Saturday in church, Caleb was overcome by a throbbing headache and overwhelming nausea—so much so that he had to lie down on the couch in the lobby. After church, when his family was enjoying their Sabbath meal at their grandma and grandpa's house, Caleb slept the entire afternoon, which was not like him at all. Nothing kept him away from his grandma's cooking. Cathy recalled another recent incident when Caleb had become violently ill with a headache—the day he was supposed to start summer camp in Puerto Rico. And now, here he was again. Something was not right with her son. She not only saw it as a physician, she felt it as a mother. Worried, she scheduled an appointment with Caleb's pediatrician who ordered an immediate CT scan. Cathy hoped with all her heart that the test wouldn't reveal anything significant.

While she waited nervously for the results, Caleb's dad took his sons to a nearby amusement park so that the boys could let off some steam. Daniel and Jacob posed for a picture as they stood in line for the Manta roller-coaster. There's always a sense of apprehension, mixed with anticipation, as you slowly wind your way to the front of the line, listening to the screams of the people on the ride as they twist and dive toward the ground. Clinton felt that, exponentially, as they waited for the test results. But a roller-coaster is safe; you're never really in danger. What they were potentially facing might be unfathomable. But he put on a brave face and prayed for the best. As they took a turn, climbing the walkway to the head of the line, Clinton got a call on his cell. It was the call that no parent wants to receive.

Straining to hear against the rumbling of the ride and the shrieks of terror, he was not prepared for what his wife would tell him about their son, who stood smiling an arm's length away.

"They saw something on the scan," Cathy said. "It's either a tumor or an aneurism." Neither one was what he expected or wanted to comprehend.

He swallowed hard, pausing to find the words to tell his son the unspeakable. But since they had always been open, he told him straight out. Caleb's only reply was: "You mean I can't go on Manta? But we waited for thirty minutes!"

Manta would have to wait.

Caleb and his family went to a nearby imaging center for an MRI. Upon seeing the results, the neurosurgeon recommended that Caleb be admitted to the hospital right away. Walking into the lobby, Caleb said that the situation seemed surreal. Despite a few headaches—although excruciating—he didn't feel that bad. What's more, he was the one carrying all of his mom's bags; if he was really sick, shouldn't he be in bed? While his mom couldn't argue with his reasoning, the pediatrician in her knew the possibilities. And, unfortunately, the MRI confirmed the worst: a tumor. Even so, they were hopeful. Medicine and the Almighty were a powerful combination. Given Caleb's age and his overall health, this was something they could conquer. And while any surgery poses risks, they were optimistic that Caleb would be fine.

On Monday, July 29, they wheeled him in for surgery. Since he had never been in a hospital before, the reality became too much, and Caleb started to cry. To calm his nerves, the doctor administered the anesthesia straightaway.

"We're going to ask you to count to ten for us, okay?" the anesthesiologist asked.

"One, two," Caleb began, "three ..." He never made it to "ten." Yet when he opened his eyes, he was in a different room. He had been out for more than eight hours, but to Caleb it seemed like the blink of an eye.

As he emerged from the grogginess, his parents told him the doctors were unable to perform the surgery because of a last-minute discussion about the scans. Concerned that it wasn't safe to do the surgery that day, the doctors opted for further testing instead.

Still shocked at how time had flown by, Caleb listened to his mother's explanation. "That's how it will be when we all go to heaven," she said. "We're going to close our eyes, and the next thing we see will be Jesus's face. We won't know if it's one year or a hundred years that our eyes are closed. But it will only feel like a blink of an eye and the next thing we will see is Jesus's face."

Less than twenty-four hours later Caleb was wheeled into surgery again—this time for real.

As the gurney was rolled away, he held out his hand. "Mami, *te amo* [I love you]," "Papi, *te amo*. Tell Grandma *te amo*; tell Daniel and Jacob I love them."

His mother's heart sank, terrified he was saying his final good-byes. But she dismissed the thought and found comfort in knowing that Caleb was being rolled away with love in his heart.

This time in the operating room, Caleb wasn't as scared because he'd been to pre-op the day before. But as he looked around the sterile room—at the beeping equipment and the doctors in their scrubs—the reality became too much and the tears began to flow. He shut his eyes and began to pray.

But he didn't have to pray alone. Seeing his fear, the three nurses and the anesthesiologist asked if they could pray, too. For just a minute, the machines and the medical degrees didn't matter as they bowed their heads to the Great Physician and asked him for help. Caleb began saying his favorite hymn to himself, *Dios Está Aquí* (God Is Here).

*"Es tan cierto como el aire que respiro . . ."*

"As certain as the air I breathe surrounds me . . ."

*"Es tan cierto como en la mañana se levanta . . ."*

"As certain as I know the morning will come . . ."

*"Es tan cierto como que le canto y El me puede oír . . ."*

"As certain that when I sing to him, he can hear me . . ."

Again the anesthesiologist instructed Caleb to count to ten.

"One . . . two . . . three," Caleb said. When he got to "four," he felt himself leaving his body. He was floating upward.

When he looked down at the operating table, he saw himself lying there and he watched the nurse shaving his head more closely. The doctor in the blue scrubs was ready to make his first incision. Caleb continued floating upward. Suddenly, all he saw was white.

Caleb was now upright, standing next to a tall man.

"Who are you?" he asked. The man answered that he was Jesus, but Caleb knew this anyway, because the man was radiant and pure.

"Am I dead?" Caleb wondered aloud.

"No," the man said. "This is just a vision."

Whether it was a vision or a dream, Caleb began confessing his sins.

"Your sins are forgiven," Jesus said.

Suddenly Caleb felt lighter. The man told Caleb to walk with him. Caleb was now standing before God, Jesus, and the Holy Spirit, which appeared before him as a large white dove. Caleb was enveloped by a feeling of peace.

He knelt and asked God to forgive his sins. Once again, he was told that his sins were forgiven, the omniscient Voice surrounding him with a feeling of safety and warmth. Caleb felt lighter still.

"You are going to wake up now, but just remember, Caleb," the Voice said, "everything is going to be all right. Everything is going to be all right."

For eight long, heartrending hours, the Acostas sat vigil for Caleb, with friends and family gathered in the waiting room and in the nearby chapel. As they waited, they remembered the words of the attending doctor who had advised them to be prepared. "Caleb's memory might be affected, as well as his speech, so don't be alarmed if he doesn't remember you when he wakes or if he isn't able to speak. It's a common side effect from the surgery itself."

Then, as the day stretched into night, casting shadows on the walls of the recovery room, Clinton and Cathy saw their son rouse from his sleep. He opened his eyes. "Mami, *te amo*," "Papi, *te amo*." *He knew them! He could speak!* They hugged their son. To Cathy, he was the most gorgeous she had ever seen him. Possibly not since the day he was born did he seem so perfect to her. She leaned in to touch him, to smell him, to feel his presence even closer.

"Mami, Mami," he said, still groggy but excited. "I had a dream. I want to tell you my dream." Clinton and Cathy listened to their son recall his dream in awe and with gratitude that he was okay—that he recognized them and that he was speaking, and quite articulately. They thanked the surgeons and the Supreme One who had helped him through the difficult surgery to remove the tumor.

But despite the jubilation, the surgery revealed grave news. The tumor was a glioblastoma, an aggressive stage-IV cancer. The surgeon had successfully removed all of it, but Caleb would need six weeks of chemotherapy and radiation. Yet even with the news, Caleb was confident and strong. *Because everything would be all right.* Where his prior day under sedation had been a blur, on this day Caleb experienced a life-affirming vision—a vision that transformed him outwardly and inwardly.

In the following weeks, as he braved his recovery and his treatments, his parents noticed an aura about him. But Cathy said it first: "Clinton, he's different . . . he has a glow about him. You can see it in his face. He's *just different*." And he was.

He exuded an inner confidence and wore a constant smile. He had a different way of being when he interacted with his brothers. Everyone saw a light in him; a spark from within. And while he had always prayed, now he was having direct conversations with God.

Caleb soldiered through six weeks of chemo and radiation, during which time the smile never left his face. And thankfully, after six weeks of treatment, Caleb was full of energy, had regained his appetite, and looked healthy and vital. The family said good-bye to the oncologist and left for Disney World, eager to celebrate.

The Acostas braved the Mount Everest ride, and Caleb laughed hysterically as a human *Toy Story* soldier made his mother do jumping jacks and told his brother to drop and give him ten push-ups. But it was when they were running through Hollywood Studios that Caleb said, "Mom, I can't feel my butt."

Cathy assumed he was just being goofy or acting like a typical teenager. After all, he and his brothers were racing through the park with energy she only wished she had. But the next day Caleb said his legs felt like they were falling asleep. Something was very wrong. The Acostas watched helplessly, and in a matter of three days, their son lost the ability to move the lower part of his body.

An MRI confirmed their fears: The brain tumor was back and there was a new tumor in Caleb's spine. When his mother told him the news, he shrugged his shoulders. "Everything's going to be all right," he assured her. "You know, Mom," he said with a quiet smile, "I'm going to heaven. . . . We all are someday."

His faith astounded her. She asked herself how her fifteen-year-old child could possess more strength than she did.

Caleb faced another emergency surgery to decompress his spinal cord and joked about his "new wheels"—the wheelchair he now needed for mobility. While many people would get angry or lose hope that it appeared they were getting worse, Caleb did not. Regardless of the medical treatment plan, Caleb was trusting in God's plan.

During this setback, the Make-A-Wish Foundation contacted Caleb's mother about fulfilling a wish for him, and with heavy hearts, the doctors advised that she make it happen as soon as possible. With its wide-reaching benevolence, the foundation helps make dreams come true for children with life-threatening medical conditions, and the wish-granter was eager to accommodate Caleb.

"Do you want to meet a sports star?" she offered, aware that Caleb was an athlete. "How about a trip to a really cool place or a shopping spree?"

But it was Caleb's aunt Cynthia who thought of something else entirely. She recalled seeing a video of a surfing dog named Ricochet who helped kids with disabilities. Intrigued, Caleb looked up the footage on the Internet and watched in awe as this cute little golden retriever surfed with a boy named Ian who had suffered a brain injury during a car accident in which his parents had died.

*How cool would it be to surf with that dog?*, Caleb thought. *Very cool.* Because Caleb couldn't walk and had lost a lot of mobility, he knew that Ricochet would be able to help him. His aunt agreed. She pointed out that surfing with Ricochet would be even more special because it was something Caleb could do that most other people could not. It was settled: Lebron or Kobe? A race car driver? Caleb chose Ricochet. Cynthia made two phone calls—the first to the Make-A-Wish Foundation to ask them if they could make this happen and the second to me to see if Ricochet and I were available. Of course, we both said "Yes."

The night before the surf, Caleb's mom tossed and turned in their California hotel. *What if Caleb falls off the surfboard? What if he can't right himself?* She knew it was silly, but her instinct as a mom was to keep her kids safe from real or imagined dangers, from monsters under the bed, to bullies, to unthinkable diseases with complicated names. And yet there are some things beyond our control. Even though Cathy trusted our surf day would be okay, she still wore her bathing suit under her clothes the next day, just in case.

That morning, our volunteers began arriving, eager to help make Caleb's dream a reality. It was a picture-perfect day—a bright blue sky with scant, puffy white clouds, as if the beach were a divine canvas with colors carefully chosen and placed from a palette just for Caleb.

When I sent out an email asking for helpers, I wasn't sure we could find enough people since the outing would take place during the week, but the response was overwhelming. Our volunteers came out even more enthusiastic than usual, all wanting to be a part of this special day. Dave came, along with a diverse crew of veteran water helpers: Max, Prue, John, Patti, Josh, Larry, Devyn, and Ryan, who got special permission to skip high school to come help. Most of them had been involved in adaptive surfing for a long time and knew that it was all about going beyond labels, defying odds, and breaking barriers of what people thought was possible, which was exactly what Caleb's journey was about. Many of them had children of their own—and they hugged them a little tighter when they left that morning—and a few were teenagers themselves, so they felt compelled to make this a memorable experience for Caleb and his family.

As we were assembling our gear, the Acosta's SUV pulled up. Caleb's parents climbed out of the vehicle and two dark-haired boys, Jacob and Daniel, spilled out with shy grins. Amid a flurry of news reporters, Caleb's dad wheeled him over the sand and he greeted us with a smile that was even more radiant in person than it was on his Facebook page, with his deep brown eyes reflecting an unexplainable glint.

"Hi, Caleb, it's nice to meet you," I said. Ricochet didn't miss a beat even with the commotion. She walked right over to Caleb and sat dutifully beside him. As he patted her head with a very gentle touch, she accepted his kindness as an invitation, nuzzling into his hands.

"Hey, Ricochet," Caleb said. The two sets of brown eyes met for a second of knowing—a pause in time that was 2,500 miles in the making. Sometimes you don't need to scream to be heard, and the two connected quietly in the sand as the cameras clicked away. Caleb was quickly getting to know Ricochet on a heart-to-heart level and their bond was instant. As Caleb petted Ricochet's head, he could feel immediately that she was a good dog and that he could trust her. He said she reminded him of his family's dog, Sunny, a golden retriever that they had when he was younger.

Devyn and Ryan introduced themselves, and I smiled as the trio talked and laughed with ease, like three water-loving spirits who had known one another forever.

"You caught a fish at the pier?" Devyn asked Caleb. "That's so rad. That's my hometown, and I've never caught a fish."

She and Ryan gave Caleb the rundown for the day, which was to make this experience whatever he wanted it to be. They would surf as much or as little as he wanted.

"Okay, who's ready to surf?" Dave asked.

With that, Caleb's mom leaned down and gave her firstborn a touching send-off: "I love you and I'm proud of you. Have fun, my love." Then she kissed him on his head. It was heartwarming to see the care that Ryan demonstrated in wheeling Caleb down to the water, two boys just two years apart in age, brought together by Ricochet. Ryan and Devyn told me they felt extremely honored that they would be assisting Caleb for his inaugural surf, and from their gentle ways, I knew he couldn't be in better hands. As they slowly helped Caleb out of his wheelchair, he turned his head and blew a kiss to his mother, who waved back, her eyes crinkling with love. The water was cold by any standards—about 60 degrees—and even though Caleb was wearing a wetsuit and booties, as the volunteers gently helped him into the water, it was a chilly wake-up call for the uninitiated, especially a Floridian.

"Think 'warm,' Caleb, think 'warm,'" Ryan said as they stepped out. "Pretend you're in Florida, or better yet, think 'Costa Rica' where it's super-warm." They all laughed.

"No, this is great!" Caleb said. "It's perfect."

As they adjusted Caleb on the board, I sensed that he was feeling some pain. Add to that a dog, an uncomfortable wetsuit, helpers, and cold water. And yet he didn't utter one word of complaint or hesitation. He let them manipulate him on the board and then position Ricochet on the back.

"All right, Caleb," Devyn explained. "You're going to be cold, you're going to get saltwater in your face, and it will be uncomfortable for a few seconds, but once we turn you around and push you into the wave, we're going to give you the ride of your life." Surfers, I'm told, approach every wave as the ride of their lives. Each time they're out there, scanning the horizon, they're looking for what could be the ride of their lives. This was the magic we hoped would happen for Caleb.

"Game on! I trust you guys 100 percent," Caleb said as they led him out into the deeper water. Once he and Ricochet were situated, the three helpers turned their heads to the horizon to pick the best wave, while the other helpers positioned themselves in the shallower water, much like the line of a fire brigade, to catch Caleb if he fell off. When Dave leaned in to whisper something in Ricochet's ear, I knew they were ready to launch the board.

"Okay, Caleb," Ryan instructed, "we'll send you on this one, all right?"

"Let's do it!" Caleb chimed.

The volunteers had described to me the magic that happens on shore when they pitch the board. Even though they are standing behind the person and can't see his or her face, the reaction of the bystanders on shore mirrors the reaction of the surfer, much like a mirrored reflection on the water. It's nothing short of magical. At first, the parents and siblings stand watching nervously, arms crossed, sometimes shifting their weight back and forth as though they themselves are balancing on the board. Then, as the person they love sails into shore, and the waves break on the beach, their pensiveness changes and erupts into cheering and clapping, laughter and smiles.

And that's the way it was for Caleb as he coasted in with Ricochet, his arms strong and firm, and a smile plastered wide across his face for the entire ride as he zoomed past the breaking waves and past the volunteers, shooting into shore in a spray of white foam. I'd seen this look before. It's beyond just happiness—it's sheer joy. There's something about Ricochet, the water, and the wind on the waves that has a healing effect. But with Caleb I saw something extra. It was a purity, the kind of purity I've experienced with Ricochet. Gliding into shore, his expression was one of genuine knowing; he seemed to be communing with everything and everyone around him as he coasted in, taking in and feeling his surroundings with every pore of his being.

Caleb's mother and I stood in the soft sand, side by side, not talking but listening to the sound of the crashing waves mixed with laughter, watching her son having fun, just being a kid again. The wind whipped her hair around. She brushed a wayward strand away from her eyes as she wiped back tears. While I've had so much loss in my life, I couldn't possibly know what the last year had been like for her. Mothers want to protect their children from harm and pain, but sometimes something swift and strong, and completely unexpected, takes them from their arms, and sometimes the people we love are called back to the light before we are ready to let them go. I knew that all too well. When I was about Caleb's age, I was faced with trauma and grief, and I came to believe that the world was not safe or dependable. Realizing I had no control, I retreated into myself. Yet Caleb was doing the exact opposite, sharing and connecting with an open heart.

Caleb himself was light, and I admired his mother's strength while he continued his fight. I was honored that Ricochet could play even a small part in bringing joy to Caleb and his family. Perhaps for a brief moment in time, as he coasted in, his parents forgot about the tests and the treatments and just basked in the wonder of their son.

"Great job, Caleb!" his parents yelled to him, their smiles radiant.

"You did it, Caleb!" his brothers cheered, jumping up and down.

As the Acosta family celebrated with Caleb from the shoreline, I looked out at my extended family, the water handlers whose excitement and jubilation was just as celebratory, just as heartfelt. They were whistling and hollering; some were wiping their eyes, and it wasn't because of the salt spray. Later, Larry and John told me that, in decades of surfing, they had never seen or felt a moment so special. I know I hadn't.

"That was so amazing!" Caleb shouted. "Let's do it again, Ricochet!"

And she agreed by wagging her wet body back and forth before spinning around to head back out.

While Ricochet is always focused when she surfs, on this day she was doing more than focusing: she was nurturing, caretaking. At one point, she was trying to reposition herself as they got closer to shore, and she had to jump off, but since Caleb was still on the board, she ran back to him to make sure he was okay. At the end of another ride, she reached the shoreline where she would have normally jumped off, but she waited until the handlers had Caleb safely situated off the board.

I noticed something else, too. All of the water handlers know that Ricochet is very serious when she surfs, and we joke that almost every photo of her surfing shows that focused, determined expression. But as I watched Ricochet and Caleb floating on the board near the shallows, I had to do a double-take: not only was Caleb smiling. . . but *Ricochet was smiling, too!* An actual open grin that perfectly matched Caleb's expression. To me, it was obvious that she was mirroring him, and what she was reflecting back was pure joy and positive energy. Two kindred spirits—cosmic cousins—enjoying the ride, connecting in an organic, effortless way.

Caleb and Ricochet rode a few more waves, and on one of the very last waves, he wanted to try sitting up on his knees. They positioned Ricochet on the front of the board, and, using her back for support, Caleb found the strength and balance to lift himself to his knees. Cheers and whistles echoed in the water and across the beach as he rode halfway into shore before he wiped out. The volunteers whisked him up, high-fiving him and reminding him that wiping out is the sign of a true surfer.

After Caleb's wipeout and spending ample time in the ocean, they headed out of the water to warm up. Prue and Josh helped Caleb out of the water, his face beaming with pride and happiness.

On shore his exuberant family ran to meet him, enveloping him with hugs and showering him with kisses and kudos.

Upon Max's suggestion, we had brought jugs of warm water to pour down Caleb's wetsuit. Apparently the heat would stay in the suit, acting like a thermos for his entire body. Dave and Ryan pulled on the back of his wetsuit, and Max poured the warm water over Caleb's head. As the warmth cascaded down his body and Caleb's expression became one of complete satisfaction, the helpers' eyes came upon a stark reminder of something we had all but forgotten on this carefree day on the beach—a fresh scar that ran down the entire length of Caleb's back. It was a humbling reminder of his struggles—the day-to-day reality that had faded away in the water for this amazing boy who never complained—a boy who we now considered part of our extended family. I touched my hand to my chest, thinking of my scar that remained from open-heart surgery— and how all of us have scars, some visible and some not—but the way Caleb persevered in spite of the monumental challenges he had faced was truly remarkable. I thought back to my open-heart surgery and how scared I had been. *How was this young boy being so brave?*

Caleb continued warming up with his parents, so Patti made a sandcastle with his youngest brother, Jacob, while Ryan and Devyn took his other brother Daniel out surfing. Daniel showed he could hang ten with the big kids, standing up and wiping out multiple times, although he seemed to enjoy the dismounts on the wipeouts better than the actual surfing itself.

"That was awesome!" Daniel yelled. "It was the most fun thing I've ever done!"

As Caleb cheered his little brother on from the shore, I realized that now both brothers could share a surfing connection and both would claim bragging rights over who had the biggest wipeout in California.

Once Caleb was rejuvenated, he gave interviews with several news crews that had descended on the beach. Apparently a story about their old friend Ricochet and Caleb's fighting spirit had resonated with them. Caleb never had a bunch of microphones in front of his face before or people bandying personal questions at him. For a minute or two, he felt like a celebrity being swarmed by paparazzi. Yet Caleb answered the questions with an ease, grace, and sincerity that was a testament to his authenticity and his beautiful spirit.

"Today with Ricochet, I feel almost normal again," Caleb shared. "I feel free."

The onlookers were touched, and even some of the veteran reporters wiped tears from their eyes. "It was great to not have to worry about anything," he said.

As he spoke, Ricochet was by his side, ever vigilant and very still. His hand never left her fur as he stroked her head. At one point, she put her front paws up and over him, seemingly protecting him, comforting him like a blanket. Two pure souls, each with their own divinely inspired message to share with the world, both radiating love and light. To watch them interacting was living proof to me that there is something far more powerful at work in the universe than just ourselves. The press hung on Caleb's every word.

"I just want everyone to know, it doesn't matter if you have cancer, or major pain, or some other struggle. There is always hope," he said. "You just have to trust that everything is going to be all right. I believe I am going to beat my cancer and that God has a plan for me."

Caleb's hope was a brilliant light that mesmerized us all—the kind of light that shines so bright that when you shut your eyes you can still see it, a light that reaches into your soul in such a way that you're inspired to love more, do more, and try in absolute earnest to be the best version of yourself. He was such an inspiration—and he was only fifteen.

When most of the reporters had left to file their stories, I turned to see Cathy and Clinton sitting down near Ricochet. I was touched to see Cathy patting Ricochet because she told me she is not typically a dog person. She saw me stifling a laugh.

"I couldn't help but love her," she said. "She just leaned into me; she was very pet-table. As strange as it seems, I really felt like she was allowing me to show her my love and appreciation for this day she has given us."

I told her it didn't seem strange at all.

"You know, Judy," she said, "that smile you've seen today . . . it's always there. It's what keeps us lifted up. Our son is stronger than we are. When Caleb went into the water I got very emotional," she shared. "To see him on the surfboard full of so much joy, I was crying tears of joy. It was overwhelming."

She stood up and wrapped her arms around me, enveloping me in a hug. I felt her gratitude and joy in the embrace, and in meeting her eyes that were now welling with tears, I saw the same purity that I'd seen reflected back in her son's eyes. As parents, she and her husband had given Caleb the greatest gift—perhaps the only gift that any of us really need—a safe harbor from which to begin his passage through life, unconditional love, and a strong faith to buoy him through even the roughest currents.

"Judy," she said, "we will never forget this. Caleb said it was the ride of his life."

Now I had tears, too.

"Yes," Clinton added, "Caleb told me earlier that this was the best day of his life."

"Well," I sniffed, "the next time we do this, we will come to Florida and surf."

"It's a deal," Cathy laughed, and we both wiped our eyes. "You have given so much to us, but I hope that in some way you have received something as well. I hope that you and your team got to see Caleb's spirit."

And indeed we did. Everyone in attendance, from the water helpers and friends, to the photographer and videographer, was touched by Caleb. While most of them had surfed hundreds if not thousands of waves, these few with Caleb held a special poignancy. In fact, Devyn had mentioned to me that she'd recently filmed an elite surfer riding waves in one of Maui's biggest breaks and today she was surfing with someone she'd never met who'd never surfed before—a boy whose desire was to catch *one* wave. They were both equally important experiences to her—both equally special memories. Today, scores of diverse people from disparate paths united to help one person catch a few waves, but those few waves were incredibly impactful to us all, just like Ricochet's first surf with Patrick.

When Ricochet jumped from her board and onto Patrick's, demonstrating to me so clearly what her purpose was, she would, on that day, begin a tide of change from which I never looked back. All because she saw things differently. It was a deliberate move—but also a symbolic one—the start of a wave of love radiating out from one dog to a human, and then another, and another, until waves of love and purpose caused a ripple effect that traveled around the world in an amazing triumph of what was possible.

Ricochet and Patrick proved that with faith and determination, anything is possible. Ricochet's journey had started with Patrick, and today it had come full circle with Caleb.

Through Caleb's example, I felt as if I were watching a human representation of Ricochet—a young boy who embodied purity, trust, and unconditional love. And if our lives are a story that we tell through our daily endeavors, Caleb's ode was strength and peace. Just as adversity changes us, it can also reveal us. What Caleb revealed to me was a hero's heart. He had what most people wait their whole lives to get, and what some will never grasp: He had found serenity—the quiet courage to trust in something larger than himself and in the knowledge that everything would be all right. It's what Ricochet had taught me on this journey. It's what surfers know when they go to catch a wave: that they need to trust—to give up control to find their bliss. I knew this, and I had for some time, but to see and feel Caleb's energy, as a living, loving human equivalent of Ricochet, crystallized it.

None of us know how long we have on this earth, whether it's the dawn or the sunset of our lives; our time is finite, and all of our journeys are but a blip in the grand scheme of the universe. But this incredible boy with unwavering faith showed us all how to *be*—just like Ricochet taught me how to *be*—and how to reach out in love to live our true purpose. Today was a celebration of having faith and fortitude and believing in infinite possibilities.

"Ready for another wave, Caleb?" Dave asked.

Of course we knew the answer would be an enthusiastic yes, so Larry retreated to his car to find a pair of gloves so Caleb could surf without his hands getting too cold.

And so Caleb geared up for what would be his last wave of the day.

I watched with gratitude and clarity as two pure souls were led out into the ocean, the sun flickering and dancing off the waves, a lone white bird sailing overhead.

I focused my sight to see Caleb smile . . . and Ricochet was smiling, too. A snapshot of joy and goodness.

And then they were launched, a boy and a dog, riding one wave together, lost in a moment in time, surrounded by love. Love flows through everything, but sometimes it needs a messenger to deliver it or awaken it from sleep. And in the coming days and weeks, Caleb, the boy who was loved very deeply by a circle of people would see the circumference widen exponentially. The story of Ricochet and Caleb would ripple outward, from one person to another, just like Patrick and Ricochet's story had, touching hearts far and wide. It would cross oceans to distant shores with a message of hope that would flow beyond time, beyond religions, race, or language. Within days, thousands of people from around the globe would send love, prayers, and words of encouragement. No matter their language or dialect, their sentiments were the same: "We love you, Ricochet," "We love you, Caleb," "Keep the faith," "Anything is possible," "Miracles happen," "Let go and let God." And just like Ricochet's first surf with Patrick, the ripples of love born that day would be forever flowing—a lasting legacy of inspiration.

We're all riding the waves of life. And as we navigate through our journeys, we often find ourselves scanning the horizon for the "perfect" wave. But perhaps it's less about venturing out very far to find it; perhaps we need to venture within to discover which wave brings us the most joy, because it's from there that we will find our true purpose. Because the perfect wave is different for everyone; to one person, it might be an exhilarating twenty-foot wave, while to another it's a gentle two-footer. But even though the wave is different, the secret to riding it, at the very essence, is about letting go and trusting; it's about having patience and surrendering to the momentum of the wave instead of trying to control it or predict where it will wash into shore. When you learn to embrace the wave, your fears will be overpowered by joy and contentment, and it will feel effortless. You won't think about the future and you won't look back. You truly will be living in the moment, moving forward and trusting that everything is going to be all right. This was the way that Ricochet taught me to live, and the way that Caleb was living as well.

Just as there is an ebb and flow to the ocean, there is an ebb and flow to our lives. Sometimes we will coast with a gentle wind, sometimes we get stuck in a rip current, and other times a sudden squall may rage like a tempest. None of us knows what will greet us on the horizon, but we must paddle out anyway, trusting that wherever the wave brings us, everything will be all right. But what Ricochet has taught me is that we need to ride the wave for all we can, even if the ocean is tumultuous or the salt stings our eyes. Some of us may stand tall on the board, while others may need to lie down or kneel—and sometimes we may even wipe out—but the trick is to ride it as if it's the wave of our lives. Because it just might be. And maybe, just maybe, the "perfect" wave is the one we're riding right now. We just need to embrace it and trust that wherever it takes us is exactly where we are meant to be. How do I know for certain? Because Ricochet told me so. And I listened.

And the wave rolls on. . . .

Both Caleb and Ricochet smiling.

©KillerImage.com

The amazing water helpers.

©KillerImage.com

Ricochet, 100 percent focused even with birds nearby.

©KillerImage.com

©KillerImage.com

Ready to surf.

Max giving Caleb the great warm-up.

©KillerImage.com

Caleb and Ricochet surf successfully to shore.

©KillerImage.com

©KillerImage.com

Ricochet with
the Acostas.

©KillerImage.com

Caleb and
Ricochet.

# To Surf with Love . . .

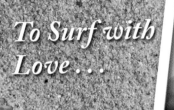

©Robert Ochoa (Pawmazing)

©Heather M. Moana

PAY TO THE ORDER OF Ian McFarland          $7500.00
DATE 6/20/10                                10735
Seventy five hundred and 00/100          DOLLARS
MEMO                          SURFice dog Ricochet

©Robert Ochoa (Pawmazing)

©Barbara McKown

©Larry Brambles

*I have loved every minute* of working and surfing with Ricochet. It's an interesting experience to be able to help people by doing something you love. In our case it's surfing. There is no doubt that we share a mutual trust of each other and passion for the ocean. The idea of continuing to inspire people through our surfing is very exciting.

—Patrick Ivison

*Never in a million years* did I know how drastically meeting Judy and Ricochet would change our lives.

—Jennifer Kayler

*Ricki has touched so many people's lives*, either through making it possible for a little boy to surf, or raising money so a teenager could go to therapy so he could walk at his graduation. I feel so blessed to have been a part of this amazing journey.

—Samantha Ivison

*From the moment* that I set eyes on her it was clear that Ricochet was not an ordinary dog but an extraordinary dog. The service she provides to all, in the water or on land, has opened up a new world for a lot of people who may not have otherwise had the same opportunity. I am happy to have been a part of such moments and proud to call her my friend. She's awesome!

—Zac Burns

*I love you, Ricochet!* Thank you for being my friend. I love surfing with you!! You will always be my best friend.

—Ian McFarland

*Ricochet and Judy* have forever changed our lives! I am overwhelmed with the gratitude in my heart.

—Melissa Coleman, Ian's aunt

*I love Ricochet* because she is the best dog I have ever seen or heard of. When I got to surf with Ricochet, I felt so happy! I had wanted to for so long watching Ian. And Judy is my BFF!!! She is so nice and caring to all of us.

—Lauren McFarland, age 8

*Ian is really lucky* to surf with Ricochet because Ricochet is such a good dog. I like to play with Ricochet. Ricochet makes me feel happy.

—Luke McFarland, age 7

*When we try to inspire* others it seems that all too often the human language is our greatest limitation. For reasons I don't claim to understand there are times when Ricochet transcends this limitation and inspires others to push themselves a little further. To be quite honest, it's something I needed to witness firsthand to believe.

—Max Moore

*Ricochet is an inspiration;* she generates an excitement in the water that nothing in this world can replicate. I can remember Ian McFarland wouldn't even get into the water without Ricochet, and now he loves the water. There are countless other people that Ricochet has inspired.

—Kate Moore, age 12

*Ricochet came into Ian's life* at the perfect time. I had felt one of the most important healing stages for Ian would be on the emotional and social level. The trauma that Ian went through creates a form of inner retraction—emotionally, energetically, and so much more. It was lovely seeing Ricochet help draw Ian out further so he could engage, connect, and trust in a deeper way. Something so simple as a doggie lick and riding waves created a special bond for the two of them.

—Prue Jeffries, healing practitioner and ex-professional surfer

©KillerImage.com

©Robert Ochoa (Pawmazing)

©DL Photos

©Kristianne Koch Riddle

©Jefferson

©KillerImage.com

*Ricochet is my best friend* and she makes me feel calm. I want Ricki and Rini (that's what I call her) at our house for Christmas so they can watch me open presents. I also like to help Randy and Dave because I just want to be a helper.

—West

*Meeting Ricochet* set off a chain reaction in West's life. He looks at life differently; he treats animals differently. To West, Ricochet is his, and I believe when they are in the water he is hers.

—Lauren Chavez, West's mom

*When I surfed with Ricochet,* I felt like I was standing on a cloud. It was just me, Ricki, and the water. All my stress and worries vanished. It had to be one of the best experiences of my life. Ricochet inspired me to try new things and to have no fear.

—Reese, West's sister

*Fun, smiles,* getting everyone together for a surf reunion, families, love.

—Jake Benarth

*I will never forget* when Jake met Ricochet. Ricochet came up to Jake and put her head in his lap and looked up at him. Jake had the biggest grin and he felt a real bond with her. Surfing with Ricochet is one of the happiest memories for Jake. He surfed all the way into shore and had the time of his life. He considers Ricochet a very good friend.

—Mary Benarth, Jake's mom

*When I think of surfing* with Ricochet, it's a warming thought that means getting our family together to bring out smiles for all involved. It brings out the very best in everyone, and is a special time for all.

—Larry Benarth, water helper

*I'm a strong believer* in the ocean's power to heal. It's why I got involved with helping those with disabilities into the water. Each time I'd jump in the water to aid a new friend in catching some waves, it'd be a transforming experience for all. When Ricochet got thrown into the mix it was nothing but an expansion of this fact. I'll still never forget the first wave we got with Ric and how originally skeptical I was about having a dog on the surfboard. But with one puff of Cheez Whiz for Ric, a push into the wave for Patrick, they were gone. The rest is history. Surfing is healing. Dogs are healing. It's actually quite meant to be.

—Devyn Bisson, water helper

*The ocean is* to West as Professor Hinkle's magic hat was to Frosty the Snowman. The instant that West's feet touch the ocean he becomes animated and full of life. West's smile and enthusiasm are infectious! You can't help but smile when you see him on the board with Ricochet wearing an ear to ear grin and offering high-fives to everyone he passes. Ricochet provides a calming reassurance to West. He loves to surf, but he wants to surf with Ricochet.

—Debbie J. Spoonhour, water helper

*Thank you, Ricki,* for saving my life. I was looking for a way to fill my heart once my kids left home and you guided me to it. I love the ocean; it makes me come alive, and I love to share this feeling with others. Surf sessions with you and your awesome participants are so inspiring; they fill me with joy and make my heart sing! I am honored to be a small part of your village.

—Patti Walsh, water helper

*Think of a child unwrapping a gift,* knowing inside it will contain some of the happiest moments their life. . . that is what I see every time Ricochet approaches a child with special needs. Ricochet loves the child unconditionally and enables them to do something they would never dream of doing alone. We can all learn by Ricochet's actions: love unconditionally and give generously.

—Doan Hohmeyer, water helper

©Larry Brambles

©KillerImage.com

©Heather M. Moana

©Laura Ann Fisher

©Robert Ochoa (Pawmazing)

*When I take Ricochet* out in the water she responds in two different ways. When she surfs with people she is very focused and is all business. She is always adapting to the ever-changing conditions and providing balance. In contrast, when it's just her and I, she is playful and much more carefree. Ricochet isn't like other dogs. She has a keen awareness that I have never seen before, an intuitive response in and out of the water. Our connection has been set for a long time: it's about trust, love, and an overall bond that can't be broken.

—Dave King, water helper

*Ricochet has touched my heart* by showing me how much of a difference she can make. People with disabilities and special needs and wounded warriors give all of their love to her and she makes their day better. She creates a very welcoming and friendly atmosphere. She is helping to change people's lives.

—Austin King, water handler

*When I first met Ricochet* and learned that she was a "surfing dog" I didn't believe that was even possible! Now, after being given the opportunity to be one of her water care takers, I am touched and feel privileged to be part of such a magnificent group of people and such an inspirational dog whose focus is to truly benefit the lives of other people. Each and every time I enter the water with Ricochet, I leave feeling overwhelmed with inspiration, happiness, and a desire to continue to help the lives of others.

—Ryan Almon, water helper

*Ricochet is the epitome* of unconditional love. Even if months go by without me seeing her, she always greets me with love. But more important is the influence she has on all the children that she interacts with. She has an ability to instill a calm and confidence in children that helps them overcome fear and doubt. I have seen children who are initially afraid to get on a surfboard, overcome their fear of the ocean and even request to go back out and catch more waves. She breaks down barriers in every child that she interacts with and shows them that they can accomplish anything that they set their mind to. What's even more amazing and inspiring is that she does all of this without uttering a single word.

—Grant Kobayashi, water helper

*The affinity between man* and man's best friend is simple and yet so profound. Ricochet's non-verbal communication speaks of love and loyalty, and her liveliness is inspiring. Anywhere she goes, her presence radiates warmth and joy, bringing out the best in anyone! It's been an honor to be a part of her journey.

—John Jefferson

*To be in the water* with such a dynamic team of amazing people and one incredibly special dog is not only life-giving but transforming physically, spiritually, and emotionally. One of my favorite memories was when Ricochet and I were out on my standup paddleboard and several children were waving to her from the beach, many of whom were a little apprehensive to get on a board. When we came in, the children rushed over to her and I heard things like, "Well, if a dog can do it then so can I!" Then one small voice said, "I will only go if she can come with me," and off the three of us went. The young man held on to Ricochet as he was telling her, "Everything is better now; I knew I could do this." The experiences are so profound, they are always with me. She is definitely more than just a dog!

—Terri Wargo, water helper

*Seeing Patrick* and Ricochet surfing together for the first time was amazing! To this day, after surfing with Ricochet many times, I am still amazed at the excitement and sense of hope that Ricochet brings to people. She brings happiness to kids with special needs and their families with each sloppy wet kiss and bug. She offers encouragement and security for these special kids to do things that maybe seemed impossible. I am so honored to call Ricochet and Judy family and look forward to many more years of helping others break boundaries and set new goals because of one special dog.

—Cory Staley, water helper

*My greatest memories with Ricochet* are from the old days when we used Cheez Whiz on Patrick's helmet. I remember being in the water and three of us all had cans in our pockets to get

©Robert Ochoa (Pawmazing)

©KillerImage.com

©KillerImage.com

©Heather M. Moana

©Robert Ochoa (Pawmazing)

*Ricochet to ride the waves. Now, of course, no one would realize we had to do that since she has become such a pro.*

—Ted Canedy, water helper

*The first time Hunter* met Ricochet he was a shy five-year-old boy, but his eyes lit up and his playful personality came out, which wasn't something that happened very easily. Over the next three years, Hunter buried Ricochet's paws on many occasions at the beach, rode at the skate park together, and hung out at the ball park. Hunter still lights up whenever we talk about Ricochet or he gets to see and play with her. Because of her gentle ways, Hunter is no longer shy around dogs and is really looking forward to the day he gets his own dog to be his companion and helper.

—Jacqueline Pochop, Hunter Pochop's mom

*I love surfing with Ricochet!* I also love to play with Ricochet at the beach. She is LOTS of fun!

—Hunter Pochop, age 8

*When Ricochet and I catch some waves, it is magical . . . actually spiritual.* I feel totally connected to her and I can feel her love to serve someone who needs her help. Her compassion resonates through me. Ricochet as a surf partner provides a profound experience. She is so clearly full of love and devotion to her mission to help those in need. When you look into Ricochet's eyes, you see a deep soul. She understands that nothing matters more than love and compassion.

—Julie Carruthers

*Being a dog lover* myself and with the faith of the healing power of surfing with the disabled, Ricochet showed me that courage is not the absence of fear, but rather the judgment that something else is more important than fear—that judgment is to aid and protect the rider.

—Brad Howe, water helper

*After watching Ricochet's* inspirational video on YouTube, I decided to e-mail her to see if she thought that a woman without arms could surf. Ricochet e-mailed me promptly back and simply said "Yes, come to California and we will surf together." I will never forget the lesson this beautiful golden retriever taught me: the seemingly impossible can become possible with hard work, focus on a positive outcome, and perseverance.

—Sabine Becker

*The energy in the water* when we surf with kids of all abilities is so pure—pure joy and pure happiness. The children gain confidence and courage while watching each other surf. It is magical. The depth of Ricki's influence is endless, therapeutic, and inspiring even when you least expect it.

—Jen Arave Volz, water helper

*Ricochet inspired me to surf.* Actually it wasn't only Ricki who inspired me; it was people like Patrick and Ian. They are so brave and they make surfing look easy. From watching them, I decided I might want to take a whack at it. One day I got on the board with Ricki, and it was the most fun experience ever!

—MJ, age 10

*Ricochet is fun and cute.* She is sweet and well trained and nice.

—Lexi

*Ricochet is* a very cool dog.

—Gina Gill

*The day I met Ricki,* I had no idea how much of an impact she would have on my life. Ricki has given me the confidence to work through PTS and to not give up hope on having a "normal" life again. Ricki brought me from a very dark place that at the time I thought I couldn't escape, to seeing a light in the distance. She saved my life.

—Tisha Knickerbocker

*The first time* I met Ricochet, we had this special connection; it was an energy vibe shared between us like nothing I have ever experienced before. I have chronic pain and combat-related PTS. She could pick up on my anxiety when I was around too many other people. Even when

©Barbara McKown

©KillerImage.com

*I was trying to hide it, she knew me and would help me in ways that are unexplainable. It never mattered how bad of a week I was having; when I met her, everything would just go away. It seemed as though my pain, anxiety, PTS, and all the worries in the world would vanish. She inspired me to get up and get back out there and work hard and push myself to get better from my injuries. She has truly affected my life in the utmost positive way.* —Andrew Michael Gonzalez

*Ricochet is my battle buddy and has been since we first met. She is truly an angel and means more to me than any words could describe.* —Randy Dexter

*Ricochet has done what only an angel could do by saving our family. She is an angel in disguise as a dog.* —Rebecca Dexter, Randy's wife

*We always wear pink together. I love her kisses. She's so sweet. She likes to shake her paw for me and I love her.* —Selena Dexter, Randy's daughter, age 3

*Our friend Ricochet has touched our lives in countless ways in the water and out. From her first magical tandem surf with Patrick in 2009 to her ongoing fund-raising efforts to help so many people and animals; she puts her heart into everything she does!* —Rosanna & 80 Messick

*I love spending time with Rina. When she looks at me she can reach down in my soul and make me feel so loved. She inspires me to be a better human.* —Carrie Madrid

*Rina fills my heart with joy and happiness. She is an angel with fur.* —Maggie Richmond

*The dogs have played a huge role in our lives. Ricochet is the most joyful, playful dog you would ever know, and it makes us so happy that we have a star dog next door! Rina is a calm, caring, loving dog, and she makes us feel good if we are ever sad. We love those dogs so much and couldn't imagine life without them both. They are all part of our extended family.* —The neighbors

*I have a picture of Ricochet on my fridge from when she was just a little bundle of fur. When she got older, she had some of her first swimming sessions in my pool and now she is a surfing star, bringing joy to so many!* —Michelle Takagi

*We were so excited to have Ricochet join the cast of Make A Film Foundation/Rina Goldberg's Film, The Magic Bracelet. Her mission in life matched our daughter Rina's attitude to "love life, dream big, and be positive." When we learned that Ricochet's sister was named Rina it was a clear sign we were meant to be connected with Judy and her fabulous dogs. Rina, the dog, was a strong physical presence on the set representing our Rina, who passed away on December 29, 2010, from mitochondrial disease prior to production. Rina, the dog, seemed to know her purpose on set.* —Ari and Stacy Goldberg, parents of Rina Goldberg (12/16/95–12/29/10)

*Ricochet is an ambassador of love and sweetness. Firsthand, I've seen her connect with and calm a number of children with special needs, and help give them the confidence to take part in real-life adventures including surfing, outrigger canoeing, and stand-up paddling. Judy's professional and compassionate, always with the children's best interest at heart. It's an honor to have them at any event.* —Max Montgomery, co-founder/executive director, Tommie Cares Foundation, co-founder/former executive director, Best Day Foundation

©Robert Ochoa (Pawmazing)

©Robert Ochoa (Pawmazing)

©Allison Shamrell Photography

©Tamandra Michaels

©KillerImage.com

*We have been blessed* to have Ricochet participate in a number of Best Day at the Beach events. Ricochet's surfing skills and engaging manner are a perfect fit in assisting volunteers helping the kids with special needs that we serve feel safe and comfortable stepping into new and exciting experiences such as surfing. There is a special magic that is evident in the extra radiant smiles that Ricochet stimulates from all of our participants. We look forward to each and every opportunity we have to share a day at the beach with Ricochet.

—Brooks Lambert, co-founder, Best Day Foundation, Inc.

*Ocean Healing Group* has had the pleasure of working with Judy and Ricochet going way back to the creation of our foundation in 2007. Their consummate passion and drive for helping others has been a fantastic source of inspiration and empowerment to so many. We're so thankful to have them in our lives and are very much looking forward to the day when we can surf together again!

—Christiaan Bailey, co-founder, Ocean Healing Group

*In 2010,* I had the distinguished pleasure of meeting one of the world's most inspirational dogs, Ricochet. I continue to utilize her incredible story during my Pay It Forward speeches because of the emotional impact it makes on the audience. Ricochet's compassion and dedication to selflessly help others demonstrates that absolutely anyone can partake in the Pay It Forward concept, which is why she is such a beloved ambassador for the internationally celebrated Pay It Forward Day.

—Donovan Nichols, Pay It Forward Day international co-coordinator and inspirational speaker

*The story of Ricochet* is amazing in its own right: man's best friend turned helper. Does it get any better than that? The joy that Ricochet brings to everyone that she comes into contact with is contagious. Watching Ricochet help paralyzed athletes surf again is one of the most beautiful sights you will ever see. I know that we at Life Rolls On Foundation are forever grateful for the joy that Ricochet brings to all of the disabled athletes during our They Will Surf Again programs.

—Jesse Billauer, founder and executive director/CEO of the Life Rolls On Foundation

*As I walked down the beach,* I remember thinking, "That dog is smiling." With a wag of her tail and a gentle nudge, Ricochet and the young marine from the Wounded Warrior Battalion at Camp Pendleton walked into the whitewash and the gentle rolling waves beyond, accompanied by an experienced surf teacher from JMMF. Five minutes later, it was the marine who had the smile on his face as he rode his first wave to the shore. It was a moment of sheer joy and release—a positive new memory, shared with his new surfing buddy, Ricochet. There have been many memorable days at JMMF Ocean Therapy, but watching Ricochet in the water and on the beach remains a shining highlight in our quest to heal ourselves and others, one wave at a time. Thank you, Judy and Ricochet, for sharing your stoke and golden paws on the surfboard and off, with your JMMF family.

—Nancy Miller, Jimmy Miller Memorial Foundation

*I am often asked* how being on the TV show Survivor changed my life. My reply is: "I have met many amazing people that I may never have met otherwise that have enhanced my life's journey incredibly." Meeting Ricochet has been one of those blessings and inspirations. The day we met we both knew we had a mission, and that was to make a difference using who we were. Ricochet became the Spokes-Dog for Reality Rally, and worked her magic helping spread the word and raising funds for men and women fighting for their lives with breast cancer at Michelle's Place. It has been an honor being part of Ricochet's life.

—Gillian Larson, *Survivor Gabon*

*When my son Spencer Fox* was thirteen years old he joined a club nobody wants to be a member of: he was paralyzed with a spinal cord injury. Once in this club, you cannot help but be overwhelmed at the generous and determined people and animals you meet. Judy and Ricochet top this list. We met Judy and Ricochet through adaptive surfing. They make faces light up with pure joy and Judy is my inspiration as I witness her "dogged" commitment to raising awareness and funds for needy animals, kids, and causes. The world is so blessed to have Judy and Ricochet. So am I.

—Celia A. Brewer

*I was with Judy* the day she started molding this great adventure which would capture Ricochet's special gifts and also help persons with disabilities in a unique way. That day, we rode together to Huntington Beach to watch Patrick surf during the US Open of Surfing. Judy's dream evolved slowly during that ride home afterwards and it seemed she never looked back. It is such an honor to have experienced the start of Ricochet's unique career.

—Carol Davis, Paws'itive Teams

*I remember holding Ricochet* when she was barely one week old. I remember her first steps onto a full-sized surfboard while Patrick watched from the shoreline. It is a privilege to remember the many spectacular moments when the magic began.

—Denise Moossa

*Ricochet is such an amazing being.* She has helped so many people to feel better and discover what they are capable of. I had her work with one of my human clients and he experienced a huge breakthrough that started him on a whole new path to healing.

—Nedra Abramson, Reiki for all Creatures

*In your lifetime you will meet many animals* and some of them are special and touch your heart, but then there are those that are extraordinary that you will never forget. . . and that is Ricochet. Ricochet and Judy have changed literally thousands of lives with their message of hope, compassion, companionship, and lifetime devotion against all odds. I know that everyone who has had the opportunity to interact with them over the years is better for having met this amazing duo. I personally want to thank them for all they have done for Helen Woodward Animal Center and the orphaned animals in our care. Their partnership has helped to build Surf Dog Surf-a-thon and raised thousands of life-saving dollars.

—Renee Resko, HWAC

*Everyone sees Ricochet* as a special dog. I just see her as a friend of mine doing what she wants to do. She's also named after me. That's cool.

—Rick Thomas

*Josh Billings* said, "A dog is the only thing on earth that loves you more than he loves himself." This is one of my favorite quotes and is the epitome of Ricochet. Ricochet's love of others and the joy she brings to the world is inspiring.

—Teri Meister

*Ricochet continues to amaze me* with her care for others with her surfing and charity. But Ricochet is amazing because of the support she has to be herself. That's a lesson so many can learn from her to make our world a better place!

—Shaina Shaver, Facebook supporter

*I'm a professor* at Seattle University and I showed Ricochet's video to graduate students getting a master's in relationship and pastoral therapy. Many teared up when watching. We are all looking for purpose, and she showed us that real meaning comes from giving to others while being your true self.

—Christie Eppler, Ph.D., Facebook supporter

*Ricochet has inspired* me to remember that it's not how we start, but how we finish. There is more than one path to fill your mission in this life; you just have to be passionate, caring, and willing to let go of what you think you have to be. We are at our greatest when we can be just who and what we are.

—R. VanVleet, Facebook supporter

# About the Author

**J**udy Fridono rose above the physical challenges and losses she faced in her childhood when Rina and Ricochet came into her life and showed her unconditional love. Judy channeled that energy into helping others overcome their own perceived limitations.

Judy worked in healthcare administration/business development before her passion for training dogs was ignited. She has a degree in service-dog training and has also received certificates from San Francisco's Hearing Dog Program and the Marin Humane Society's Canine Behavior Academy. As a former certified professional dog trainer, she knows the value of education, so she stays current on the latest training techniques. However, it's the puppies who have taught her the most.

Judy founded the nonprofit organization Puppy Prodigies Neonatal and Early Learning Program to train service dogs for people with disabilities.

She is the guardian of Ricochet, the only SURFice dog in the world who surfs with people with disabilities, kids with special needs, wounded warriors, and veterans with PTS as an assistive aide.

Judy is committed to continuing her journey with Ricochet and sharing her messages for as long as they continue to inspire, give hope, provide a positive effect, and help others.

Judy lives in San Diego with Ricochet and her service dog, Rina. Judy and Ricochet's unique and inspiring work can be found at *www.surfdog ricochet.com* and *www.puppyprodigies.org.*

**Giving back: A percentage of the proceeds from the sale of this book will go to Ricochet's causes fund to help humans and animals in need.**

# About Ricochet

Ricochet is a female golden retriever who was born on January 25, 2008. An ordinary dog with an extraordinary spirit, she is a canine good citizen and a registered therapy dog with Therapy Dogs Incorporated. She's also a certified therapy dog with the American Kennel Club (AKC) and a certified goal-directed therapy dog with Paws'itive Teams.

She's the only SURFice dog in the world who surfs with people with disabilities, kids with special needs, wounded warriors, and veterans with PTS as an assistive aide.

Ricochet also surfs for fun and competition. She has typically placed as one of the top three winners in the contests she's entered. She's tried her paw at stand-up paddleboarding, but also enjoys surfing solo with children, adults, pros, celebrities, other dogs, and even a goat! When she's not working, she enjoys dock jumping, lure coursing, and chasing squirrels and birds.

Ricochet has held more than fifty fund-raisers and raised more than $300,000, which benefited more than 150 human and animal causes. She's also held campaigns to help feed homeless animals, which have resulted in more than 1 million bowls of food being donated.

She's won several fund-raising awards and top dog awards, including the AKC Award for Canine Excellence, the American Humane Association's Hero Dog Award, and the ASPCA's Dog of the Year (see the Resources page for a full list).

Ricochet is an advocate for antibullying in schools. She offers comfort, support, and acceptance, empowering kids to be their authentic selves.

Ricochet is living proof that if you let go of your expectations, and let others be who they truly are, things may turn out better than you could have ever imagined. She would like to remind people that if they are caring for a dog, a cat, or any other animal (or human being), please give them a chance! Give yourself a chance: live your life true to yourself and not the life others expect of you.

If Ricochet can influence one child, change one mind, or save one life, she will have accomplished what she's on this earth to do. Visit Ricochet at the following:

**Email** *pawinspired@aol.com*
**Ricochet's Web site** *www.surfdogricochet.com*
**Ricochet's Facebook Page** *https://www.facebook.com/SurfDogRicochet*
**Ricochet's Twitter** *https://twitter.com/SurfDogRicochet*
**Ricochet's YouTube Channel** *www.youtube.com/user/docchat*
**SURFice Dog Video** *http://youtu.be/BGODurRfVv4*
**Various Videos of Ricochet in Action** *www.surfdogricochet.com/ricochets-book.html*
**Ricochet's Pinterest** *www.pinterest.com/surfdogricochet*
**Ricochet's Fund-raisers** *www.surfdogricochet.com/donors--beneficiaries.html*
**Puppy Prodigies** *www.puppyprodigies.org*

# About Rina

Rina is Judy's service dog, but more significant, her once-in-a-lifetime dog. She's a female golden/Lab mix who was born on April 20, 2003. She is the wind beneath Judy and Ricochet's wings. She's wise, happy, and accommodating, and she always has a smile!

Rina is a registered therapy dog with Therapy Dogs Incorporated, a certified therapy dog with the American Kennel Club (AKC), and a goal-directed therapy dog with Paws'itive Teams, where she works at a school with at-risk children.

Her favorite activities are sniffing on trails, rolling in smelly stuff, and stealing shoes and remote controls and leaving them outside. Her absolute favorite thing to do is pick up packages from the bottom of her 100-foot-long driveway when a delivery truck drops them off. She tends to be a pickpocket and will bring Judy things from her friend's bags if they're left with easy access. She especially likes to scrounge through bags to find Biscuits by Lambchop, her favorite treat (they even make special shoe-shaped biscuits for her). On one occasion at the beach, Rina brought Judy a bag of Cheetos. Thankfully, she doesn't rip open the packages; she just delivers them to Judy.

If Rina could, she would live outside. The highlight of her day is when the neighbors give her a treat. If they are late, she will sit in the yard, looking up at their window, and let out a "Woof" every couple of minutes. Her favorite toy is an orange plush monkey that she sleeps with every night. As one of Ricochet's fans said, "Rina is one cool breeze blowing through our lives."

# About the Writer

**K**ay **Pfaltz** is the author of *Flash's Song: How One Small Dog Turned into One Big Miracle*, *Lauren's Story: An American Dog in Paris*, and *The Beagle*. Her works have appeared in numerous publications. Kay donates profits from books to animal rescue. For a list of charities please see *www.kaypfaltz.com*.

# About the Photographers

**Larry Brambles** of Pacific Piers Photography is a fine arts photographer specializing in photography immersed in the coastal community culture of the West Coast. His photos of Ricochet were taken while working on a photographic art exhibit called "Doggies at the Beach," which was featured in several art galleries in Southern California. Now located in beautiful Astoria, Oregon, Larry is photographing a new Pacific Northwest coastal portfolio. To view his work and contact him, visit his Web site: *www.ILovePacificPiers.com.*

**Sean Callahan** is a lifestyle photographer and videographer based out of San Diego who specializes in Southern California coastal events, places, people, and landscape-based photography. With over 1,200 videos on Youtube.com/socalbeachesmagazine and thousands of images indexed online on various Web sites and blogs, (including "SocalBeachesBlog.com"), Sean can be found photographing and videotaping anything and everything along the coastal cities of San Diego, as well as Orange County and Los Angeles.

**Diane Edmonds** has had a lifelong infatuation with the ocean which led to a career as a pro surf photographer. In addition to shooting everyday surfers at their everyday breaks and surfing dogs, she frequently volunteers her photography skills to capture the stoke of people with disabilities enjoying the ocean with groups including Life Rolls On, Best Day Foundation, Wheels2Water, and others. Diane has captured some of the special milestones in Ricochet's journey as a Surf-ice Dog. Visit: *www.YourWavePics.com.*

**Laura Fisher** is not a professional photographer, but she most definitely has their enthusiasm for the art, especially when it comes to the bond between dogs and humans. There is something so pure and genuine with our canine companions, and she loves capturing that in pictures, most particularly with her own rescued dogs, Marley and Piffer, and those of her friends, such as Ricochet.

**Jessica Hecock** enjoys taking pictures of all things related to dogs. She spends most weekends doing agility with her golden retrievers. You can find out more information at: *www.margoldgoldens.com.*

**John Jefferson** was born and raised in California. He's called Huntington Beach home for more than forty years. Local to the surf scene and having graduated high school in the area, surfing was in his blood. Injured in a head-on collision in his twenties, he turned to photography and his love for the ocean as therapy and healing, and has enjoyed it ever since. Meeting Judy and Ricochet through a mutual friend, he loves watching the changes and happiness they've brought to so many.

**Kristianne Koch** received her BFA in fine art photography and then set out on a life-changing adventure with her husband. They sailed across the Pacific Ocean in a thirty-eight-foot cutter rig sailboat. She currently lives with her family in the California surf town where she grew up and works as a commercial and fine art photographer specializing in ocean lifestyle and portraiture. Visit: *www.kristiannekoch.com.*

**Dominique Labreque** is a professional photographer based in Carlsbad, California, who has been creating captivating images for over twelve years. Growing up in Hawaii, he appreciates beauty and strives to capture these special moments in Southern California. Starting out shooting weddings, he is well versed in all areas. Dominique has been an avid waterman for over twenty years and has a love and passion for the ocean, and wants to share his love with everyone. Visit: *www.DLphotos.net.*

**Carol Martin** is the top dog at Sit 'n Stay Global and loves to take pictures of her favorite dogs in her free time. Sit 'n Stay is a group of corporate flight attendants, pet whisperers, in-flight chefs and pet nannies who offer exquisite human and pet pampering on private jets globally. Carol is also an avid advocate in the fight against K9 cancer and provides support and information to those fighting the fight through her angel dog's "Buddy's Be The Dog Life" Facebook page. Mostly, she just loves the extraordinary lessons dogs teach, and sometimes even catches a few of them with a camera. Visit: *www.sitnstayglobal.com/.*

**Barbara McKown** is a hobby photographer drawn to nature, birds, dogs, and children. Sometimes she is fortunate enough to capture the shared emotions between people and dogs. Some of her photographs have been published in the newspaper and in magazines, and several have appeared in calendars. Combining her love of dogs and photography enables her to capture a lot of puppy cuteness and many special moments, including the day when Ricochet and her siblings were born.

**Julie Megill**'s career in photography began nearly ten years ago when she started shooting at her sons' baseball games. As her children grew, so did her passion for her craft. She takes great pride in her attention to detail, but what she's the most proud of is seeing the smiles on the faces of the families that come back year after year, and the children that she gets to see grow up. From cake smashings to senior pictures, and everything in between, she feels fortunate to have the best job in the world. Visit: *www.julsmegill.blogspot.com, julsmegill@aol.com.*

**Tamandra Michaels** is known for images that are evocative and emotional, and capture and celebrate the essence of the human-animal bond. Born with a physical disability, she experienced early on the healing power of animals. Her love for photographing dogs was inspired by her relationship with her beloved "heart dog," Borias, a German shepherd with a colorful and expressive personality. His passing from cancer deepened Tamandra's passion and insight for capturing the depth of connection possible between dogs and their humans. She is currently owned and adored by a young Shepherd boy, Justice True. Visit: *www.heartdogphotography.com.*

**Heather Moana** enjoys photography as a hobby. She also enjoys traveling and has had the opportunity to take photos in many beautiful places around the world. One of her travel photos received an Honorable Mention in the Documentary category at the 2013 San Diego County Fair Exhibition of Photography. Visit her Web site with travel photos and stories at: *www.heathermoana.com.*

**Robert Ochoa** has been a pet photographer for a number of years. Since 2008 PawMazing has made clients across Southern California realize the value of pet photography. Robert's love and patience for pets allows him to capture ever lasting memories of families' most beloved pets. Visit: *www.PawMazing.com, www. facebook.com/pawmazing.*

**Dale Porter** photographs people, places, and events in the San Diego area as "Killer Image." He also pilots three small drone aircraft and offers aerial photography services. Contact: *Dale@KillerImage.com* or visit *www.KillerImage.com.*

**Allison Shamrell** is a professional photographer in San Diego, California, who specializes in working with pets, especially dogs. Her style is natural, playful, and soulful, and her custom photo sessions take place all around San Diego and in her private studio. For more information, visit the Allison Shamrell Pet Photography Web site at: *www.AllisonShamrell.com.*

# Resources

## For More Information About Ricochet

Email *pawinspired@aol.com*

Ricochet's Web site *www.surfdogricochet.com*

Ricochet's Facebook Page *https://www.facebook.com/SurfDogRicochet*

Ricochet's Twitter *https://twitter.com/SurfDogRicochet*

Ricochet's YouTube Channel *www.youtube.com/user/docchat*

SURFice Dog Video *http://youtu.be/BGODurRfVv4*

Ricochet's Pinterest *www.pinterest.com/surfdogricochet*

Ricochet's Fund-raisers *www.surfdogricochet.com/donors--beneficiaries.html*

Puppy Prodigies *www.puppyprodigies.org*

## Causes Ricochet Supports

Allen & Linda Anderson/Angel Animals Network *www.angelanimals.net*

American Humane Association *www.americanhumane.org*

Animal Rescue Corps *www.animalrescuecorps.org*

Asia Voight Animal Communicator *asiavoight.com*

Assistance Dogs International *www.assistancedogsinternational.org*

Best Day Foundation *www.bestdayfoundation.org*

Biscuits by Lambchop *www.biscuitsbylambchop.com*

Caleb Acosta's Facebook page *www.facebook.com/PrayforCaleb*

Carson Events *www.carsonevents.com*

Chase Away K9 Cancer *www.chaseawayk9cancer.org*

Dr. Marty Becker *www.drmartybecker.com*

Eldad Hagar *www.eldadhagar.com*

Fido Friendly *www.fidofriendly.com*

Free Kibble *www.freekibble.com*

Friends of Bethany *www.friendsofbethany.com*

Going the Distance *www.Goingthedistance.info*

Golden Retriever Meetup Group *www.meetup.com/goldens-33*

Helen Woodward Animal Center *www.animalcenter.org*

Help Patrick Walk *www.helppatrickwalk.org*

Hero Dog Awards *www.herodogawards.org*

Ian McFarland *bit.ly/HelpHopeLiveIanMcFarland*

International Association of Assistance Dog Partners *www.iaadp.org*

Jennifer Skiff *www.JenniferSkiff.com*

Jessie Rees Foundation *www.negu.org*

Jimmy Miller Memorial Foundation *www.jimmymillerfoundation.org*

K2 Adventures *www.k2adventures.org*

Kindred Spirit Animal Communication *www.kindredspiritsanimalcommunication.com*

Life Rolls On Foundation *www.liferollson.org*

Living the Dream Foundation *www.ltdfoundation.org*

Loews Coronado Bay Resort Surf Dog Competition *www.loewssurfdog.blogspot.com*

Lone Survivor Foundation *www.lonesurvivorfund.org*

Lucky Dog Rescue Blog *www.facebook.com/luckydogrescueblog*

Marc Bekoff *www.marcbekoff.com*

Markham Woods Church *www.markhamwoodschurch.org*

Make a Film Foundation *www.makeafilmfoundation.org*

Mary Lelle, Energy Medicine Specialist *www.marylelle.com*

Michelle's Place|Breast Cancer Resource Center *www.michellesplace.org*

Military Veteran Project *www.jamiejarboe.org*

Morris Animal Foundation *www.morrisanimalfoundation.org*

New Jersey SPCA *www.njspca.org*

No Means Go–The Barney Miller Story *www.nomeansgo.com*

Ocean Healing Group *www.oceanhealinggroup.org*

Patrick Ivison *www.helppatrickwalk.org*

Paws'itive Teams *www.pawsteams.org*

Pay It Forward Day *www.payitforwardday.com*

Pet Pardons *www.petpardons.com*

Pets for Patriots *www.petsforpatriots.org*

Pipeline to a Cure *www.pipelinetoacure.com*

Project Walk *www.projectwalk.org*

Puppy Rescue Mission *www.puppyrescuemission.com*

Purina Pro Plan Incredible Dog Challenge *www.proplan.com/community/incredible-dog-challenge*

Rancho Coastal Humane Society *www.rchumanesociety.org*

Reality Rally *www.realityrally.com*
Reiki for All Creatures *www.reikiforallcreatures.com*
Rina's Magic Bracelet Movie *www.rinasmovie.com*
San Diego Humane Society *www.sdhumane.org*
Seth Casteel *www.littlefriendsphoto.com*
So Cal H2o Rescue Team *www.facebook.com/SoCalH2ORescueTeam/info*
Spencer Fox Recovery Fund *bit.ly/SpencerFox*
Surfers for Autism *www.surfersforautism.org*
Surf City Surf Dog *www.surfcitysurfdog.com*
Surf Divas *www.surfdivas.com*
Surfers Healing *www.surfershealing.org*
The American Dog Magazine *www.theamericandogmagazine.com*
The A.skate Foundation *www.askate.org*
Tommie Cares Foundation *www.tommiecares.org*
US Open of Surfing *www.usopenofsurfing.com*
Victoria Stilwell *www.positively.com*
Warrior Canine Connection *www.warriorcanineconnection.org*
Wendy Diamond Animal Fair *www.animalfair.com*
Wheels 2 Water *www.wheels2water.org*
Wounded Warrior Project *www.woundedwarriorproject.org*
W. Bruce Cameron *www.brucecameron.com*

## Ricochet's Titles, Awards, and Honors

Canine Good Citizen
Certified Therapy Dog
Registered Therapy Dog
AKC Certified Therapy Dog, THD
Appeared as an extra in the movie *Marmaduke*
2009 DogTipper, Top 10 Dog Stars of 2009
Featured in the 2010, 2011, and 2012 Surf Dogs Calendar
Won the 2010 Helen Woodward Billboard contest with fellow surFURS, Nani, Dozer & Toby
2010 *USA Today* Dog Hero
2010 Petopia TV, Pet of the Year
2010 Dogswell Wag Award "Most Charitable Story"
2010 Morris Animal Foundation K9 Cancer Walk, Top Fundraiser

2010 Arthritis Walk with Leash Your Fitness, Top Fundraiser

2010 American College of Veterinary Internal Medicine Foundation, honoree

2010 Helen Woodward Surf Dog-A-Thon, 1st Place "Top Fundraiser"

2010 The American Kennel Club Humane Fund Ace Award for Canine Excellence for Exemplary Companion Dog

2010 Dog Town San Diego's 3 Dog Walk for Breast Cancer, Top Fundraiser

2010 Nominated for three humanitarian awards in the *American Dog Magazine*: Spokesdog for a charitable cause, Service/Therapy Dog that gives unconditionally & Role Model/ Philanthropist

2010 won 1st Place in *American Dog Magazine*'s Humanitarian Awards for Role model/ philanthropist, 2nd Place for Spokesdog for Charitable Cause & 2nd Place for Service/ Therapy Dog that gives unconditionally

2010 Named Best Dog of the Year in DogTipper.com's Best Dog & Cat of the Year contest

2010 Nominated in *USA Today*'s 2010 Top Dog Hero contest

2010 Made it to the finals in the Natural Balance parade float tryouts for skimboarding

2011 Awarded the Gold Standard Award from the Golden Retriever Club of America

2011 Featured in five books

2011 Named *Fido Friendly*'s Best of 2011

2011 Working Class K9 Hero Award Pet Sitters International & Take Your Dog to Work Day

2011 American Humane Association Hero Dog Awards, emerging hero category

2011 Dog of the Year, ASPCA

2011 Top Ten Most Memorable Dogs of 2011, A Place to Love Dogs

2011 Top 25 Pet People of 2011, Petside

2011 Top 10 Unsung Heroes of 2011, Take Part

2011 Top 10 Dogs of 2011, Cesar's Way

2012 PAWS Companion for Life Award!

2013 San Diego Humane Society's Animal Compassion Award

## Surf Dog Competition Medals

2009 Purina Incredible Dog Challenge Surf Dog Competition at Dog Beach in San Diego: Third Place Large Dogs

2009 Helen Woodward Surf Dog Surf-a-Thon in Del Mar, California:
First Place Large Dog Heat
Second Place Overall

2009 Surf City Surf Dog Competition in Huntington Beach, California:
First Place Large Dog Heat
Second Place Large Dog Finals

2010 Loews Coronado Surf Dog Competition in Imperial Beach, California:
First Place Tandem

2010 Purina Incredible Dog Challenge Surf Dog Competition at Dog Beach in San Diego:
Third Place Large Dogs

2010 SPN Surf Dog Competition, in Huntington Beach, California:
Second Place

2010 Helen Woodward Surf Dog Surf-a-Thon in Del Mar, California:
Second Place Large Dog Heat

2010 Surf City Surf Dog Competition in Huntington Beach, California:
First Place Large Dogs
Third Place Large Dog Finals
Best Wipeout!
Best Crowd Pleaser

2011 Purina Incredible Dog Challenge Surf Dog Competition at Dog Beach in San Diego:
Second Place Large Dogs

2011 Helen Woodward Animal Center Surf Dog Surf-a-Thon
First place, Large Dog 2nd Heat

2012 Purina Incredible Dog Challenge Surf Dog Competition at Dog Beach in San Diego
Second Place, Tandem category

2012 Loews Coronado Surf Dog Competition in Imperial Beach, California:
First Place, Large Dogs
2nd Place, Tandem with Cameron Mathison

2012 Helen Woodward Animal Center Surf Dog Surf-a-Thon
1st Place Large Dog 2nd Heat
1st Place Best of Surf Finals
2nd Place Doo the Dah
1st Place Highest Fundraiser—$7,340

2013 Loews Coronado Bay Resort Surf Dog contest, 3rd Place Large Dogs

2013 Loews Coronado Bay Resort Surf Dog contest, 3rd Place Tandem

2013 Helen Woodward Animal Center Surf Dog Surf-a-Thon—1st Place Large Dog
category

# Acknowledgments

Writing the acknowledgments has been the hardest part of this book. There are so many people who have crossed our path on this journey. Some have imparted wisdom with a quick interaction. Others have changed my course completely. If I've excluded your name, it's not because you haven't made a difference; it's because my memory failed me within the window of time I had to prepare this.

This book couldn't have been written without the help of so many people. More important, this journey could have never gotten to where it is today without the selfless, kindhearted people who have helped along the way. I am eternally grateful.

To Patrick, for trusting Ricochet. Thanks for being the yin to Ricochet's yang. The milk to her bone! If it wasn't for you, Ricochet may have never been able to live her purpose.

To Jennifer, for being open to my dog surfing with your son. No matter where the road took us, you were always willing to go. You have such a way of making things happen.

To Denise, for making dreams come true.

To WebMD Health Foundation, for making Ricochet's first fundraiser so successful, and to the Rose Foundation for making Patrick's dream a reality.

To Dave, for always being there for us. Thanks for loving Ricochet and keeping her safe. We could not have accomplished the things we have without you, my friend. Your compassion and commitment is truly a gift to us.

To all of the families of the kids and people Ricochet has surfed with. Thank you for not only trusting my dog, but for inviting me into your families.

To all of the siblings of the kids that Ricochet has surfed with, you are exceptional and I love you.

To my parents, grandparents, aunts, and uncles who I've loved and lost. Our time together was much too short.

To my sister, Maria, and brothers, Bobby and Frankie, for always supporting me and giving me strength during a time of profound grief. Thanks also to Terry, Jill, Lisa, and Andrea for being part of our family.

To all my relatives from around the country, thank you for your support, and for keeping my parents alive in your hearts.

To all of my childhood friends, thank you for teaching me street smarts and always having my back.

To Phil, for showing me there was a world beyond Huron Street.

To Frank, for being there during the worst time of my life.

To Steve, for being one of the best things that ever happened to me. Unfortunately, it was before I was able to realize what goodness was.

To Rina, for giving me the courage to overcome my irrational fears. You are my rock. Your sense of humor and love for life brings me such joy. You have been the ever-accommodating one, and because of your low-maintenance personality and willingness to help others shine, you encouraged me to go forth and make a difference. You are the wind beneath not only my wings but Ricochet's, too.

To Ricochet, for remaining true to yourself no matter how I tried to detour you. You have taught me so many lessons and showed me a new way to live my life. Although I didn't like your bird obsession at the beginning, I truly enjoy watching you run full speed down the beach. Your sense of freedom is liberating.

To all the puppies, who were my best teachers.

To Carol, for supporting me and accepting me into the Paws'itive Teams family. You were the catalyst to many things on this journey.

To all the trainers and volunteers at Paws'itive Teams. Thank you for welcoming me to San Diego with open arms.

To the Golden Retriever Meetup Group for welcoming me into your group when I first moved to San Diego, even though Rina was only half golden!

To Dr. Joy, for gifting me with a life that went on to touch millions of other lives.

To Charli, for helping me with ten little miracles.

To Rebecca, Asia, and Mary, for communicating with my dogs before I opened my heart and could do it myself.

To Robbie, for trusting me and Ricochet the first time she jumped on Patrick's surfboard.

To all of the volunteers who came out to help the first time Ricochet and Patrick surfed together.

To the service members and veterans who have so graciously shared their lives with us. Thank you for your service, but more important, thank you for being our friends.

To Barbara for helping me connect with Ian, and for all the wonderful segments you've done that have not only touched my heart but America's as well.

To Max, for coordinating everything with Ian and his family.

To Melissa, for being one of the most selfless people I've ever met.

To the media: without you, we couldn't have raised the amount of awareness that we have, raised the funds, or helped the number of humans and animals in need.

To Sarah and Rob, thanks so much for trying to make my dream come true.

To Patti, for helping me understand book contracts. Your guidance and generosity went above and beyond.

To Lisa, for legally protecting my and Ricochet's best interests.

To Eddie and Sonny, for saving my life. And to Bill for saving Ricochet's.

To Glenda, for taking such good care of me. You're always right there whether it's to hold Rina's leash, grab a water, or share your wonderful heart.

To Vernon, your ability to capture once-in-a-lifetime moments on video is amazing.

To all of the adaptive surfing organizations and other organizations that allow Ricochet to be part of your efforts.

To all of the animal organizations that allowed us to raise awareness and funds for them. Thank you for saving lives.

To the Make A Film Foundation and *Rina's Magic Bracelet Movie*: thank you for casting Ricochet as Melvin, the cheese-obsessed dog, and for not losing your patience when she climbed trees instead of acting out scenes.

To Cathy and Carson Events, for giving me the platform to see Ricochet's talents, which began a completely new journey.

To all of the donors who donated to Ricochet's fund-raisers. Without you, she couldn't have raised more than $300,000 and helped so many humans and animals in need.

To all of Ricochet's Facebook supporters: Thank you for coming together for the greater good and proving that an ocean is made up of single drops of water all blended together to make something beautiful. Thank you for your continued support, sharing, liking, posting, and commenting.

To all of the celebrities who have helped me further my cause.

To all the organizations that awarded Ricochet special honors, awards, and accolades for her work.

To Hotel Indigo Del Mar, for helping us make dreams come true by extending your hospitality.

To Go Pro, for your kindness and generosity. There is no better feeling than to see the kids' reactions to themselves surfing on film.

To all of the sponsors that have donated funds or donations in kind to support Ricochet's work.

To Charlotte, for assisting me with Rina so that I could pursue my education. Your love for her made my time away from her much easier.

To all of my friends who rallied together to help me out when I had open-heart surgery. There are no words to describe how grateful I am.

To the Pay It Forward Day Foundation, for allowing Ricochet to be an ambassador for the Paw It Forward movement.

To Surftech, for helping us with one of the most important items: a surfboard.

To all of my Southern California friends, for supporting me on this journey and understanding Ricochet's unique mission.

To all of my friends back in Chicago and around the country. Thanks for supporting me. Although we may be separated by geography, you are still close to my heart.

To everyone who doesn't care that Ricochet chases birds, even if it's in the middle of a live broadcast.

To Charmaine, for pointing me in the right direction.

To the photographers who not only took amazing photos, but bestowed their generosity on me by donating their photos of the once-in-a-lifetime experiences Ricochet had with the individuals she surfed with: Allison, Amy, Barbara, Bobbie, Brandise, Carol, Caroline, Charli, Dale, Diane, Dina, Dominique, Heather, Jessica, John, Juls,

Karen, Kristen, Kristianne, Larry, Laura, Maggie, Manny, Michael, Nicole, Rob, Sean, Seth, and Tamandra.

To my friends and neighbors, who spoiled Rina at home while Ricochet and I were at her events. There is no greater gift than loving my dogs, and you all made her feel so special, and help ease my guilt: Ben, Carol, Carrie, Jessica, Maggie, Michelle, Rick, Robin and her whole family, and Rosanna & 80.

To all of the water helpers: Ricochet wouldn't be able to fulfill the surfing part of her SURFice dog role without the selfless water helpers who personify the essence of helping others with no agenda while instilling the pure stoke of surfing. Your love, high-fives, encouragement, and skill act as the foundation to the pure stoke and joy that manifests in the water: Ali, Austin, Brad, Cory, Courtney, Dave, Deb, Devyn, Doan, Grant, Jen, Jennifer, John, Josh, Kaley, Kate, Lara, Larry, Mary, Max, Patti, Prue, Richelle, Rick, Robbie, Rosanna & 80, Ryan, Sam, Ted, Terri, Tony, Travis, Zac, and all the others whose names I may not have gotten, thank you for keeping Ricochet and the people she surfs with safe.

To all of the people and kids Ricochet has surfed with. Thank you for bringing me such joy: Amanda, Caleb, Cameron, Christiaan, Dana, Gillian, Gina, Guy, Hunter, Ian, Jake, Jo, Lexi, MJ, Patrick, Randy, Reese, Sabine, Taylor, Tisha, West, and all of the others who have shared your love.

To all of the people in this book who not only shared their stories with me, but shared their lives.

To Allison, who believed in me and Ricochet from the beginning and never gave up even when I wanted to quit several times. You're one of the most patient people I know.

To Kay, for reaching deep within my soul and listening to me tell the story of my journey while writing it with your heart.

To Allen, Jamie, Jennifer, Linda, Marc, Marty, Robin, Seth, Susan, Victoria, and Wendy for believing in me and Ricochet and writing endorsements. You all are my role models.

To W. Bruce Cameron, for writing the foreword to this book. I knew you would understand where I was coming from.

To Teri and Danny, for being guided by your guardian angels, which kept Ricochet safe.

To Dr. Shikhman, for saving my life.

To Michelle, Kristen, Jonathan, Deb, and Annette, for reading the manuscript and giving me such great input.

To the Klassen family, for helping Patrick and Ricochet surf.

To the surfers at Torrey Pines Christian Church, for your willingness to help Patrick and Ricochet surf.

To Bob and Janice, for being so welcoming and loving. Your support and kindness is so appreciated.

To Nedra, for helping to balance Ricochet's energy so she could continue to work with the military with PTSD. And for always being willing to balance me and Rina out, too.

To Cynthia, Caleb's aunt, for taking the initiative to call me, and for being my source of support whenever I had questions.

# Book Club Questions

I n chapter 3, Judy calls Rina her "once-in-a-lifetime dog" whereas Ricochet "belongs to everyone," showing that each dog we come to know will have a different connection with us and will play a different role in our lives. Think about the dogs you have known over the course of your life and what they have meant to you. Describe how they helped you grow or shaped you to be the person you are today.

In chapter 7, Judy learns to let go of her expectations of Ricochet. Have you ever placed unrealistic expectations on someone else (pet or person)? How did it feel when you learned to let them go, or are you still having difficulty surrendering?

Throughout the book, there are recurring themes of synchronicity: Can you share a time when something happened to you that was not just coincidence but something divinely predestined?

Throughout the book, the uncommon name "Rina" keeps occurring in Judy's life. Have you ever had a special name, number, or color—or "something"—that keeps repeating in your life? Do you think it is a sign that you are on the right path or just a coincidence?

🐾 Rina likes to steal Kleenex and Ricochet chases squirrels. What are your pet's idiosyncrasies and what helpful—or hilarious—ways have you tried to "fix" them?

🐾 Do you believe that people can communicate with animals as the animal communicators did with Ricochet and the others? Have you ever had an experience with one? If so, what happened?

🐾 Do you believe that our pets or animals can communicate with us? Have you ever had an experience in your own life when your pet was trying to tell you something?

🐾 Do you see any parallels between Judy and Melissa? Lauren and Jennifer? How are they similar? How are they different?

🐾 What choices did Judy make that changed her path and broke the cycle? If she hadn't made those choices, how might her life be different?

🐾 In the beginning of the book, Judy sees the world as bad and dangerous. By the end of the book, her view has changed. What's your perspective? Are you an optimist or a pessimist? Do you think that your upbringing has a big impact on that? Can you change? How?

🐾 Randy, Patrick, Judy, and Ian were all struggling with a life-defining adversity at one time. How has adversity changed you?

🐾 A general theme in the book is that we are happiest when we are living our purpose. Do you agree? Are you living yours? If not, how could you?

🐾 In trying to name Ricochet, Judy had some options like *Que Será, Será*, Destiny, and Chance. What is your favorite dog name? What was the name of your first dog?

🐾 Judy made an unexpected move from Chicago to California. Have you ever done something like that? What was it? Was it a good choice?